IMAGINARY POWER, REAL HORIZONS

The Practicality of Utopianism

Richard Gilman-Opalsky

AK PRESS

Imaginary Power, Real Horizons

ISBN: 978-1-84935-555-1
E-ISBN: 978-1-84935-556-8
Library of Congress Control Number:2023948366
AK Press
370 Ryan Ave. #100
Chico, CA 95973
www.akpress.org
akpress@akpress.org

AK Press
33 Tower St.
Edinburgh EH6 7BN
Scotland
www.akuk.com
ak@akedin.demon.co.uk

The above addresses would be delighted to provide you with the latest AK Press distribution catalog, which features books, pamphlets, zines, and stylish apparel published and/or distributed by AK Press. Alternatively, visit our websites for the complete catalog, latest news, and secure ordering.

Cover design by Josh MacPhee
Printed in the USA on acid-free paper

For my children and the imaginations of children everywhere. For a world of dignity worthy of your dreams.

CONTENTS

INTRODUCTION

A Question of Imagination: What Can it Mean to Be a Communist Today?

The question of what it can mean to be a communist today is a question of the imagination. This is because it cannot mean today what it has meant to earlier generations of communists, anarchists, and various anticommunists and because communists today must ground communism in the present reality. Communists must also confront past failures and catastrophes as well as ongoing ideological vilification. We know the least imaginative route: to acquiesce to failures, catastrophes, and vilifications and to abandon a rich revolutionary history and theory—now full of anarchist insight and influence—to the unimaginative dead conclusions of our enemies. To speak of communism without any imagination is to speak of a corpse or to try to reanimate one. With some imagination, we can see other possibilities, some grounded in real struggles and concrete practices of the here and now. Imagination may exceed reality without abandoning it. That is one of the central themes of this book.

Clearly, the word *imagination* demands further definition, especially because of its simultaneous implication of both the real and the unreal, or not-yet-real. On the side of the already- and actually existing, imagination is a capacity of the human brain to form and reconceive ideas and images. That definition of imagination dates to the middle of the fourteenth century and captures the human faculty of thinking that can create a concept or idea of something that does not exist as such. Perhaps the easiest examples are in creative writing about fantasy creatures and worlds. The imagination puts things together to make something new. From the old French *imaginacion*, imagination indicates a concept or idea but also a hallucination. With the Latin *imaginationem*, we mean the fanciful power to form a new idea out of things already represented. What I want to emphasize is that imagination contains yet exceeds reality and in many ways is a power that makes new things out of real experiences in the world. In the present book, imagination involves looking closely at the world as it is and using a peculiar power of the brain, joined with a sense of the desirable and the possible, to move beyond the existing reality toward the conceptualization of real horizons.

Before attempting to answer the question of what it can mean to be a communist today, I should say that I am myself a communist, and I will offer an answer from a communist point of view. Not *the* communist point of view, for there is not only one of those; communists often disagree. However, I shall answer from one communist point of view, which is mine, because I think it is the best of the bunch.

Perhaps obviously, the place to begin is with Karl Marx's definition of communism as he and Frederick Engels provided in *The German Ideology*. I keep close to Marx's original definition of communism, which many communists don't do and which *all* anticommunists ignore in order to preserve their demonstrably wrong views of communism. Ok, so what did Marx say?

> Communism is for us not a stable state which is to be established, an *ideal* to which reality will have to adjust itself. We call communism the *real* movement which abolishes the present state of things. The conditions of this movement result from the premises now in existence.[1]

The first sentence is a negative definition, or statement of what communism is not. Marx says communism is not a stable state to establish. Communism is not something you establish and name like a government or a building or some other artifact or noun. Communism is rather something *we do*, a process, not an end state. Marx also says it is not an *ideal*. Therefore, it is a process but not an ideal process that we only imagine. He says exactly this in the second sentence, the positive definition, or statement of what communism is. He says it is a real movement. This means communism is an actually

---

1. Karl Marx and Frederick Engels, "The German Ideology," cited in *The Portable Marx*, ed. by Eugene Kamenka (New York: Penguin Books, 1983), 179.

happening movement or historical process but not just any real movement or historical process. Communism is only the movement that abolishes the present state of things. Therefore, it cannot be a process of merely improving things, of making the insufferable a bit more sufferable. It cannot be reformist. For example, communists would not want to make slavery kinder and gentler for the slave but would prefer a movement for the total abolition of the slave system, which Marx did in fact prefer and even communicated in writing to Abraham Lincoln.[2] Communism is an abolitionist movement and what it abolishes is something defining of the present reality. That part is tricky because today's present reality is not that of 1846, and if communists are for the abolition of the present state of things, they have to rethink their targets as the present never stays the same. This indicates a materialist grounding for our imaginary efforts. Consider the question: What must we abolish today? It requires that we think both about what is and what is not yet.

Finally, Marx adds, "The conditions of this movement result from the premises now in existence."[3] For him, this meant looking at the conditions of class conflict in globalizing industrial societies where the gap between the haves and have-nots was becoming an opposition between "two great hostile camps," as he wrote two years later in *The Communist Manifesto*.[4]

A few sentences from Marx get us pretty far in answering our opening question: What can it mean to be a communist today? A communist must think about present conditions of life that cannot be reformed and that therefore require abolition. It means to think about really existing premises that give rise to really happening movements. For example, a communist in the United States in recent years will think about resurgent white supremacy, killer cops, Black Lives Matter uprisings, and a whole range of activism surrounding ecology, sexuality, and gender. Communists take sides with real movements when we cannot participate in them directly. We never side with those who defend the existing conditions of life.

That is why, even if we would ourselves like to storm the Capitol Building in Washington, DC, we oppose the so-called insurrection of January 6, 2021.

---

2. Robin Blackburn, *An Unfinished Revolution: Karl Marx and Abraham Lincoln* (New York: Verso Books, 2011).

3. Marx and Engels, "The German Ideology," 179.

4. Karl Marx and Frederick Engels, *The Communist Manifesto* (New York: Prometheus Books, 1988), 210.

This so-called insurrection was a tantrum of the status quo, a paramilitary deployment of a sitting president, resisting a scarcely imaginative transition of office from Donald Trump to Joe Biden. Aside from the fact that we prefer insurrections aimed at heads of state not commanded by them, many in the mob action of January 6, 2021, would have preferred to go backward to the US of the 1950s (or Germany in the 1930s or 1940s) than forward to some new form of life.

Further, among those who actually do want to change things, whether that means addressing problems of racism, capitalism, ecological destruction, sexism, etc., we take the abolitionist or most radical position, the one that calls for transformation at the root causes. That is important because Marx understood communism as a revolutionary process. To be a communist is to be a revolutionary.

Communism is an active abolitionist opposition to the world such as it is. Even though we are not confronting the same Manchester capitalism of Marx's life and times, the world is no less governed by the logic of capital, no less ruled by money, and class society has never seen as much global inequality as exists today. Whatever else has changed, capitalism still describes the social, political, and economic realities in most of the world, and communism still entails an effort to overthrow the rule of capital. I therefore understand communism as movement toward healthy human relations. This is the communism of what Marx called the *Gemeinwesen*, the community, communal being, or common sensibility.[5]

Because I focus on forms of life instead of forms of government and because I favor uprisings to their settling down, I am the kind of communist that Vladimir Lenin diagnosed in 1920 as having an "infantile disorder."[6] I am the kind of communist who distrusts and ruthlessly criticizes all ruling classes and political parties, including those that claim to be proletarian. Marx himself, in one of his last major works, *Critique of the Gotha Program*, took great pains to insist that left-wing political parties calling themselves "communist," specifically those that had just drafted a program that would create the Social

5. Marx retained Hegel's fixation on the *Gemeinwesen*, which we see throughout Marx's work from 1844 onward.

6. V. I. Lenin, *"Left-Wing" Communism, An Infantile Disorder* (Peking: Foreign Languages Press, 1970).

Democratic Party of Germany, was nothing but a line-by-line betrayal of his entire philosophy.[7] Marx understood long ago that men like Bernie Sanders were not communists nor even socialists. There is a long line of communists like me after Marx too, stretching back to Anton Pannekoek and Sylvia Pankhurst, to Cornelius Castoriadis, C. L. R James, and Raya Dunayevskaya, on up to the Autonomia movement from Italy; there is a long history of efforts to distinguish, as Antonio Negri and Félix Guattari called it, *Communists Like Us*.[8] It turns out that communists like me have more in common with many anarchists than with so many socialists, yet we insist on the ongoing necessity and urgency of the word and idea of communism.

One way I make the case for communism is to invoke Marx's dream for a better *Gemeinwesen*: "From each according to their ability, to each according to their needs."[9] In my work, including the present book, I try to locate the communist *Gemeinwesen* in real activities and relations. Wherever we find real people expecting from others what is in line with their abilities, desires, and interests, and wherever we find people wanting others to have what they need, independent from anything that they do, I find a communist logic at work in the world.

In my book *Precarious Communism*, I wanted to think about what it means to be a communist today.[10] We who are "precarious communists" retain a communist identity, disposition, and active commitments without any strident confidence in our ability to abolish the present reality. What makes us *precarious* is the fact that we do not know how to get where we want to go. The time of dogmatic communism is over. Communists who claim to know what to do belong in the dustbins of history. What makes us *communist* is that the only thing about which we have a good deal of confidence is the violence, racism, immorality, and unsustainability of capitalism. That capitalism has to be opposed for existential, ethical, and ecological reasons is adequate grounding for communism.

---

7. See Karl Marx, *Critique of the Gotha Program* (New York: International Publishers, 2002).

8. Félix Guattari and Antonio Negri, *Communists Like Us*, trans. Michael Ryan (New York: Semiotext(e), 1990).

9. Marx, *Critique of the Gotha Program*, 27.

10. Richard Gilman-Opalsky, *Precarious Communism: Manifest Mutations, Manifesto Detourned* (Brooklyn: Autonomedia, 2014).

Many reading this would rightly demand a confrontation with the political problem of communist movements in history turning into the opposite of communism. There are many examples of this, from Russia to Spain to Hungary. Raya Dunayevskaya wrote powerfully about the real communist movement in Russia becoming capitalist counter-revolution, for example.[11] The question is irresistible: Is there something in the idea of communism itself that tends toward its opposite? To this, I will suggest that the problems of the so-called communist projects of the twentieth century becoming opposite are not intrinsic to anything in the word or idea of communism.

Earlier generations of communists did not take the theory of power of the anarchists seriously enough. Marx was himself in constant dialogue with anarchists and made some traceable concessions to their strongest points in his own work. Michael Bakunin accounts for some of that in his book *Statism and Anarchy*, where Bakunin also made his famous statement that "anyone who is invested with power by an invariable social law will inevitably become the oppressor and exploiter of society."[12] Because of the fate of the 1871 Paris Commune and the historical conditions of revolutionary politics in the late nineteenth and early twentieth centuries, many generations of Marxists, for too long, were able to disregard or even mock anarchist insights about hierarchy, consolidated and concentrated political power, representation, etc. Shortly into the twentieth century, however, real events appeared to vindicate anarchist concerns about power, party politics, and representation. Communists uncritical of power and hierarchy could seize both and defend themselves as the ruling class while simultaneously denying they were a ruling class at all. This occurred in many of the so-called communist countries, and continues today, not only in revived anticommunist ideology but also in the absurd notion of functional communism in China.

Communists today need to adopt more anarchist sensibilities as communists, not because of deficits in the word and idea of communism but because of real history. However, a communist with anarchist sensibilities about the state is still a communist. Marx's opposition to Ferdinand Lassalle

---

11. Raya Dunayevskaya, *Russia: From Proletarian Revolution to State-Capitalist Counter-Revolution: Selected Writings*, eds. by Franklin Dmitryev and Eugene Gogol (Leiden, NL: Brill, 2017).

12. Michael Bakunin, *Statism and Anarchy*, trans. Marshall S. Shatz (Cambridge: Cambridge University Press, 1990), 134.

was largely due to the former's distrust of state power and party politics, which is especially clear in *Critique of the Gotha Program*. Marx was himself concerned that communism could become its opposite, and already in the nineteenth century wrote warnings about the so-called communism of the twentieth (which he did not live to see).

In any case, communists today must refuse to look at problems from the perspective of state power, not only because of Marx's preference for real movements and revolts over party politics but because of a real confrontation with communism becoming its opposite in the last century. If you say you are a communist today, you have to explain what you mean by that. People no longer simply assume you are a Stalinist, Maoist, or a statist of any kind. The most common of these assumptions is that you are a statist, though that assumption mainly comes from highly ideological anarchists and right-wing conservatives, who often strangely share a perspective on communism. Some may say that, with so much confusion surrounding what communism means, it is better to drop the whole thing and adopt a new language. However, if lack of clarity were the measure, we would have to run just as fast away from the words and ideas "socialism," "anarchism," "freedom," and many others that we may not wish to jettison for lack of clarity. We cannot afford to abandon good ideas that we need, no matter how maligned by misunderstanding or by enemy vilification. We have to fight for the words and ideas that define us, that describe what we want and imagine, and especially when they come under attack. That they are so attacked, maligned, and vilified by our opponents should give us special pause in their abandonment.

It is also necessary to confront the fact that capitalism remains the dominant ideology of the world and that the problems of the world—including authoritarian resurgences in West Africa and Europe, inequalities in health care, the climate crisis, open white supremacy, and many other problems—are problems of the existing reality. People prefer to imagine all the problems that communists cannot solve, but rarely do they pause to notice that the whole litany they conjure—crime, violence, poverty, and war—are already reliable features of the society they defend.

We have to use the language of communism and capitalism for as long as it is useful. As long as we can continue to understand the existing reality with the help of this discursive apparatus, we cannot abandon its language. For as long as the logic of capital governs the world, for as long as life is ruled by money as a power of human freedom and exploitation, we have to continue to speak about capitalism. For as long as we want to juxtapose to such a world, the idea of a radically different *Gemeinwesen* grounded in the logic of health and well-being, we have to continue to speak of communism. Describing the world differently does not change it.

One of the more interesting examples of the enduring relevance and necessity of communism is found in the work of Kohei Saito. Born in 1987, Saito is a young professor of philosophy and political economy at University of Tokyo. He wrote an openly Marxist bestseller in Japan, one of today's most hyper-capitalist societies. Saito's book, *Marx in the Anthropocene: Towards the Idea of Degrowth Communism*, sold half a million copies shortly after its publication in late 2020.[13] The book is widely discussed throughout Japan, and Saito, who reasonably expected to be a more or less obscure academic, ended up a minor celebrity. The early popularity of the book pertains only to sales of the original Japanese edition, so we can say that the idea of communism resonates in the Japanese belly of the beast.

Saito argues that capitalism requires perpetual growth. From a capitalist point of view, insufficient growth means economic and political sickness; degrowth equals death. Saito argues that the growth/extraction imperatives of capitalism exacerbate climate crisis. Degrowth may mean the death of capitalism but is necessary for the continuation of life on Earth. Saito warns, "If we don't stop capitalism by our own hands, the history of humanity will come to an end."[14]

If degrowth is antithetical to capitalism, a movement of degrowth would occupy one position of communism today. Like me, Saito insists that communism is nothing close to the statist or productivist so-called communism of the Soviet Union or China. (It is worth noting that in 1953, in his short piece "On State Capitalism," Mao himself called China a capitalist country with a capitalist economy.) Ecology is one place where we can see what it means to be a communist today. There are other examples. We can be communists in abolitionist movements against white supremacy, against fascism

13. Kohei Saito, *Marx in the Anthropocene: Towards the Idea of Degrowth Communism* (Cambridge: Cambridge University Press, 2023).

14. Cited in Ulv Hanssen's review of Saito's book in *Marx and Philosophy Review of Books*, July 18, 2022, https://marxandphilosophy.org.uk/reviews/20369_hitoshinsei-no-shihonron-capital-in-the-anthropocene-by-kohei-saito-reviewed-by-ulv-hanssen.

(i.e., Antifaschistische Aktion, a militant antifascist group in the Weimar Republic from 1932–33, which was started by communists), mass incarceration, sexism, racism, all of which serve concrete purposes in reproducing the capitalist reality. Obviously, many who join these movements do not call themselves communists, and that's okay. Black children who walk around with a carceral consciousness of their lopsided likelihood of being imprisoned or harassed by cops may not care if those who work to abolish racism call themselves communists.

However, words matter. Liberals may want to hold killer cops accountable for murder but tend to think that Derek Chauvin is more the problem than the white supremacy that reproduces him in other cops with different names and bodies. Liberals cannot imagine a world without police, even though most of them could live several lifetimes without ever needing the cops and do not know there are places like Denman Island that have no cops and little crime to speak of.[15] Conservatives don't even want to hold killer cops accountable, for they are prone to defending them and spend lots of time searching under every rock for reasons to blame the victim.

In this book, I shall argue that human imagination—*imaginary power*—is utterly indispensable to real revolution. I follow Drucilla Cornell on this basic premise. Cornell claims that revolution is "a continual interplay—we could even call it a 'dialectic'—between the materiality of struggle and the imagination: the future to which the struggle aims can only be imagined and never known in advance. . . . What revolution 'is' is created, again and again, by people in struggle who transform both who they are and what they imagine they could become. Any future beyond colonial-racial capitalism and the limits of the knowable that it imposes on us . . . will therefore only be brought into being by the creative power of people as they imagine it in the struggle for it."[16] We are, in other words, talking about the radicality of a creative political imaginary emergent from struggle.

From fourteenth-century etymology, in the Latin *radicalis*, the word "radical" refers to a root in the ground. The word "radish," for a root vegetable,

15. Denman Island is one of the Northern Gulf Islands of British Columbia, Canada. The island is also known by its Indigenous name, *Sla-dai-aich*, which locals still use today.

16. Drucilla Cornell, *Today's Struggles, Tomorrow's Revolutions: Afro-Caribbean Liberatory Thought* (Lanham: Rowman & Littlefield, 2023), 30.

is no accident. It is radical to address problems at their root causes. Are you really addressing problems if you ignore their roots? Communism is a long, international history of radical thought and action, which continues to be necessary. To keep on being communists means to keep on with the radical imagination. Insofar as communism is about abolishing the present state of things, we have to imagine other things. Imaginary power is the ability to do that, an ability we cannot take for granted. "Impractical" is the name given to anyone who imagines something radically other than what exists. However, when we begin to practice the impractical, possibility widens. That is the first premise of the argument that imaginary power is real power. In the diverse chapters of this book, we shall explore the relationship between imaginary power and real horizons.

CHAPTER 1

Theory as an Everyday Thing

Marcelo Starcenbaum: *I would like to ask you, first of all, about your beginnings.*[1] *You currently teach at the University of Illinois but studied at The New School for Social Research in New York. How and why did you approach political theory and philosophy? Can you share a bit about your intellectual origins?*

Richard Gilman-Opalsky: When I think about my beginnings, it is perhaps unsurprising that I would think about my parents. My parents had no university education. My mother came to the United States from Russia and Poland when she was a teenager. My father was born and raised on the Lower East Side of Manhattan. Going into academia always turns one into a strange creature, and it certainly made me into a kind of space alien in my family. My father's idea was to work to live, not to study. He had no known father himself, and he thus thought of his role as essentially one of financial obligation to his family. He was a good man, though very nervous and precarious throughout his life. My mother had similar sensibilities to my father about the alien world of academia, and, in general, they were mainly concerned that I would perish as a philosopher. Such concern was appropriate. In our

1. This chapter was originally published in Spanish as "Capitalismo, revuelta y comunidad. Entrevista a Richard Gilman-Opalsky" in the journal *Sociohistorica*, no. 47 (February 2021), http://dx.doi.org/https://doi.org/10.24215/18521606e133. The interview was conducted by Marcelo Starcenbaum, professor at the Institute for Research in Humanities and Social Sciences at University of La Plata, Argentina. I have expanded and revised my answers to Marcelo's interview questions for the purposes of this book.

society, to be a philosopher is very close to the decision to be a poet or a jazz saxophonist or a painter. Capital is not kind to such people.

I believe there was something in my parents' acceptance of living in order to live that I was reacting against. I did not want to accept that the purpose of a life is merely to go on living, and I was drawn at a young age to throwing the basic assumptions of such a life into question. I found a certain questioning of normal life first in music and then in philosophy. Philosophy helped me to develop and articulate certain disaffections as I was "coming to voice," as bell hooks would say.[2]

I became interested in philosophical problems during some classes I took as an undergraduate. I expected to be bored and then was shocked and unsettled as I confronted questions about the meaning of a life and the justice of the world. I was especially shaken by a professor at Hofstra University, David Cernic, who began his course on existentialism by writing, "God is dead" across the blackboard in giant letters. I was on the edge of my seat and had never felt that way in a classroom. I remember some students dropping the class after that because they found it offensive. It was then that I first felt ideas could move people, upset their composure, and change their comportment.

After graduating, I wished to avoid academia and work. I did not succeed for long and eventually went to The New School for Social Research, one of the few places in the United States where one could study critical theory and could take courses with Jürgen Habermas, Jacques Derrida, and Julia Kristeva. I was surprised when I realized that while I could study critical theory, there were not many opportunities to do so, and none of my professors were teaching Marx. I began to study Marx outside the institution's curriculum and was eventually invited to design and teach a course on Marxist theory at The New School, which I did. I still teach a version of that course today.

Because you asked about intellectual origins, this is just the intellectual piece. There is also a political side, which I arrived at in relation to the social movements of my time. I will leave the details of that story aside here, but it is important to say that I immediately identified academic theory as, at its best, an accomplice to social and political struggles. Academic theory is not itself

2. bell hooks, *Teaching to Transgress: Education as the Practice of Freedom* (New York: Routledge, 1994), 148.

revolutionary but it can aspire to aid and abet struggles in some minor ways. Fortunately, there is also theory from below, which does not happen inside the academy.

Your first book, Unbounded Publics, *focuses on problems of the public sphere.*[3] *It is somewhat surprising that you approached a topic that is not generally of interest in radical politics or culture. In what context did you take this up? How do you define a Marxist or critical approach to the problem of the public sphere?*

Unbounded Publics was not only my first major research but also the work in which I decided that theory had to learn from and follow real struggles in Latin America. The book offers an anticapitalist intervention into debates about the public sphere, which entered the United States late by way of the English translation of Jürgen Habermas's book *The Structural Transformation of the Public Sphere.*[4] Originally published in German in 1962, it was decades before English-reading scholars took it up, and by 1989, Habermas's international popularity made the English publication of that work a major event. The question of the public sphere remains important because it frames the question of political power as something generated in civil society, outside of and often against the state. For Habermas, this was mainly a power for the legitimation of the state, but not for me. I approached theories of the public sphere as a way to theorize power from below, which, you are right, is not the usual orientation.

However, in Germany there had already been a Marxist appropriation and radical redeployment of the theory of the public sphere by two great thinkers, Oskar Negt and Alexander Kluge.[5] Negt and Kluge's study was also not available in English until much later. A lot of the literature on the public sphere is a legacy of liberal political theory, taking its point of origin in Immanuel Kant's Enlightenment conception of the public use of reason

3. Richard Gilman-Opalsky, *Unbounded Publics: Transgressive Public Spheres, Zapatismo, and Political Theory* (Lanham: Rowman and Littlefield, 2008).

4. Jürgen Habermas, *The Structural Transformation of the Public Sphere: An Inquiry into a Category of Bourgeois Society*, trans. Thomas Burger (Cambridge, MA: MIT Press, 1989).

5. Oskar Negt and Alexander Kluge, *Public Sphere and Experience: Toward an Analysis of the Bourgeois and Proletarian Public Sphere*, trans. Peter Labanyi, Jamie Owen Daniel, and Assenka Oksiloff (Minneapolis: University of Minnesota Press, 1993).

from the late eighteenth century.[6] Kant's idea was that the freedom to publicly criticize guardians in the churches, government, military, and science would make public criticism into a progressive historical force and lead to social and political advancement. Habermas and other thinkers of the Western European tradition gravitated to Kant's cosmopolitanism, the ultimate destination of enlightenment, especially since they were thinking in the darkness of the nationalist nightmares of Nazism and World War II. Habermas himself, living through that period and living to see the creation of the European Union and its so-called democratic aspirations, felt that Kant's time had finally come.

As you know, that is not how I relate to the concept of the public sphere. Studying politics in the United States means thinking about the ruling class. The main trend in American political science and political theory is to think of politics as the business of the state, as what institutions of government do. Liberated from its liberal confines, the concept of the public sphere offers an alternative way to think about politics. To think of power as something generated in real-world gatherings of everyday people is to think of politics as something in civil society, to think of voluntary associations and agonistic assemblies, and to say that when we think about power we do not need to think solely about the ruling class.

Therefore, I came to the public sphere as a political theorist interested in thinking about politics from below, and it is important to point out that Habermas has always claimed a connection to both Kant and Marx, and he did have a critique of capitalism in his writings in the 60s and 70s especially. Nonetheless, I was interested in how Kant's original theory of the public use of reason led inevitably to a cosmopolitan horizon in the public sphere. Habermas produced his first works shortly after the Nazi defeat, and he was not at all thinking about a cosmopolitan horizon at that time. He was thinking about the legitimacy of the German state, of nation-states in general. He was thinking about issues like transparency and reciprocity between the German state and the German people. That is why he said, in an interview with Peter Dews, that only after the Nuremberg trials did the Germans realize that they had been living in a criminal political system. Reflecting on his personal

6. Immanuel Kant, "An Answer to the Question: What Is Enlightenment?" in *Kant's Political Writings,* trans. H. B. Nisbet (Cambridge: Cambridge University Press, 1999).

experience with the Holocaust and learning about what was really happening in his youth, Habermas recalls: "I think we were too inhibited at the time to convert our own personal shock into a direct family confrontation. I was in the Hitler Youth; at fifteen I was sent to man the western defences. Our situation was completely different from that of today's youth. Our own history was suddenly cast in a light that made all its essential aspects appear radically different. All at once we saw that we had been living in a politically criminal system. I had never imagined that before."[7]

Habermas understood that the public sphere had been targeted by propaganda for purposes of political manipulation. There is no mystery, then, in his becoming a student of Theodor Adorno and Max Horkheimer. But you can see in this example that Habermas was thinking about the legitimacy of a nation-state supported by manipulated public opinion. He was thinking about dangers of nationalism and state-led programs of propaganda aided by rapidly evolving mass media technologies.

I found something else in Zapatismo coming out of the rebellion in Mexico in the 1990s. I found in Zapatismo, in the spirit and sensibility of the Zapatista rebellion, a different theory of the public sphere. What I found there was absent in European political philosophy. With the Zapatistas, the public sphere was neither national nor transnational but both national and transnational at once. As the name suggests, the Zapatista Army for National Liberation (EZLN) was about national liberation. At the same time, however, they held meetings of "intergalactic" gatherings, or *encuentros*, in which they spoke of insurgent humanity rising up against neoliberalism. This aspect of Zapatismo was about understanding the situation of Indigenous people *both* within the framework of the nation and in the neoliberal context of post–Cold War capitalism. There is no Zapatista movement without a politics of the public sphere. The Zapatista movement forcibly, that is, by insurrectionary means, framed and raised questions about how to think about transformative politics and thus radically redirected political thought and action on the anticapitalist left.

Therefore, I wondered: What if instead of doing what theorists usually do, instead of applying theoretical literature to the analysis of a case, we try to

7. Jürgen Habermas, *Autonomy and Solidarity*, rev. ed., by Peter Dews (London: Verso Books, 1992), 78.

understand the intelligence of the movement itself? It seemed to me that we did not need to explain the Zapatistas with a Eurocentric theory of the public sphere but rather that the uprising was directly producing and expressing a theoretical understanding of current problems and that theorists should theorize from those lessons. We must never assume that the philosopher, because they deal in ideas, is the great wellspring of the imaginary.

Theorizing in this way flips the script on academics. It involves thinking not about how a theory explains an event but about how the event develops a theory directly in its activity. This specific way of approaching Zapatismo accompanied me from that point on. All of my research begins in the real movements of real people. I begin every written work with the conviction that the most interesting forms of theorizing do not come from the university but from the everyday struggles of everyday people.

Your second book, Spectacular Capitalism, *offers a new reading of the work of Guy Debord.*[8] *How did you arrive at your own articulations about the theory of the spectacle? What are the political implications of Debord's incorporation into the conceptual universe of Marxism?*

I think the most significant and controversial aspect of that book is that it takes Debord seriously as a major theorist and suggests that while Marxists generally ignore Debord's theory of the spectacle, they need it. One of the problems one faces in such a project is the worldwide cult of Debord, which is full of people who want to protect Debord from heterodox readings and radical interpretations. Such "Debordians" simultaneously mock the idea of Debord as a museum piece and act as his museum guards.

I was a student of Jacques Derrida's at The New School, and I never agreed with those conservative professors who claimed Derrida disrespected philosophers when he read them in unorthodox and creative directions. I think such an approach, but not necessarily deconstruction, is necessary when we want to take Debord's theoretical work seriously. In the United States, an anarchist group and publisher in Detroit called Black & Red were among the first to translate, read, and proliferate Debord's theory of the spectacle. Fredy

8. Richard Gilman-Opalsky, *Spectacular Capitalism: Guy Debord and the Practice of Radical Philosophy* (Brooklyn: Minor Compositions, 2011).

Perlman, a very interesting theorist and activist, translated and distributed cheap copies of *The Society of the Spectacle*.[9] When I first read Debord's *The Society of the Spectacle* it was almost impenetrable to me as I could not understand what he was doing. For years, I wanted to understand that book but simply could not. When I returned to his work after a long interlude of reading other things, what struck me most was that Debord understood Lukács, Hegel, and Marx with exceptional insight. I had not grasped previously—and I think neither had Perlman's group—the depth with which Debord had studied and intervened in Marxist philosophy. On the other hand, Marxists did not take Debord seriously either; they mostly ignored him. Debord's closest readers, for a time, worked on art history. Debord appeared as something of a footnote to the French revolt of May 1968. Mainly, because of his work as a filmmaker and his close company with artists and poets and his interest in aesthetics, he had become influential in the art world. His best biographer, Anselm Jappe, changed this and made a major contribution to the seriousness of Debord's study of Lukács and Marx.[10] Although Jappe's book did not aim to move beyond intellectual biography, it did so very well and offered an opportunity to begin new inquiry into the meaning that the theory of the spectacle could and should have for revolutionary theory today.

You asked also about the political dimension of that research, which I will link to the trajectory of French critical theory contemporaneous with and immediately following Debord. We could think of Jean Baudrillard, who wrote about Debord and published in Situationist journals. Baudrillard was originally working in Marxist political economy and sociological theory, and he wrote a wonderfully critical book on Marx in the early 1970s, *The Mirror of Production*.[11] However, after this point, French critical theory, and much of what is often called postmodern theory, appeared to lose faith in any transformative political project. This historical abandonment is to some extent related to the frustrations of ultra-left tendencies of figures such as Jean-François Lyotard. Baudrillard aligned himself with a post-political

9. For a beautiful account of some of this history, see Lorraine Perlman, *Having Little, Being Much: A Chronicle of Fredy Perlman's Fifty Years* (Detroit: Black & Red, 1989).

10. Anselm Jappe, *Guy Debord*, trans. Donald Nicholson-Smith (Berkeley: University of California Press, 1999).

11. Jean Baudrillard, *The Mirror of Production*, trans. Mark Poster (St. Louis: Telos Press, 1975).

nihilism, according to which only catastrophes and viruses could change things. What I found in Debord was precisely the moment prior to this cynical depoliticization. Debord was like the final paroxysm before that, as he sought connection with revolutionaries trying to assemble international networks that could confront the problems of capital in various creative ways. The fact that Debord was not very good at seeing that through, that he was ultimately more divisive than uniting, is another matter.

In any case, what I proposed—and to some extent still propose—is a sort of rescue mission for the revolutionary theory and imaginative praxis of Debord. Why? The answer is political. I believe that the theory of the spectacle helps us to understand current *impasses* in the twenty-first century. This is because we still have to deal with the difference between things as they are in fact and as they are presented in ideological myths; we still need to distinguish democracy from its spectacle form, communism from its spectacle form, capitalism from its spectacle form, anarchism from its spectacle form, and so on. Moreover, how is it possible that we can know, almost instinctually, that a world that commodifies everything, governed by capital, is a bad scene and yet still have no idea how to change it?

Debord can help us with such problems. Debord was not a classical or conventional Marxist—we don't need classical or conventional Marxists these days. However, instead of wanting to abandon revolutionary politics, Debord wanted to imagine revolutionary alternatives to classical revolution. That is, he wanted to think through and experiment with revolutionary alternatives to revolution that are still revolutionary. That is where we need to activate our imaginary power. Can we imagine revolution in forms other than those meant by Edmund Burke or Karl Marx? Someone may say that Debord's commitment to rethinking revolution in imaginative new directions is also in the works of Michel Foucault or Gilles Deleuze and Félix Guattari. I can agree with that, but Debord is doing something different in that he is critically engaging Marxist theory and developing Marx beyond Marxism in order to face impasses that Marx himself could not predict, such as that we know capitalist society is fatally wrong yet we don't know how to overcome it and that so much of what we think and speak about is not the reality so much as an ideological understanding of it. Debord's approach takes seriously nontextual terrains like visual art and other creative, playful activities, including film, graffiti, and civil disobedience.

Look on the walls of any capitalist city. Look around this city of La Plata, Argentina. Cities governed by money, life ruled by capital, and exchange relations at every human interface, but at the same time, look on the walls, and what do you see? Countless expressions that reflect the discontent of life in the capitalist world of the city. We know we live in a capitalist society, and we know it is unacceptable, and yet we accept it. We go on accepting the unacceptable. We simultaneously accept and do not accept capitalism. The sidewalks lead to commerce yet the walls are full of protest. There is something explosive just beneath the surface of this form of life, and it is something we can see with the help of Debord's theory of the spectacle.

Your fourth book, Specters of Revolt, *is devoted to the analysis of a series of political processes, including uprisings in Spain, Greece, and Turkey; Occupy Wall Street; and Black Lives Matter upheavals in Ferguson and Baltimore.*[12] *What led you to attempt a global understanding of this heterogeneous set of revolts?*

It took some time to figure out Derrida's relationship to Marx. Many philosophers wanted to know about this relationship, and so there was much anticipation when Derrida's book *Specters of Marx* appeared after the end of the Cold War.[13] As with most of Derrida's books, the debate about this one went on for years.[14] While I was studying Derrida's *Specters of Marx* between 2009 and 2012, a cycle of revolts was opening up globally in Spain, in Turkey, and in the so-called Arab Spring. Perhaps most surprisingly, in the United States, the Occupy Wall Street movement reanimated what would be years of discussion about the problems of capitalism. That was especially interesting, since capitalism had not appeared in protest slogans in the United States since the end of the 1960s. After this wave of uprisings, I considered that perhaps we are not so much haunted by specters of Marx as we are by specters of revolt. These revolts are not, themselves, Marx's theory or a self-conscious resurgence of communism, but they seem to haunt the present capitalist reality.

---

12. Richard Gilman-Opalsky, *Specters of Revolt: On the Intellect of Insurrection and Philosophy from Below* (London: Repeater Books, 2016).

13. Jacques Derrida, *Specters of Marx,* trans. Peggy Kamuf (New York: Routledge, 1994).

14. See especially, *Ghostly Demarcations: A Symposium on Jacques Derrida's* Specters of Marx, ed. by Michael Sprinker (London: Verso Books, 1999).

I begin *Specters of Revolt* with an anecdote of a trip I made to New York after the reoccupation of Zuccotti Park in lower Manhattan. I had heard that activists reoccupied the park while I was making the trip from Illinois to New York. By the time I arrived in the city and walked down to the park, I found that there were only a few cops there. I asked one of the cops where the people were. He told me, "They all went home." I asked why there were still police there. He responded, "Because they always come back." That police presence in the absence of Occupy activists yet in anticipation of them coming back was indicative for me of the haunting of revolt, of its spectral character. Security forces are always preparing for something that is not yet happening but expected to happen. The cops were not thinking about Marx but about something else. The perspective of power was concerned with preempting or containing the disruptive potential of uprising. If they did not think the revolt was a threat, they would not be deployed against it, even in its absence.

What is a revolt? First, a revolt is not a revolution. In fact, sometimes a revolt appears as a desperate attempt to reform things, change laws. For example, if the Black Lives Matter movement in the United States sought only to put cameras on the bodies of police, only to hold individual killer cops accountable, that may be important, but it is not revolutionary. Those initiatives fundamentally center on reforming policing. I think classical concepts of revolution have been off the table in most countries for a while, and we are far more likely to see revolt, which actively haunts and happens reliably around the world. The question is, can revolt move beyond reform toward revolution? I think the answer is yes, but not in terms of classical revolutionary thinking—that is, not in terms of what Edmund Burke or Karl Marx thought of as revolution. Enrique Dussel's position seems more relevant here. In thesis seventeen of his *Twenty Theses on Politics,* Dussel argues that we should juxtapose transformative politics with reformist politics today. Dussel claims that "the real opposition" is between "'reform' and 'transformation,' with revolution as a radical form of the latter."[15] We should think about that. There are always elements inside the revolt that want to radically transform the society, not just hold "a few bad apples" accountable and get bodycams onto cops. For example, inside Black Lives Matter there are also abolitionist tendencies that

15. Enrique Dussel, *Twenty Theses on Politics,* trans. George Ciccariello-Maher (Durham: Duke University Press, 2008), 110.

call for defunding police forces, abolishing mass incarceration, and addressing the deep structures of white supremacy and institutional racism.

In various ways, a revolt always calls into question the morality and justice of the existing reality. We could say that a revolt may contain reformist elements and simultaneously exceed them in its transformative aspirations. Individual uprisings are different from each other but all of them question the justice and reality of the world where they take place. All of them point to some condemnable immorality or material travesty of the existing state of affairs.

The other central point I wanted to make was that the same goes for good philosophy. Good philosophy always questions the justice and reality of the world in which it develops. Philosophy should compel us to interrogate and rethink the world we live in. Therefore, whatever else it may be, the revolt is also always a philosophical event. There is a crucial connection with Marx here. In *The German Ideology*, when Marx states directly what he means by communism, he calls it "the *real* movement which abolishes the present state of things."[16] Insofar as communism is a real movement that wants to transform the reality to create a new reality, the revolt does participate in communism. This is crucial especially because, today, our materialist imperative is to think more about revolt than revolution. Revolts are happening and seemingly insuppressible, and so we have to start from there. We imagine possibility, the not-yet, from what is happening now. If we had lived toward the end of the nineteenth century and the beginning of the twentieth century, our materialist imperative may have been to think more about revolution. However, here in the twenty-first century, thinking about revolution in classical terms (which for Burke and Hegel and Marx was the iconic example of the French Revolution) can feel disconnected from what is happening in the world. We do see many revolts, however, so I think it is better to consider the connection of such social eruptions to transformative and revolutionary aspirations and imaginations.

How is your conception of revolt as an interruption of the existing order related to the theoretical proposals of newer Marxisms? I am thinking above all of the

16. Karl Marx and Frederick Engels, "The German Ideology" cited in *The Portable Marx*, ed. Eugene Kamenka (New York: Penguin Books, 1983), 179.

concept of "the event" in Alain Badiou or the idea of politics as an interruption of police order in Jacques Rancière.

I find many resonances and insights in both Badiou and Rancière. Rancière's work, especially, has great importance in *Specters of Revolt.* Badiou is more important in my research on love. Regarding Badiou, I appreciate how he is capable of producing analyses concurrent with revolts as they are taking place. Every time there is an insurrection, Badiou reliably weighs in to help us understand what is happening without, of course, ever condemning the event as irrational violence. Rancière, however, was more influential to me because in his work I find perhaps the only theory of democracy that may retain some of the vital meaning of that tired and abused concept. I am drawn to Rancière's idea that, when the *demos* is dissatisfied and disaffected, it will express its discontent outside of election cycles. This is to say that, for Rancière, democracy is in the uprising in Tahrir Square, in Gezi Park, Taksim Square, or in Mexico City. For Rancière, democracy is not in the state, for all states are oligarchic, and even Aristotle—who hated democracy—knew that oligarchy was not democracy. If we did not have such an anemic and procedural conception of democracy, we might realize that the most vital activity of democracy is in the event of revolts.

Let me give an example from recent politics in the United States. Those of us on the anticapitalist radical left, or in its near orbit, have had little choice but to find in Bernie Sanders the only practical possibility of achieving some of what has been achieved here in Argentina as a result of left-wing Peronism. Specifically, having a universal public health system, free education, etc. Now, while you and I are having this very discussion, Sanders is being defeated by Joe Biden in the final moments of the Democratic primary. Biden is, without a doubt, the least interesting and most inactive candidate that the Democratic Party has had as a finalist in the last forty years (possibly ever). He descends only in the final moments after a year of contested primary fighting and gives some speeches to tiny audiences gathered in cars because of COVID-19 precautions. What mobilizes so much support for Biden as opposed to for Sanders, who has been exhausting himself before throngs of young supporters for years?

The first thing we must accept, which is a bit stunning, is that there is ample support for Biden. Of course, he was vice president during Obama's presidency, but this new energy for Biden does not come from his own campaign for president. The reality is that energy for Biden comes from fear of Trump on the one hand and fear of Sanders on the other. Most in the United States do not want full-blown fascism. However, it is no less certain that most in the United States see anything "socialistic" as an equal, albeit different danger than fascism. Many do not even know the difference. The desire to defeat Trump and Sanders can put Biden into the White House.[17] Above all, I would argue that what mobilizes the most support for Biden is what Rancière calls "the hatred of democracy."[18] People are genuinely afraid of anything other than the status quo, which both the left and right may challenge. Liberals in the United States are, for the most part, unmoved by mass rallies filled with young people opposed to racism, class inequality, and debt. In the face of Trump, they demand status quo conservatism. The entire so-called "democratic" system is not set up to appreciate protest or revolts but to silence them. The basic idea is that, if the revolt is reasonable, its message can and should be converted into some legible demand for capitalist elections. In short, following Rancière, to be reasonable, democracy must capitulate to oligarchy. That is the basis of what Rancière calls "hatred of democracy." Rancière has much to say about the vitality of democracy in our response to revolts. Where procedural democracy overrides the *demos*, the revolt may be the only thing truly outside of and against the oligarchy.

Your most recent work, The Communism of Love, *proposes a critical reading of the capitalist system mediated by love as a disruptive force.*[19] *I would like to ask you about this idea of love, which, with a few exceptions—Badiou's latest works, for example—is difficult to find in political science and in the social and human sciences in general. Furthermore, it has a rather negative connotation in the discourses of critical theory or radical thought. What are you looking for with the introduction of this idea? In what sense can love be a force against the logic of capital?*

Let me return to Enrique Dussel, especially as we are talking together here in Argentina. When Dussel thinks of love, he is thinking mainly of romantic

17. Indeed, it did.

18. Jacques Rancière, *Hatred of Democracy*, trans. Steve Corcoran (New York: Verso, 2006).

19. Richard Gilman-Opalsky, *The Communism of Love: An Inquiry into the Poverty of Exchange Value* (Chico: AK Press, 2020).

love and sexual relations. That is not just a tendency in Dussel's work but was already in Socrates and Plato. Dussel wrote only a little about love relations in *Philosophy of Liberation,* but he wrote of closeness to others, of "action directed toward proximity . . . I am not speaking about going toward a table, a chair, or a thing . . . to take it, buy it, sell it, or use it . . . I am speaking about approaching a person, of shortening the distance between someone who can accept or reject us, shake our hand or injure us, kiss or kill us."[20] Inasmuch as love shortens the distance between people, it is a praxis, "an approach to proximity."[21] Dussel argued that "the ethos of liberation is other-directed . . . it is love of the other as other."[22] Dussel devotes sections of *Philosophy of Liberation* not only to erotics, proximity, and liberation but also to the question of alienation. "The praxis of liberation . . . puts the system into question—not just as a possible or ideational questioning but as a questioning that opens a world from itself, its own road from within itself."[23] What Dussel means is that we cannot only think about how to destroy the existing order but that our idea of liberation must be grounded in practices and experiences that follow a different logic and *reveal* different ways of being-in-the-world, different possibilities for human relations beyond capitalist alienation. Dussel says that we must find an emancipatory path from what we know—that is, from our life experience.

For me, all of the above makes it obvious that we have to think about love if we are to think seriously about emancipatory politics. However, the truth is, as you say, that most radicals and revolutionaries have doubts about love, and most—not all—reject love as a political concept.

So, let me explain a bit about how I came to my theory of love. I was thinking about the engagement of critical theory with love, especially vis-à-vis Erich Fromm and Herbert Marcuse, when I came across a different book by Maurice Blanchot, *The Unavowable Community,* which has a chapter titled "The Community of Lovers."[24] What Blanchot talks about in this

---

20. Enrique Dussel, *Philosophy of Liberation,* trans. Aquilina Martinez and Christine Morkovsky (Eugene, OR: Wipf and Stock Publishers, 1985), 17.

21. Dussel, *Philosophy of Liberation,* 17.

22. Dussel, *Philosophy of Liberation,* 64.

23. Dussel, *Philosophy of Liberation,* 63.

24. Maurice Blanchot, *The Unavowable Community,* trans. Pierre Joris (New York: Station Hill, 1988).

chapter on lovers is the French revolts of 1968. I wondered what love could have to do with revolt. Now, as I was saying, there *was* an effort in critical theory in the mid-twentieth century—in Marcuse and mostly Fromm—to think about what I call "the communism of love." It was interesting to me that, after that period, political theory only lightly touched on love as a political concept because I think that Fromm framed important questions about love and capitalist society that called for further development. In books such as *The Sane Society*, *The Art of Loving*, and *To Have or to Be*, Fromm understood love not as a possession but as practice. He was interested in the question of what actually happens in the practical activity of love. Fromm reaches a conclusion that I accept: "The *principle* underlying capitalistic society and the *principle* of love are incompatible."[25] The practice of love is an active relation that is not an exchange relation and, thus, indicates human relations organized by logics contrary to the logic of capital. We do not treat people in love according to the logic of capitalist exchange that governs so much relationality in capitalist societies. The beloved other is not someone you own but rather someone you actively relate to in a particular way. The question is not merely sexual or romantic, for one must consider also how one actively relates to beloved friends, comrades, or other kindred spirits.

After Fromm, I read the major sociological theories on love but was frustrated when I continually came across narrow conceptions of love as one-to-one monogamous romantic and sexual relationships, as for example in the work of Eva Illouz. But much else happened in between Fromm and Illouz. For example, in 1962, Hannah Arendt scolded the Black writer and activist James Baldwin for talking about love as a political concept.[26] More or less reliably throughout political theory and philosophy, stretching all the way back to Plato's *Symposium*, love appears as a concept for the private affairs of romance and sex on the one hand or as too immaterial and inchoate for politics on the other.

However, what if we think of love not as a private relationship between two people, or of a small family, but as a noncapitalist logic of life. For

25. Erich Fromm, *The Art of Loving* (New York: Harper Perennial, 2006), 121.

26. Hannah Arendt, "The Meaning of Love in Politics: A Letter by Hannah Arendt to James Baldwin," cited at https://www.hannaharendt.net/index.php/han/article/view/95/156.

example, you mentioned to me that 40 percent of the Argentine population fully support neoliberal policies. Nearly half the population not only does not criticize capitalism but even wants more capitalism. Yet, what is happening in the privacy of their little love relations? There, in their friendships, the relationship to a child, to a lover, exchange relations would offend these same Argentines. They cannot accept that their young children should work for the right to food or that their partner should exchange sexual activity for money or anything else. In these private spaces, they would defend the communism of love but, of course, would never think about this different logic as communist. I claim that the reason the communism of love eludes so many people is because we do not think enough about both love and the meaning of communism. If people thought a little more about what love means in their own lives, they may realize that the best things that happen in the capitalist mode of life are the least capitalist things. If you think about your children, your friends, your comrades, all your relationships . . . If these relationships are healthy, then they are not based on exchange. You cannot tell a friend going through a hard time that you will agree to talk with them only in exchange for twenty dollars an hour. That would contradict the principle of friendship and could destroy the relationship. Capitalist relations do not govern the healthy relations within a typical family in Argentina. Exchange relations are not the relations of the family life and friendships of a significant percentage of people who are against communism.

Here is where Dussel's idea of starting toward emancipation from what we know seems to me so important. What if more people saw the communism of love in their everyday lives? Imagine if everyday people understood this and understood why they must defend their dearest human relations from the perverse logic of capitalist exchange relations. Furthermore, what if we could think of love—and this is perhaps a bit dangerous to suggest—as something like a universal aspiration, something like dignity and freedom? Who does not aspire to love? If love is necessarily and irreducibly communist, can we say that communism is a universal aspiration?

What is the relationship between this conception of love and the idea of communism in Marx? How does this interpretation of love dialogue with other readings, for example, in the field of liberation theology?

In relation to the idea of communism, an important part of *The Communism of Love* is dedicated to my study of *Grundrisse*. There, Marx speaks of communism often in terms of the *Gemeinwesen*, which in German refers to "community," "common sensibility," or "being-common in the world." In *Grundrisse,* Marx consistently thinks of communism as something destroyed by mercantile relationships. He thinks of communism when he attempts to understand how social relations are broken apart and replaced by commercial relations. He tries to understand *what happened to us*. For example, he marvels at how it came to pass that one only trusts another if that other leaves a deposit. Money replaces trust, or rather, stands in where trust is absent. "The individual carries his social power, as well as his bond with society, in his pocket."[27] In other words, money functions as social power and social bond: the more you have in your pocket, the more power and social trust you can leverage. However, it was not always that way. Earlier forms of life were not governed by money or by capitalist exchange relations. Toward the end of *Grundrisse,* just before the manuscript breaks off, Marx writes, "Exchange begins not between the individuals within a community, but rather at the point where the communities end—at their boundary, at the point of contact between different communities . . . The system of production founded on private exchange is, to begin with, the historic dissolution of naturally arisen communism."[28]

It is clear from *Grundrisse* that Marx's project, at its most fundamental level, is about actual and possible forms of life, so it is not surprising that Marxists continued to think about forms of life. If you read Rosa Luxemburg or Alexandra Kollontai, for example, you see that love has participated in the theory of communism in the past and that both love and communism are fundamentally about forms of life.

When Marx says in *Grundrisse* that exchange relations begin at the border between two communities, he means to say that they are alien inside the communities of naturally arisen communism. I argue, then, that thinking through the communism of love is not breaking with Marx's theory but rather reconnecting with the original ideas of communist theory, which go

27. Karl Marx, *Grundrisse,* trans. Martin Nicholaus (New York: Penguin Books, 1993), 157.

28. Marx, *Grundrisse,* 882.

back to Marx's own concerns about forms of life and the *Gemeinwesen*. Some would say—the Althusserians, for example—that this is too humanistic. I do not agree. What Marx wrote about forms of life and the *Gemeinwesen* should not be characterized as an idea belonging to a particular "school." When one reads the *Grundrisse*, one reads about forms of life. When one reads Marx, one reads a writer facing the political and economic reality of Manchester capitalism. Industrial capitalism was radically transforming life and society. Therefore, communism is inextricably linked to fundamental questions about forms of life. In that context, the question of love is neither naïve nor romantic; it is exactly the opposite. The question of love is a question of concrete experiences of real people in the real world. It is a question of what is desirable and possible.

Regarding the question of religion, in his book *The Soul at Work* Franco "Bifo" Berardi argues that Marxists and revolutionaries have long been afraid to talk about the soul because we believe the subject of the soul is the private property of theology.[29] However, Berardi explores a materialist conception of the soul as the living energy that animates the body. We could think of the soul in materialistic terms, as the energetic life activity of a human person. Berardi wondered why we would surrender the problem of the soul—insofar as we may think of the soul as an emotional or intellectual energy, or as the intensity, for example, in a work of art or musical performance—entirely to theology. I find something similar in Dussel's approach to historically religious questions. Dussel observes that all the world's religions contain substantively socialist and communist ideas and commitments and that all the world's religions contain emancipatory thinking about other possible worlds. We can find Marxist ideas in the story of Moses. This was crucial for Dussel, given his attention to Latin American contexts, liberation theology, and decolonizing theory. People will not come to the same purposes in the same ways.

> To be born among pygmies in Africa or in a Fifth Avenue neighborhood in New York is . . . to be born in another world; it is to be born spatially into a world that predetermines—radically, though not

29. Franco "Bifo" Berardi, *The Soul at Work: From Alienation to Autonomy,* trans. Francesca Cadel and Giuseppina Mecchia (Los Angeles: Semiotext(e), 2009).

> absolutely—the orientation of one's future *proyecto*. The one born among the pygmies will strive to become a great hunter of animals; the one born in New York will strive to become a great entrepreneur (a hunter of persons).[30]

Is Marxism only sensible in New York? Perhaps not so much to the capitalist entrepreneur, but what about to Indigenous people in Chiapas, Mexico or throughout Africa? No one would suggest that capitalism has no bearing in Argentina, Chile, Ghana, or Liberia. Dussel argues that there are both ontological and epistemological differences that make different locations into different worlds, yet no place on Earth does not need a philosophy of liberation. The question of liberation theology is, in part, how to reach ideas about emancipation through religion, and that means not barricading Marxist ideas from religion; and with Berardi's project, it means not barricading religious ideas from Marxist thought.

How does this relate to the question of love? We should not surrender the concept of love to theology, poetry, or to the private and ineffable. If we think that love is a useful concept, as I argue, that it is an experience with a communist logic of human relationality, then we must not be afraid to take it up and think it through. Anyway, no one wants to live a life without love, even if everyone defines that word differently. What could the practice of love mean beyond the private lives of individual homes, beyond the musings of poets and theologians? There may be something universal in the human aspiration to love, an everyday sort of thing, and no philosopher can ignore that.

30. Dussel, *Philosophy of Liberation*, 25.

CHAPTER 2

Inversion and Abolition

Upside-Down

The capitalist world is upside-down.[1] A world governed by capital is a world organized and ruled by fatal logics. Logics of profit and private property continue to govern everyday life from childhood to death (from childcare to the death and dying industries). Our ability to pay largely decides our ability to secure the most basic things, from food and shelter to education and healthcare. However, we are at a historical juncture where not even ability to pay can secure the psychosocial health of children and a livable planet for future generations. Concentrations of wealth determine the form and content of political power. Children around the world are taught—and know well—that money should not determine life. Yet it does.

The current situation is a thoroughly documented catastrophe. "Close to half of humanity subsists on less than $5.50 per day. The world's few billionaires own more than the poorest 60 percent of the planet. Wealth taxes are at historic lows for the rich and corporations. Twenty percent of the world's children—more than a quarter of a billion—cannot attend school. Ten thousand people die unnecessarily every day, from causes directly related to poverty."[2] These are some of the economic features of the capitalist

1. This chapter is based on a short essay originally published in the journal *Theory in Action*: "Inversion and Abolition: On the Upside-Down Logics of Wealth, Poverty, and Capital," *Theory in Action* 11, no. 3 (July 2018). To develop it into the present chapter, I have substantially expanded it with new research.

2. China Miéville, *A Spectre, Haunting: On the* Communist Manifesto (Chicago: Haymarket Books, 2022), 2.

present, related to ecological crisis, too. China Miéville locates one antithesis to ecological health and well-being in capital's logic of accumulation. "In the ruthless pursuit of profit over the needs of the biome or humanity, capital accumulation has led to cataclysmic upheaval and death. Whatever the desires of any individual capitalists, whatever the pious declarations about 'corporate responsibility,' at a social level that fundamental dynamic toward accumulation is definitional, and will always be stronger than any other tendency . . . it's overwhelmingly likely that this capitalist dynamic will fail to adequately address the climate crisis."[3] Indeed, how could a logic of constant growth, expansion, and extraction do anything but exacerbate the ecological predicament, the latter of which calls for the exactly opposite orientation of degrowth, sustainability, and conservation?[4]

Harder to see, and less commonly addressed, are the psychosocial harms of the capitalist world order. Recently, Gabor Maté has accounted for some of this often-invisible side of the problem:

> Although the world's most advanced capitalist country evinces the rawest individualistic ethic, leaving the majority of its people mired in insecurity, we are not speaking of a uniquely American trend . . . The Organization for Economic Co-operation and Development reported that pressures on the middle class around the world have increased since the 1980s. Thus on the very terrain in which capitalism stakes its greatest claim to success—economic achievement—we find many people in a state of chronic uncertainty and loss of control, subject to stress-inducing fears that translate into disturbances of the hormonal apparatus, of the immune system, and of the entire organism. No wonder, then, that insecurity about work or the loss of it can instigate disease.[5]

Maté studies how emotional stress, growing anxiety, and intensifications of insecurity in everything from pandemics like COVID-19 to war and the

3. Miéville, *A Spectre, Haunting*, 149–50.

4. See Kohei Saito, *Marx in the Anthropocene: Towards the Idea of Degrowth Communism* (Cambridge: Cambridge University Press, 2023).

5. Gabor Maté, *The Myth of Normal: Trauma, Illness and Healing in a Toxic Culture* (New York: Avery Books, 2022), 281.

forced migrations of refugees are connected to the globalization of a capitalist form of life. Capitalists know how to benefit from the stressors they generate too. "The corporate elite, served by its amply compensated minions in the fields of science and psychology, well know how to profit off the stress generated by the system that gives them power. They wouldn't be doing their jobs if they didn't."[6] Unsurprisingly, massive layoffs and exoduses of outsourced labor are usually boons of windfall profit for capitalists, as are pandemics for pharmaceutical companies and wars for the oil and gas industries and for security, arms, and defense corporations.

One upside-down perspective views capital as wealth, but it is not. Capital is a power, whereas wealth is a certain property (or a composite of aggregate properties). Poverty specifies a relative absence of properties, including those properties needed to secure some of the most basic things mentioned above. It is remarkable and absurd that capitalism has come to be associated with wealth. Global macroeconomic data shows that capitalism and its neoliberal growth have in fact increased income inequality and intensified the brutal exclusions of poverty.[7] It is upside-down that we do not associate capitalism with inequality and poverty. It is upside down, for example, that we do not associate inequality and poverty in India, Liberia, Haiti, Honduras, Indonesia, Colombia, and El Salvador with the ruthless and rampant capitalism there. Although we should think of these countries (and other so-called third world countries) as perfect images of capitalism, we tend to make capitalist icons out of the things we like *best* in the US and Western Europe, such as our preponderance of high-tech gadgetry and affluent infrastructure. Meanwhile, capitalist culture and economic analysis continue to proliferate some form of David Ricardo's apologetics to rationalize and excuse the things we like *least* in the US and Western Europe, such as ongoing racism and growing inequality.[8]

At the same time, even from the more narrow economistic perspectives of Thomas Piketty and friends at the Paris and London Schools of Economics, it would make more sense to associate capitalism with poverty. Recently,

6. Maté, *The Myth of Normal*, 304.

7. Saskia Sassen, *Expulsions: Brutality and Complexity in the Global Economy* (Cambridge, MA: Harvard University Press, 2014).

8. See Karl Marx, "Crisis Theory" in *The Marx-Engels Reader: Second Edition*, ed. Robert C. Tucker (New York: W. W. Norton & Company, 1978), 444, 448–49.

OXFAM reported, "Since 2015, the richest 1 percent has owned more wealth than the rest of the planet" and that "eight men now own the same amount of wealth as the poorest half of the world."[9] Compare this report from 2017 to the more recent account given above by Miéville in 2022, and the old capitalist saw of "things getting better" is quickly debunked. A longer comparative account, such as that of Piketty, shows the same tendencies of worsening and multiplying crises.[10] Despite all of this, common understandings remain so upside-down as to imagine capitalism as causally related to wealth—a total inversion of the reality. Capitalism is far more responsible for poverty than wealth.

The Poverty of Wealth (First Inversion)

In Plato's *Republic,* Socrates claims that a healthy city must defend itself against wealth. Wealth "produces luxury, idleness, and innovation."[11]

Socrates worries about *luxury* as a subversion of the more vital concern for human needs and social health. Luxury shifts the focus to what Guy Debord would much later call "pseudo-needs."[12] Socrates worries also about *idleness* as the inactivity of those deprived of their basic motivations for doing anything. His example is that of the "potter who's gotten rich" and comes to care less about their craft.[13] Socrates wrongly assumes that the potter's only motivation is money. The evidence of his error can be found in a long history of art created in a world of unpaid artists who are almost invariably punished by capital for their creative activities. Parents everywhere tremble in fear at the prospects of their children trying to make a life out of pottery, poetry, music, philosophy, painting, or performance art. For good reason

9. See "An Economy for the 99%," OXFAM Briefing Paper, January 2017, https://www.oxfam.org/sites/www.oxfam.org/files/file_attachments/bp-economy-for-99-percent-160117-summ-en.pdf.

10. Thomas Piketty, *Capital in the Twenty-First Century*, trans. Arthur Goldhammer (Cambridge, MA: Harvard University Press, 2014).

11. Plato, *The Republic of Plato*, trans. Allan Bloom (New York: Basic Books, 1991), 422a, 99.

12. Guy Debord, *The Society of the Spectacle,* trans. Donald Nicholson-Smith (New York: Zone Books, 1995), 33.

13. Plato, *The Republic*, 421d, 99.

too, because anyone who has lived a little in the capitalist world sees how the star system rewards precious few artists (often not the greatest ones, lest you think that capital only appreciates the best) and makes casualties out of most of the world's artists. Finally, *innovation*—a term always celebrated by capitalists—is condemned by Socrates as one of the evils of wealth. With innovation, Socrates worries about all the experiments in doing new and dangerous things that come from wielding wealth beyond any regard for real human needs. Here, we may think of long histories of war and political corruption, urban and suburban developments of ecological destruction, and isolation ameliorated (and simultaneously exacerbated) technologically by social media in an anxious, lonely world. Not every innovation is good news.

His mistakes notwithstanding, Socrates was right to be worried about the poverty of the wealthy society. Indeed, one has to wonder if we will continue to envy our wealthy societies as they continue to kill us. One key question of the imagination is whether we can wrest the concepts of wealth and poverty from their capitalist designations and reconceive them in better directions.

The Wealth of Poverty (Second Inversion)

Socrates also condemns poverty as something against which every healthy city should guard. No one on Earth wants to be impoverished. That alone is sufficient reason to abolish poverty and the whole class of concentrated impoverishment, just as generations of revolutionaries have imagined.

Socrates says that poverty produces "illiberality and wrongdoing as well as innovation."[14] By *illiberality,* Socrates means the "vulgarity" of the absence of cultural or scholarly refinement, which he dislikes. He also worries about *wrongdoing,* including the whole field of criminality. Once again, *innovation,* which he previously named as an evil of wealth, reappears as an evil of poverty. For Socrates, this is because some of the most innovative people of history are criminals, rebels, and other so-called "wrongdoers." Long before the empirical vindications of criminology, Socrates understood that crime was less the cause of criminals than the conditions of life that are crime's *raison d'être.*

14. Plato, *The Republic,* 422a, 99.

Socrates could not, however, understand the contemporary condition of poverty as so eloquently described by John Berger: "The poverty of our century is unlike that of any other. It is not, as poverty was before, the result of natural scarcity, but of a set of priorities imposed upon the rest of the world by the rich. Consequently, the modern poor are not pitied . . . but written off as trash. The twentieth century consumer economy has produced the first culture for which a beggar is a reminder of nothing."[15]

In contrast to Socrates's fear of what poverty produces in the impoverished, I see a potential wealth that is not the property of the powerful. As Berger observes, the ruling class may despise and write off the poor, but a long international history of revolts reveals that poverty also generates forms of being-against the existing reality.

John Holloway has written about a different kind of richness than that of the capitalists. He rethinks our richness as not what encloses us but rather "the force that can break that enclosure," defining our richness as "our absolute working-out of our creative potentialities, our absolute movement of becoming. Start from *us,* not from *them* . . . from our overflowing against that which contains us."[16] In short, we can and must think about the powers of the supposedly powerless, about what impoverished people can do—not with the capital they do not wield but with hope and indignation instead.

Abolitionist Perspective (Inversion of the Inverted)

Socrates wanted a society guarded against the twin evils of poverty and wealth. A capitalist society could try to guard against poverty and wealth with, one might imagine, a minimum and a maximum wage, a global tax, or by way of some other regulation. However, after more than two hundred years of failed efforts to do these things, a certain conclusion is clearer than ever: We cannot govern capital with laws that are themselves governed by capital, because capital governs the governments of the world. We cannot count on governments to turn on their master. Therefore, an abolitionist perspective is inevitable and necessary. Both capitalist wealth and poverty call

15. John Berger, *Keeping a Rendezvous* (New York: Pantheon Books, 1991), 227.
16. John Holloway, *Hope in Hopeless Times* (London: Pluto Press, 2022), 6.

out for abolition, and we need an abolitionist orientation that rejects all of the inverted logics of a world governed by capital. This means, among other things, that—*everywhere we are able and know how to do it*—we must bring to light the root causes of our problems and the material necessity (and ethical obligation) of a total opposition, of a total inversion of the inverted.

Ruth Wilson Gilmore is right to observe the utopian dimension of an abolitionist comportment. "To me, abolition is utopian in the sense that it's looking forward to a world in which prisons are not necessary because not only are the political-economic motives behind mass incarceration gone, but also the instances in which people might harm each other are minimized because the causes for that harm (setting aside, for the moment, psychopaths) are minimized as well."[17] Essentially, Gilmore is an abolitionist who wants to deal with mass incarceration and crime by getting to their root causes. To do this, we have to extend the same abolitionist logic to the root causes of capitalist wealth and poverty. Abolitionist politics is radical, and appears inevitably as utopian, but this utopian horizon is—paradoxically of course—also practical, as we shall see.

Gilmore is not only an abolitionist but also a geographer. Her idea of "abolition geography" concretizes the positive dimension of abolition. "Abolition geography starts from the homely premise that freedom is a place. Place-making is normal human activity: we figure out how to combine people, and land, and other resources with our social capacity to organize ourselves in a variety of ways, whether to stay put or go wandering."[18] Abolition geography is not about getting rid of what we oppose but about the creation of new spaces and places of human freedom. Human beings are always looking for spaces and places to be and to become, and abolition geography juxtaposes such places of freedom and open possibility to spaces of confinement, repression, and punishment.

An abolitionist may do many things. The being-against of global uprisings is one thing. Other things may include artwork, writing, printmaking, music, discussion circles, protest, disobedience, sabotage, and a wide range of expressions of disaffection fueled by our radical imaginations. An abolitionist does

17. Ruth Wilson Gilmore, *Abolition Geography: Essays Towards Liberation* (New York: Verso, 2022), 468–69.

18. Wilson Gilmore, *Abolition Geography*, 474–75.

not want to conserve the status quo, or defend what already exists (like a conservative, or the pseudo-insurrectionists of the January 6, 2021 paramilitary deployment of Donald Trump's presidency). An abolitionist does not adopt a politics of accepting the unacceptable, as do practical capitalist liberals. Abolitionists today want to recover and enliven practices of resistance and revolt that emerged around the same time that the anarchist and communist trajectories took off: "Slave resistance was everywhere in the in the 1830s. When the *Amistad* revolt took place, everybody saw it as part of something much bigger. The abolitionists saw it that way; the Africans saw it that way; that was part of its power. To situate the event in a larger field of struggle is important."[19]

According to Marcus Rediker above, slave resistance understood itself as part of a larger field of emancipatory struggle. The 1830s and 1840s were also a time of burgeoning revolutionary theory, as communist and anarchist imaginaries ignited around the globe shortly thereafter, in the second half of the nineteenth century. Slave revolts and theories of revolts were animated by abolitionist hopes.

Angela Y. Davis has long argued for the continuation of abolitionist politics after the legal abolition of slavery. Davis picks up the term "abolition democracy" from W. E. B. Du Bois's *Black Reconstruction*.[20] Following Du Bois, Davis points out that the legal abolition of slavery was the negation of a particular institution, but the larger project of which that accomplishment was one major victory would need to be ongoing. Davis argues that continuing abolitionism today demands a confrontation with the death penalty, mass incarceration, ongoing sexisms and racisms, capitalism, and empire. Following Achille Mbembe, I would add the necessity of an abolitionist confrontation with colonialism. As Mbembe puts it, the colonial world is democracy's "double," its "nocturnal face," and "no democracy exists without its double, without its colony . . . The colony is not external to democracy and is not necessarily located outside its walls. Democracy bears the colony within it, just as colonialism bears democracy, often in the guise of a mask."[21]

19. Marcus Rediker, "Native Resistance: A Conversation with Historian Marcus Rediker" in *Works and Days* 65/66, 67/68, vol. 33 & 34, 2016–2017, 100.

20. Angela Y. Davis, *Abolition Democracy: Beyond Empire, Prisons, and Torture* (New York: Seven Stories Press, 2005), 91.

21. Achille Mbembe, *Necropolitics*, trans. Steve Corcoran (Durham: Duke University Press, 2019), 27.

However, let us go back to Du Bois for a moment. An abolitionist recognizes unacceptable logics that must be opposed categorically, stem, root, and seed. Anything short of total opposition is inadequate, unjust, and morally indefensible. "The propaganda which made the abolition movement terribly real was the Fugitive Slave—the piece of intelligent humanity who could say: I have been owned like an ox. I stole my own body and now I am hunted by law and lash to be made an ox again. By no conception of justice could such logic be answered."[22] To confront the fugitive slave as fleeing humanity, and to seek, in the face of that humanity, to return fugitive slaves to dehumanizing private property, makes the case for abolition clear.

However, the disastrous limitations of reformist approaches to slavery, which Davis aims to address in ongoing abolitionist politics, was already well understood by Du Bois in 1935. "Slavery was not abolished even after the Thirteenth Amendment. There were four million freedmen and most of them on the same plantation, doing the same work that they did before emancipation, except as their work had been interrupted and changed by the upheaval of war. Moreover, they were getting about the same wages and apparently were going to be subject to slave codes modified only in name . . . They had been freed practically with no land or money, and, save in exceptional cases, without legal status and without protection."[23] White supremacy and the slave's form of life did not die with the legal abolition of slavery. Not even the slave codes disappeared, and indeed, it would take another full century before the legal end of Jim Crow segregation. As mass incarceration, racial profiling, police brutality, and recent movements against all three show, the legal end of segregation was by no means the end of the problem either. Thus, abolitionists have more to do.

This is where Davis's crucial insistence on the continuation of abolitionist politics comes in. "In actual practice, both Emancipation and the authorization of penal servitude combined to create an immense black presence within southern prisons and to transform the character of punishment into a means of managing former slaves as opposed to addressing problems of serious crime."[24] The legal abolition of chattel slavery was not the abolition

22. W. E. B. Du Bois, *Black Reconstruction in America: 1860–1880* (New York: The Free Press, 1992), 20.

23. Du Bois, *Black Reconstruction in America*, 188.

24. Angela Y. Davis, "Racialized Punishment and Prison Abolition" in *The Angela Y. Davis Reader*, ed. by Joy James (Malden: Blackwell Publishing, 1998), 99.

of white supremacy and racism. Therefore, white supremacy and racism had to find a new institution, a new central location, namely the criminal "justice" system, with growing incarceration and penal servitude. When we abolish one institution of white supremacy but white supremacy remains, it finds another institution.

Davis tracks how incarceration after Emancipation was less about crime than about racist power, containment, and enslavement by other means. "The incarceration of former slaves served not so much to affirm the rights and liberties of the freedmen and women (i.e., as rights and liberties of which they could be deprived), nor to discipline a potential labor force; rather it symbolically emphasized that black people's social status continued to be that of slaves, even though the institution of slavery had been disestablished."[25] The prison became a newfangled plantation-institution, as well as a constant reminder, and even a threat, that Black people could and would still be seized and held against their wills and freedoms.

This point is key to Davis's argument for ongoing abolitionist politics. Insofar as people think of the prison system as totally disconnected from slavery, insofar as people believe dominant disciplinary myths about the prison as a public safety institution protecting society from dangerous criminals, prison abolition may sound more frightening than prisons to many. "I emphasize the need to disarticulate notions of punishment from crime because I want to argue for a serious consideration of abolitionist strategies to dismantle the prison system in its present role as an institution which preserves existing structures of racism as well as creates more complicated modes of racism in US society."[26] According to Davis, then, it is necessary to understand *both* how the prison system maintains a racialized order of society in accordance with white supremacy and how in some ways it makes things worse by complicating and obscuring racist brutality behind the screen of "criminal justice."

One indispensable feature of an abolitionist orientation like Davis's is that it reveals how formal and legal channels of reform, including the courts and justice system, are dead ends. We cannot address the issues of abolitionists within the limits of the systems that abolitionists directly target. It is for

25. Davis, "Racialized Punishment and Prison Abolition," 100.
26. Davis, "Racialized Punishment and Prison Abolition," 105.

the same reason that Marxist abolitionists thinking about capitalism cannot address structural problems of political economy with capitalist elections. No one is surprised to discover that the abolition of capitalism is not an option on the ballots of capitalist elections. Davis is fully aware of this point. "Issues raised by abolition, especially when we consider the abolition of slavery as organically linked to the abolition of prisons and capital punishment, help us to recognize the pitfalls of abstract equality and formal democracy. One of the glaring contradictions enabled by the cohabitation of poverty and racism, on the one hand, and legal equality and democracy, on the other, can be found in the soaring population behind bars and the cavalier manner in which increasing numbers of people are put to death."[27] Simply put, liberal capitalist societies maintain all the splendor of their superficial commitments to equality and democracy simultaneously with spiraling rises in the mass incarceration of impoverished people of color. When one takes a closer look, the history and realities of the prison system blow our beloved mythologies about egalitarian capitalist democracies to smithereens.

Abolitionists, therefore, must always set their sights on what demands condemnation and requires abolition in the present. Yes, abolition is about getting rid of something, pulling it up at the roots. However, one negation is never enough. In the field of mathematics, the multiplication of negatives produces positives, and in the field of revolutionary theory, negation is not only negative. Indeed, negation is the heart of revolution in permanence. The abolitionist idea captures well what Raya Dunayevskaya called "the power of negativity."[28] In fact, Dunayevskaya wrote about abolitionist politics in a powerful way:

> The movement renounced all traditional politics, considering all political parties of the day as "corrupt." They were inter-racial and in a slave society preached and practiced Negro equality. They were distinguished as well for inspiring, aligning with and fighting for equality of women in an age when the women had neither the right to the ballot

27. Angela Y. Davis, *The Meaning of Freedom and Other Difficult Dialogues* (San Francisco: City Lights Books, 2012), 106.

28. Raya Dunayevskaya, *The Power of Negativity: Selected Writings on the Dialectic in Hegel and Marx*, eds. by Peter Hudis and Kevin B. Anderson (Lanham: Lexington Books, 2002).

> nor to property nor to divorce. They were internationalist, covering Europe with their message . . . They sought no rewards of any kind, fighting for the pure idea, though that meant facing the hostility of the national government, the state, the local police, and the best citizens who became the most unruly mobs.[29]

Like Du Bois and Davis, Dunayevskaya hoped for a second phase of abolition through which to continue revolutionary struggle, but she observed instead: "Soon after the war and the abolition of slavery, Abolitionism as a movement vanished from the scene."[30] The fact that many abolitionists saw their major aims realized with the abolition of legal slavery was catastrophic for radical politics, which could have instead trained abolitionist sights on new targets and kept on going.

We must not forget, however, that this world has never been without its abolitionists. Abolitionism, as a real movement, may be temporarily demobilized or halted. An irrepressible-repressed abolitionism may be kept down only for so long, sometimes as the result of its own despair or perhaps in search of a new form and content (a new aim and expression), but it is never gone for good. Even slavery faced abolitionists before major abolitionist movements gathered traction.

Marcus Rediker presents the rousing story of Benjamin Lay: "As the first person to boycott slavery-produced commodities, Benjamin pioneered the politics of consumption and initiated a tactic that would become central to the ultimate success of abolition in the nineteenth century. In his time, Benjamin may have been the most radical person on the planet. He helps us to understand what was thinkable and what was politically and morally possible in the first half of the eighteenth century—and what may be possible now. It was more than we thought."[31] The example of Lay demonstrates two crucial points for our purposes. First, abolitionist movement has to begin somewhere, with a certain set of claims and actions. It has to have a starting position, a particular framing, and tactics. Second, abolitionists insist on the

29. Raya Dunayevskaya, *American Civilization on Trial: Black Masses as Vanguard* (Chicago: News and Letters, 2003), 34 (original in italics).

30. Dunayevskaya, *American Civilization on Trial*, 37.

31. Marcus Rediker, *The Fearless Benjamin Lay: The Quaker Dwarf who Became the First Revolutionary Abolitionist* (Boston: Beacon Press, 2017), 149–50.

possibility of the supposedly impossible. Opponents deride abolitionists as impractical utopians until others come along and see that what is desirable and just may be possible too.

There is yet something else about abolitionist politics to retrieve and recognize. Abolitionists like Benjamin Lay, Harriet Tubman, John Brown, Frederick Douglass, and Sojourner Truth were not bourgeois philosophers or legislators of the ruling class. Rediker makes this point sharp and clear with the example of Lay. "Benjamin's revolutionary abolitionism suggests a new genealogy of antislavery, the history of which has long been associated with elites such as Voltaire and the late eighteenth-century Enlightenment. Benjamin belongs to a history of abolition 'from below,' which has a longer trajectory . . . He challenges a history that has long emphasized middle- and upper-class abolitionist 'saints,' from William Wilberforce to Lewis Tappan."[32] The idea of abolition from below demands emphasis. When we talk about struggles against colonization in India, Algeria, and elsewhere, it is important to appreciate the fact that "getting free" required an abolitionist comportment emanating from below, from the agency of the colonized. Frantz Fanon understood this well, and we must too.[33]

One thing that today's abolitionists must everywhere resist and reject is the capitalist logic that perpetuates a pathological results-orientation according to which we may only value every action, effort, or initiative by its measurable and direct outcomes. When Egyptians abolish one regime and end up with another unacceptable one, the pathological results-orientation quickly declares the revolution a failure, predictably saying, "Look! No good has come from it! It was all for naught!" Aside from the fact that such declarations of failure are demonstrably false, we must also keep in mind that the abolition of the existing world is not an activity suited for the corporate appraisal of outcomes. What abolitionists have always done throughout human history, and in every context, is not something to measure like commodity production or customer satisfaction. We cannot measure abolitionist success in terms of an accounting of direct or immediate results. Therefore, abolitionists must resist and reject the pathological results-orientation,

32. Rediker, *The Fearless Benjamin Lay*, 148.

33. See Frantz Fanon, *Toward the African Revolution: Political Essays,* trans. Haakon Chevalier (New York: Grove Press, 1967).

denouncing it as the distinguishing feature of a method of analysis that is in fact the special product and property of capital. An insidious capitalist logic holds hostage the far richer and better understanding of value that we use to appreciate our lives in their *real fullness*, and we must not subject our struggles and movements to the reductionist thinking of our enemies.

We need abolitionists to keep on going, to keep on being abolitionists. Abolitionists must consider—*situated as we are*—how we may contribute to a continuation of abolitionism in new ways. Earlier in this chapter, we reviewed the appalling realities of an upside-down world ruled by money and the logic of capital. In this upside-down world, it is commonly held that there is no wealth or richness among the impoverished, although histories of abolitionism and decolonization show that real power gathers in rising tides from below. In this upside-down world, we see the poverty of the ruling class, impoverished in terms of their ethical regard and sense of justice, incapable as they are of seeing the glaring injustice of what they possess. Today's abolitionists must put *all* our talents in the service of confronting and overturning the inverted logics that govern this upside-down world. White supremacy continues to rear its hydra heads. We know that its history and ongoing reality are part of the defense of a capitalist reality that depends on racialized divisions of labor, demographic stratifications of inequality, and a criminal "justice" system that never wanted to kiss the slave system goodbye. We do not need to stop there. We will not. We cannot stop, not until human life finally and fully betrays the logic of capital and insists on the many healthy logics of a *common wealth*.

Let us now turn to an example of the kinds of rising tides we need.

CHAPTER 3

Horizons of the George Floyd Rebellion

Ill Will Editions: *In your work, you have expressed an interest in thinking a "politics against politics," namely, a form of political experience, action, and thinking asymmetrical with the professional forms of "classical politics" in the West.*[1] *The George Floyd Rebellion has combined various orders of political action, from symbolic protest-style marches to ballistic clashes with police officers, the destruction of state-owned and corporate property trashing, burning, and looting, as well as the occupation of public spaces and the push for "autonomous zones." We have the feeling that it is a mistake to lazily conflate all of these different elements into one big "social movement." Among friends, we refer instead to the initial phase of the rebellion, marked by the material attack on capitalist and state infrastructure as the "real movement," which then (as happened already with Ferguson) devolved or was recuperated into the form of a "social movement" that coheres more tightly with the interests and agendas of established NGO's and leftist protest managers. Overall, the trend seems to be for the social movement to supplant the real movement. How can your idea of a "politics against politics" help us parse and differentiate the current cycle of struggle into its different elements?*

Richard Gilman-Opalsky: The concept of politics against politics is, in many ways, the beating heart of my work. That has been true from the beginning,

1. In the immediate wake of the George Floyd Rebellion that broke out at the height of COVID-19 lockdowns, Adrian Wohlleben interviewed me for *Ill Will* online magazine. The interview is presented here with some revisions and elaborations for the purposes of this book.

since my first book on transgressive counterpublics and the Zapatista rebellion in Mexico.[2] One way to elaborate on the concept and your question would be through what the Latin American philosopher Enrique Dussel calls "the political field."[3] Dussel finds the following three figures on the political field: *potestas, potentia,* and *hyperpotentia. Potestas* refers to the entire institutional apparatus of politics, including the police, prisons, courts, military, etc. *Potentia* refers to the heterogeneous array of people outside of *potestas.* The people of *potentia* are most everyone on Earth, since *potentia* is composed of everyone outside of the ruling class. Then there is *hyperpotentia,* which refers to the various states of rebellion and revolt that break out when sectors of *potentia* rise up to confront and contest the powers of *potestas.*

On Dussel's political field, the institutional apparatus of politics is just one factor. The problem is what Dussel calls the "fetishization of power."[4] Our pathological attraction to seeing the head of state as the locus of power leads us to think of political power as the private property of the formal institutions of government. When we think "politics," we then think of heads of state and the political class. Dussel warns against this as a corruption that fixes political discourse to elections, public policy, and concepts of justice that pass through the cops and the courts. One could say that "politics against politics" means, first of all, breaking the fetishization of the power of the official political class, the ruling class as such. Opposed to their form of politics are the active upheavals of *hyperpotentia.*

In my work, I generally agree with this, although unlike Dussel, I want to push *potestas* off the field as such. I insist that *potestas* is already the private property of capital, which means that the governments of the world are in fact already governed by capital and have been for a long time. Essentially, C. Wright Mills was right in 1956 to diagnose the entrenchment of the power elite; we have been living under grotesque permutations of Mills's theory ever since.[5] To speak of *potestas* is to speak of the toolbox of capital. The formal institutions of government are essentially subservient to and faithfully serve capital. For this reason, the politics that have always interested me are

---

2. Richard Gilman-Opalsky, *Unbounded Publics: Transgressive Public Spheres, Zapatismo, and Political Theory* (Lanham: Rowman and Littlefield, 2008).
3. Enrique Dussel, *Twenty Theses on Politics* (Durham: Duke University Press, 2008).
4. Dussel, *Twenty Theses on Politics*, 30–32.
5. C. Wright Mills, *The Power Elite* (New York: Oxford University Press, 1956).

those that materialize abolitionist forces from below.[6] According to political science, such forces are only ever pre-political because they merely aspire to become "real politics." According to some within radical milieus, these forces are "post-political," which highlights their abandoned hope in *potestas*. However, I do not think we should allow our enemies to have the concept of politics to themselves. We cannot leave it to them, so we have to think of a politics against politics.

This means we have to find other ways of mobilizing our disaffections than to channel them into legible demands for the established powers of *potestas*. In the register of legible demands, every protest against capitalist power ends up translated into something acceptable to capitalist power, or discarded as irrational violence. Contrary to this, politics against politics means shifting from asking the political class to do something to refuting its power directly; it means experimenting with politics outside of and against the institutional apparatus of politics. We are trying to think about politics by other means than politics.

This is all rather abstract, and you can end up with some kind of categorical rubric ungrounded in actual events. We cannot trade actual events for analytical rubrics. It is helpful to consider the present cycle of struggle in the US. We could say that the uprisings sparked by the murder of George Floyd mark a passage from *potentia* to *hyperpotentia*. That much is true, but what we find in the current uprisings is, as you point out, a range of very different things.

Some of those things are ultimately fettered to *potestas*. For example, calls for justice for George Floyd that center on the state's punishment of the cops do not break the fetishization of power. Demands for nonlethal weaponry and body cameras may be helpful, but they are fundamentally conservative initiatives despite the fact that they sometimes announce themselves in the streets. What is more interesting, and more dangerous from the point of view of capitalist power, are some of the other things we find in the uprisings: calls to defund the police mark a possible passageway to a more abolitionist position; riots and revolt, including property destruction or looting; the CHOP/CHAZ commune in Seattle. I think a lot of what is happening in this cycle of

6. For a definition and discussion of what I mean by "abolitionist forces from below," see Chapter 2 above.

revolt does contain some real threats to the existing state of things, an existing reality that we must abolish.

So, yes, lazy conflations are dangerous. Some of the content in this recent cycle of uprising belongs to what you call "social movement," a sustained form of public pressure to get police accountability and other things through the system, by way of *potestas*. However, there are also bigger imaginations at work there. We should not defend all #BLM activity as if it were totally pacifist in order to calm the fears of those who always denounce the so-called violence of revolts. People worried about the violence of Black revolt are never so worried about the everyday quotidian violence of white supremacy and capitalism. They have no visible opposition to looters like AT&T or to long histories of looted labor. Guy Debord understood some of these crucial points roughly sixty years ago, while thinking about the 1965 uprising in Watts, Los Angeles:

> Looting is a natural response to the unnatural and inhuman society of commodity abundance. It instantly undermines the commodity as such, and it also exposes what the commodity ultimately implies: the army, the police and the other specialized detachments of the state's monopoly of armed violence. What is a policeman? He is the active servant of the commodity, the man in complete submission to the commodity, whose job is to ensure that a given product of human labor remains a commodity, with the magical property of having to be paid for . . . In rejecting the humiliation of being subject to police, the blacks are at the same time rejecting the humiliation of being subject to commodities.[7]

Debord's brilliant analysis remains useful, however agonizing the fact that it requires fresh repetition decade after decade.

At the same time, we should be careful about a different kind of conflation, which would see the George Floyd uprisings as "the initial phase of the rebellion." Yes, it is a phase of rebellion, but it is not an initial phase. It is

7. Guy Debord, "The Decline and Fall of the Spectacle-Commodity Economy" in *Situationist International Anthology*, ed. and trans. by Ken Knabb (Berkeley: Bureau of Public Secrets, 2006), 197–98.

a resumption (not a repetition) of revolt with a long and often-interrupted history. It is not quite right to say that revolt interrupts everyday life. I think it is fair to say that everyday life interrupts the revolt, the latter of which is ongoing in a sporadic but discontinuous history of struggle. Black revolt in the US today, for example, marks a nodal point in a continuity of Black revolt stretching back to early slave revolts. There is no repetition here. It is a resumption and continuity, a picking up where earlier efforts left off. It is, to my mind, connected to the premise of ongoing abolitionism (discussed in Chapter 2). We should not be too surprised when that which is not finished keeps going.

The concept of a politics against politics is helpful inasmuch as it deepens our understanding and appreciation of the limits of the official institutions of politics, which the left and right continue to fetishize in dangerous ways. While politics against politics can help us to distinguish the demand for greater police accountability from the call for the abolition of the police, it cannot help us differentiate other elements in the current cycle of struggle, such as what differentiates property destruction from looting or an occupation from a commune. However, politics against politics does help us to look around for power, to look at each other, instead of always looking up to some kind of Hobbesian Leviathan. We should remember that the original fourteenth century idea of the Leviathan was a sea monster or Satan not from above but from below.

You've suggested that "if the sense and sensibility of capital is what we oppose, let us become capital's nonsense, its opposite sensibility." By contrast, the well-known claim that "riots are the language of the unheard" has once again been trotted out in response to the George Floyd Rebellion. Is it correct to think of acts such as rioting, looting, and fighting the police as a language? If so, what is communicated therein and to whom? Is it a good idea to view language as fundamentally communicative? If so, must we broaden our view of "communication"? Or, is language perhaps better thought of as occupied enemy territory, a field ruled by dominant forces that conducts power to and across us through nonlinguistic illocutionary factors, as Deleuze and Guattari (following Canetti) famously argued? If the latter, does it make sense to treat riots as "communicative," or should we question the allegedly communicative function of discourse as doing something other than merely communicating—maybe it's more about disciplining and controlling us?

For instance, we can look at the way the media and Trump speak of the riots: it's fairly obvious that they have little interest in understanding them but move directly to dividing and splitting them into "good" and "bad" protesters. In brief, how are we to parse power and speech, action and meaning, in the current moment? How does what you've called a "philosophy from below" approach these questions?

Yes. We must not strive to make sense according to the logic of capital. If we follow that logic, we would only hope to make sense by presenting measurable results for every action, like citing a policy change won by means of protest. The social and political sciences love to measure efficacy that way, such that the current Black-led revolt could only prove its worth if it changes laws. In order to become legible, in order to become sensible, we have to make sense to a cable news anchor who wants us to tell them what we want Trump or Biden to do about it. It is better to confuse than to satisfy such logic. It is completely offensive to conclude that the failure of Morsi simply defeats the so-called Arab Spring or that the limitations of Alexis Tsipras prove the Greek revolts false. No! We have to consider what happens to people, and especially to young people, when they participate in a revolt. Hope can be scarce and for good reasons. Not only because of capitalist insecurity but also because of global pandemics and ecological catastrophe, among other things. Nobody thinks burning a cop car will end racism, but experiences of revolt change people. Listen to what people say. They are fed up and fighting back. They are experimenting with their own powers to fight the reality that threatens them.[8] A diverse range of existential, cultural, psychic, historical, and political experiences are not nothing. In the end, they may be everything.

On the question of reading revolts or riots, I have always insisted that we must never convert them into legible texts. Martin Luther King Jr.'s claim that "riots are the language of the unheard" is important but not because he likens the riot to language. It is important because he is telling an audience in a high

8. There are dozens of excellent sources including firsthand participant accounts of experiments and aspirations of recent revolts. For a tiny start, you may consult *The 2015 Baltimore Uprising: A Teen Epistolary* (New York: Research and Destroy, 2015); Marina Sitrin and Dario Azzellini, *They Can't Represent Us: Reinventing Democracy from Greece to Occupy* (New York: Verso Books, 2014); Keeanga-Yamahtta Taylor, *From #BLACKLIVESMATTER to Black Liberation* (Chicago: Haymarket Books, 2021).

school in Michigan in 1968 that they must not see in the upheaval nothing but inchoate irrationality and barbaric stupidity. That is not only how many people thought about riots in 1968 but still to this day. People who are not communists and anarchists continue to repeat the same old strategic reduction of revolt to irrational violence. For me, the argument was never about language. That is how Hamid Dabashi wrote about the Arab Spring, but I do not agree with him.[9] No one needs to translate uprisings into a university essay. Impoverished Black people in the US know what they are experiencing, thinking, and expressing. When I write about reason and revolt, what I am saying is not that the protest needs to speak a language but that we need to learn how to hear and understand other ways of speaking. Even then, speaking is only one part of it. Sure, we could say that rioting, looting, and fighting the police are expressions of disaffection, proclamations of indignation and rage. However, they are not merely "communiqués." To say so would be to misunderstand the importance of the passage from *potentia* to *hyperpotentia*, the passage from the normal violence of capitalist society to the open revolt against it.

On the question of communication, I oppose presenting everything we like as some kind of perfectly rational "communicative action." For Habermas, much like Kant, his father, the riot does not count. Riot and revolt are not sufficiently legible to a so-called reading public, the favored addressee of Kant. Nonetheless, revolts do have something to say, and the vast mass of society outside of them (the rest of *potentia*) needs to listen and learn. You cannot simply erase all communicative content for theoretical or political reasons. It is in there as part of the revolt. I claim that the revolt exceeds language, includes communicative content yet surpasses communication.

Consider a concrete example. When the Zapatistas made their rebellion in 1994, there had been roughly seventy years of one-party (PRI) rule in Mexico. The Indigenous people in the mountains had been communicating to the Mexican state and to the people of Mexico through conventional language for decades. Yet few heard them beyond the bounds of Chiapas. As was discussed in those days, the Indigenous people lived in oblivion.[10] Therefore,

9. Hamid Dabashi, *The Arab Spring: The End of Postcolonialism* (New York: Zed Books, 2012).

10. See John Ross, *The War Against Oblivion: The Zapatistas Chronicles, 1994–2000* (Monroe, ME: Common Courage Press, 2000).

they found other ways to speak through rebellion, and people in Mexico suddenly had epiphanies about "the Indigenous problem" that they never knew existed. This shows that uprisings must exceed linguistic communication, not conform to it. This is why I have also written about art and insurrection, about nontextual expressions.[11] Of course, the Zapatistas did not only speak. They also built worlds to live inside of up in the mountains. The making of new worlds always includes and exceeds language.

I must be clear that with my concept of philosophy from below I am talking about a very particular communist notion of theory, which I try to develop and defend in my work. Against the idea that the great philosophies always issue from the heads of men like Hegel, I claim that the most provocative questioning of the reality and justice of the world (the classical purview of philosophy) comes better through the revolt than the philosophical text.

You've resisted the tendency to treat revolts as "discrete events" that start at X moment in time at Y place, last a while, then either fizzle out or are crushed. Instead, you see each new revolt as "taking up unfinished business from within the society, from where previous revolts left off." This links revolts to one another along a sort of volcanic line, where each connects with, responds to, and continues the "work" that others had done. This also allows us to frame revolt as a "specter" that "haunts" society in the interim, and against which state and extra-state forces of order continuously mobilize counter-insurgency in order to anticipate and quash them, just as leftist and liberal organizations continuously attempt to siphon off and capture the social energies of revolt and "convert them into a platform for their own political strategies," i.e., for the building of their parties. How, amidst these different contending forces, can the energy of revolt carry itself forward after the crest of clashes and battles subsides? How can revolt keep itself alive in the interim, while resisting the forces that seek to flatten or co-opt it?

When we treat revolts as discrete events that start on one date and end on another, we misunderstand them. We cut them off from a long history of struggle. In my 2016 book, *Specters of Revolt* I wrote that "The Ferguson

11. Richard Gilman-Opalsky and Stevphen Shukaitis, *Riotous Epistemology: Imaginary Power, Art, and Insurrection* (Brooklyn: Autonomedia, 2019). Much of that text appears, in revised and edited form, as Chapter 7 of this book.

revolt did not take place; the Baltimore revolt is proof."[12] I wrote that in the context of a *détournement* of Deleuze and Guattari's essay "May '68 Did Not Take Place."[13] Today, we must say that the Baltimore revolt did not take place; the George Floyd uprisings are proof. To say the event did not take place means that it was not over when it appeared to have ended. Such an approach connects the current wave of revolt with previous waves, and a good theory should help us to see that connective tissue. Why would anyone expect the revolt to end if the conditions of existence it opposes remain intact? How could we expect the revolt to find a conclusion amid the continuation of the conditions that give rise to it? That is why I argue that, when revolt is not visibly and actively happening, its specter still haunts.

To return to Dussel, we could say that the possibility of *hyperpotentia* always haunts the law and order of *potestas* and *potentia*. That is why the forces of law and order make plans for revolt even in its absence. Likewise, the wisest hospitals and governments of the world will now make plans for the next pandemic, which they fully expect to come.

Regarding the co-optation of the social energies of revolt, that is a serious question. The channeling of revolutionary or insurrectionary energies into leftist and liberal organizations is always a risk, as we have seen with what I would call the *Jacobin* (social democratic) wing of the Democratic Party in the US. There is a lot of good content in that social energy, and its energetic expressions during the Bernie Sanders campaign tell us that capitalist white supremacy is not in fact what everyone desires. However, it is long past the deadline when we should expect any real gains against capitalist white supremacy through existing capitalist institutions. They suck up and swallow everything good that we give them and then flush it into their sewers. On the other hand, our own subterranean and more radical alternatives to the mainstream institutions of the left, with all of their rhizomatic hopes, do not mobilize anything at the scale of the recent Sanders campaigns (in 2016 and 2020). What I want to say is that this is not an organizational problem with an organizational solution.

---

12. Richard Gilman-Opalsky, *Specters of Revolt: On the Intellect of Insurrection and Philosophy from Below* (London: Repeater Books, 2016), 215.

13. Gilles Deleuze and Félix Guattari, "May '68 Did Not Take Place" in *Hatred of Capitalism: A Semiotext(e) Reader*, eds. by Chris Kraus and Sylvère Lotringer (Los Angeles: Semiotext(e), 2001).

We should go back to Rosa Luxemburg's essay on "The Mass Strike."[14] In it, she argues that the "rigid, mechanical-bureaucratic conception cannot conceive of the struggle save as the product of organization at a certain stage of its strength."[15] In fact, the organizations must come out of the uprisings, Luxemburg argues, which she observed "in Russia, where a proletariat almost wholly unorganized created a comprehensive network of organizational appendages in a year-and-a-half of stormy revolutionary struggle."[16] Luxemburg insists that we "cannot keep historical events in check while making recipes for them."[17]

Luxemburg makes two crucial points here. First, existing organizations should be ready and able to aid and abet uprisings when they happen, to follow the uprisings, *not lead them*. Second, when uprisings sustain over a long period, they eventually generate organizations and organizational initiatives. In this way, I think that organizations, including the formation of parties and unions, may be very important at various points in real struggles, but they have to come out of movements and follow the lead of actual uprisings in the world. Raya Dunayevskaya later developed some of Luxemburg's ideas into a critique of state-capitalism in Russia that more resolutely grounded every major advance in the real and seemingly spontaneous uprisings of women, Black and Brown people, and workers. So I feel that we cannot teach revolt how to stay alive, how to carry itself forward. Our only reassurance is that revolt will never end unless or until we fully and finally abolish the conditions of society that give it cause. This connects my theory of revolt to my arguments about abolition in Chapter 2.

Regarding the George Floyd uprisings, I lament the fact that the COVID-19 virus coincided with this explosive wave of revolt in the US. We can only wonder how many more would have joined the uprisings—especially people with underlying health conditions and risks or those with young children and others to care for at home—all those whose hearts were with the insurrection while their bodies were quarantined. Well, we can imagine many things and we must. Whenever we confront the question of what is possible,

14. Rosa Luxemburg, "The Mass Strike, the Political Party, and the Trade Unions" in *Socialism or Barbarism* (London: Pluto Press, 2010).

15. Luxemburg, "The Mass Strike," 112.

16. Luxemburg, "The Mass Strike," 112.

17. Luxemburg, "The Mass Strike," 122.

we have to exercise our imaginary power. However, a theorist concerned with real horizons must also go to the concrete, to the actually happening. That is the only way to consider the difference and the distance between what is and what ought to be, and we have no choice but to think from there.

It is either that or theory becomes nothing but pataphysics. Pataphysics is a peculiar concept of Alfred Jarry's, a proposal for a philosophy dealing with imaginary realms, a kind of parodic mocking of science, a science of examining imaginary phenomena and recommending imaginary solutions. There is always a pataphysical dimension to philosophies, which—in opposition to the existing world—imagine other realms, other forms of life. Inside of the George Floyd Rebellion, some imaginings need no speculation, no transcribing. We confront white supremacy, cops, police brutality, mass incarceration, and racial profiling, and imagine a world without them. White supremacy, police, and racial profiling concentrate their forces on the bodies of impoverished people of color in the United States and there are always some participants in the rebellion who bring forward a confrontation with class power and capital. We imagine the abolition of all these things, but these are real phenomena, and we really rise up against them and for the imaginary realm. To avoid pataphysical traps, then, our imagining must come out of real conditions of life, real movements, and focus on real horizons. There is perhaps always a pataphysical dimension to radical thinking, but at the same time, the existing reality must end.

CHAPTER 4

Bad Imagination: Capitalism of "Communist" China

On Saturday, July 14, 2018, I arrived in Xi'an, China, in Shaanxi Province.[1] It was a two-hour flight from Beijing. The flight from Chicago to Beijing was thirteen hours. I had never before been to China, and at home in the United States I am not a China scholar.

The basic idea for this chapter follows the example of Audre Lorde's "Notes from a Trip to Russia," which consisted of edited journal entries from her two-week visit to Russia in 1976.[2] Lorde visited Russia in a different century, during the time of the Cold War and as a critic of US capitalism and its culture. I visited China in the post–Cold War twenty-first century, also as a critic of capitalism and its culture. In the United States today, many believe that the Soviet Union was the iconic example of past communism but that today, communism "still exists in China."[3]

Before saying anything else, however, I must qualify that I cannot speak about China in general terms. Many reading this chapter surely know more about China than I do. I only offer some carefully considered theoretical and political reflections drawing on (a) a specific experience in Xi'an in the summer of 2018 and (b) research in the variegated currents of

1. An earlier version of this chapter appeared in the journal *Situations: A Project of the Radical Imagination* IX, nos. 1 and 2, 2021.

2. Audre Lorde, "Notes from a Trip to Russia" (1976) in *Sister Outsider: Essays and Speeches* (Berkeley: Crossing Press, 2007).

3. See Maggie Astor, "What Is Democratic Socialism? Whose Version Are We Talking About?," *New York Times*, June 12, 2019, https://www.nytimes.com/2019/06/12/us/politics/democratic-socialism-facts-history.html.

Marxist philosophy and scholarship on China. In this essay, I draw on (a) and (b) to make some modest contributions to understanding the capitalism of "communist" China. The spectacle of communist China has evolved into a new contradiction where the Chinese Communist Party (CCP) is now one of the greatest harbingers of twenty-first century global capitalism. However, I also claim that Chinese students and workers remain capable of a politics from below that is well positioned for both a critique of capitalist and Chinese bureaucratic power. In addition to substantiating these discrete points *and their intersecting significance*, I shall critically appreciate Chinese politics and culture in relation to the purportedly rival example of the United States. In that regard, I also offer an impressionistic comparative account.

We must never speak of a nation as a model. Each nation contains a history of violence and catastrophe but never only that. Any analysis of a nation that treats it as a unified and cohesive being-in-the-world announces its failure from the start. Every nation on Earth is a complex, historically variegated and internally heterogeneous intergenerational construction. This does not mean we can say nothing at all. Some things done in some nations could and should happen elsewhere. Other things deserve ruthless criticism and condemnation. It is therefore not necessary to say nothing but to say as much as can be said, with all necessary qualifications.

I traveled to China to give two full weeks of daily lectures at Shaanxi Normal University under the course title, "Twenty-First Century Political Philosophy: New Theories, New Horizons." I lectured on Partha Chatterjee, Martha Nussbaum, Silvia Federici, Franco "Bifo" Berardi, Antonio Negri, Paul Virilio, Jacques Rancière, my own research, and some other subjects and thinkers.

My host, a Chinese political scientist, "Jinhao," had attended some of my lectures at the University of Illinois while he was a visiting professor there in 2016.[4] Having read my work and enjoyed my lectures, Jinhao had resolved to bring me to China.

4. I have changed the name of my host to avoid associating him with this chapter.

Cultural and Political Reflections on Chinese "Communism" from an Ancient City

It is common among too many Western Marxist theorists to view culture as an immaterial or epiphenomenal accumulation of signs, language, practices, and values generated by the political-economic structure of society. Such an orientation suggests that things like art, food, language, and style are superstructural contingencies of a macrosocial and political-economic reality that would change along with a structural transformation (i.e., revolution) of politics and economy. All such "miniaturizers" of culture should visit China.

In China (and of course, not only in China), language, food, and style are very consciously part of a political assertion of national identity. In China, culture often conveys a conscious resistance to globalized commercial Western culture. It is critical to note that Anglophone assumptions and Western capitalist interests swirl around China looking for points of entry and conquest. We can think of this as a kind of encroachment of Western capital, which is visible throughout China and understood as such by the people. For example, in Xi'an, Kentucky Fried Chicken (KFC) is a US export modified with local spices to appeal to culinary tastes in Xi'an. People in China know that KFC is not Chinese. Encircled and outnumbered by bustling Indigenous fare, the Xi'an KFC appeared as a corporate export that looked like a precarious business venture at best. Surrounding businesses like KFC and Starbucks, I saw Communist Party flags, portraits of Mao, hammers and sickles, and Chinese food and traditional attire. Seeing so much communist iconography adjacent to a Starbucks made me wonder if culture was a space in which some Chinese people may assert a "communistic" sensibility against the increasing marketization of life. Is it possible for a communist sensibility, or a communist aesthetic, to conceal or resist a capitalist base? In Western Europe, the United States, and in places like Singapore and Japan, there is no mainstream, highly visible aesthetic juxtaposition to the capitalism of society and life, because the brazen capitalism of those places is not encircled by anticapitalist iconography. Whereas in China, it is common to think about national identity as variously communist or Marxist in explicit and very public ways (more on this point below).

Nonetheless, let us be clear: China is a capitalist country. Increasing integration into global capitalism since the 1970s, accelerated vastly in the

1990s, has made China—and specifically Chinese production and consumption—one of the most indispensable capitalist powers on Earth. While many commodities remain inexpensive in China, and many services and institutions remain free and open to the public, capital governs China more than China governs capital, and that has been true for a long time. Subsequently, the logic of capital largely organizes and governs life in China. We see a reliable indication of capitalist rule wherever money governs daily life, work, and opportunities to do what one desires. Governments that call themselves "communist" have long been contradictions in terms, and governments that call other governments "communist" tend only to do so when deploying the term as vilification. This was the case in Russia and Romania and Hungary and elsewhere during the twentieth century, and it remains true in China in the twenty-first century, over thirty years after the Cold War's end.

Autonomist Marxists, left communists, Marxist-humanists, and others who read Marx carefully know that "communist government" is a nonsensical term. The major countries that declared themselves communist were state-capitalist bureaucracies and in fact, that remains the best frame within which to characterize China today (although not categorically). The United States government and much of its media and people like to refer to China as "communist" for the same reasons its conservative and liberal mainstream like to call Bernie Sanders or Venezuela "socialist." There is, perhaps more reliably in the United States than in any other country, an enduring reality from decades of Cold War propaganda: namely, one can still win political arguments by convincing enough people that one's enemy is communist. Moreover, since the economic crises of 2008 have shaken people's confidence in capitalism (including many capitalists), there has been a resurgent new wave of communist vilification.

China—a major and dominant capitalist power—is still regularly denounced by detractors as "communist," while internally, ongoing identification with communism is seen as a distinguishing virtue. The different signification of communism inside and outside of China allows for both an internal and external assertion of China as communist but assertions do not constitute reality. In fact, even long before China's opening up in the late 1970s to an accelerated integration into global markets, even during its most fervently communist identification, we could have spoken of capitalist China.

Raya Dunayevskaya frequently wrote about China in the four decades from the 1950s to the 1980s. In 1957, she wrote: "The Chinese Communist regime is a state-capitalist society. It was born out of the revolution against the corrupt feudal-capitalistic society under Chiang Kai-shek. There is no doubt that when Chiang and his Guomindang regime were overthrown, a much wider base was created for the new state-capitalist regime. Chinese capitalism was finally stripped of its feudal trappings and its corrupt warlords. Honest or otherwise, however, state-capitalism is an exploitative society."[5]

This is an important observation, which remains necessary for understanding present-day China. Chiang and his Guomindang regime had to be overthrown, but this was mainly a transition from one form of capitalism to another, and we know this because Chinese production and consumption were still governed by a capitalist profit-logic throughout the transition, and for that reason remained (and still remain) exploitative of the impoverished workers of the country.

Aside from the retention of a capitalist organization of life and labor, Chinese so-called communism attempted to fuse nationalism with Marxism, which constitutes a fundamental and direct rejection of Marx's consistent and committed internationalism. Marx was unwavering in his insistence that nationalism and patriotism pervert and undermine the activities and possibilities of communism in the world. However, because of nationalism and patriotism in China, people came to see the state-ownership of the means of production as the peoples' ownership, which in fact it never was. This is one of the dangerous outcomes of over-identification with the state. According to Dunayevskaya: "*That is to say, Communism tries to keep the theory of liberation known as Marxism imprisoned in its own perverse philosophy that State property equals socialism.*"[6] I observed that nationalism remains remarkably pervasive in China and that the people who adopt a staunchly nationalist point of view do not—at least not in general—perceive their nationalism as a contradiction of communism. Mao had much to do with this impossible fusion because he sought to imbue Chinese nationalism with Marxism in a new synthesis, a move about which Marx issued many warnings. Though another

5. Raya Dunayevskaya, *Russia: From Proletarian Revolution to State-Capitalist Counter-Revolution*, eds. by Eugene Gogol and Franklin Dmitryev (Leiden and Boston: Brill, 2017), 354–55.

6. Dunayevskaya, *Russia*, 360.

and more significant cause of Chinese nationalism is the country's historical experience with colonization (discussed more below).

Dunayevskaya argued "that in Mao's China, the state, *and not the people,* rules over production, in agriculture as in industry."[7] This is what some call an administered economy, but we should call it state-capitalism when the purposes of production, consumption, import, export, and the whole of agriculture and industry are carried out for profits derived from surplus labor. Today, Xi Jinping is very open about the capitalist power of China. Nothing is hidden or concealed on that front, although strangely, a discourse of Chinese socialism, communism, and Marxism continues less as a way of specifying a political or economic philosophy and more as a way to distinguish and tout the country's collectivism and purported equality as virtues preferred to individualism and personal freedom.

Nevertheless, and perhaps surprisingly, Mao himself confirmed Dunayevskaya's insights about state-capitalism in China. In 1953, Mao wrote:

> The present-day capitalist economy in China is a capitalist economy which for the most part is under the control of the People's Government and which is linked with the state-owned socialist economy in various forms and supervised by the workers. It is not an ordinary but a particular kind of capitalist economy, namely, a state-capitalist economy of a new type. It exists not chiefly to make profits for the capitalists but to meet the needs of the people and the state. True, a share of the profits produced by the workers goes to the capitalists, but that is only a small part, about one quarter, of the total. The remaining three quarters are produced for the workers (in the form of the welfare fund), for the state (in the form of income tax) and for expanding productive capacity (a small part of which produces profits for the capitalists). Therefore, this state-capitalist economy of a new type takes on a socialist character to a very great extent and benefits the workers and the state.[8]

7. Dunayevskaya, *Russia,* 367.

8. Mao Tse-tung, "On State Capitalism" from a document of the National Conference on Financial and Economic Work (1953), accessed November 21, 2022, https://www.marxists.org/reference/archive/mao/selected-works/volume-5/mswv5_30.htm.

Mao did not deny that post-revolutionary China was capitalist, but he claimed it was a capitalism under the control of the People's Government. Naming one's government "the People's Government" is simply a way to say that the government governs the economy *for* all of the people, even if it is not *by* the people. This is an attempt to make a simple endorsement, much like naming the United States a democracy even when the *demos*, whose political will is acted out through representatives, directly governs very little.

What does Mao mean when he says that the workers supervise the economy? How can a whole people supervise an economy in a nation like China through a government in which they play no role that is not vicarious? This is the same ideological nonsense spoken by all heads of state, but at least Mao was more honest than most of his Western detractors. Mao at least admits that his China is "a particular kind of capitalist economy" called "state-capitalism," which maintains its connection to Marxism in one way only. According to Mao, the capitalist economy of China is ruled to satisfy everyone's needs and not by a profit logic. If this is true, why call it capitalist at all? What is capitalism without a profit logic? Especially since, in the next breath, Mao confesses that a small part of the profits goes to the capitalists. What Mao means to say in 1953 is quite simple; the Chinese government regulates the capitalists with a socialist sensibility.

This is state-capitalism according to both Mao and Dunayevskaya. However, Dunayevskaya grasps the fact that capitalism is antithetical to communism and to Marxism, whereas Mao does not. This remains crucial to understandings today because so many continue to mistake any statist regulation of capital as communist, socialist, or Marxist. However, today such imprecators are right-wing reactionaries or neoliberal capitalists.

In the summer of 2018, some of the major news in China covered the reaction against Donald Trump's "trade war" hostility directed at China's position in the global market. One of the most peculiar features of this coverage was that Chinese media presented China as defending the free market while showing Trump's posturing against Chinese business as undue government blockage to the free flow of capital. It was stunning to see so-called "communist China" frustrated by an insufficient commitment to neoliberal capitalism by the likes of Donald Trump, a casino and resort businessman. Chinese officials and the Chinese business community were on Chinese television daily arguing for greater freedom of capital in the global capitalist market. In a twist, then, "communist China" appeared to be more committed to capitalism than the United States.

One of the most important China scholars working today, Kellee S. Tsai, has shown that China has become increasingly capitalist while becoming less and less democratic. Her book *Capitalism without Democracy: The Private Sector in Contemporary China* gives the lie to the deception that capitalism generates democracy. China may be the best example of the fact that capitalism does not cause democracy and if anything, undermines democracy more than it democratizes society. Tsai writes about adaptive informal institutions, by which she means all of the private businesses and active conduits of capital that evade, dodge, and effectively betray the socialistic character presented by China's formal institutions of government. "Although most observers focus on the formal institutions governing China's political economy, the emergence of adaptive informal institutions represents a significant part of the story about how capitalists could thrive in an authoritarian regime that claims to adhere to a socialist ideology."[9]

Economically, China may end up having a good run of influence and control over global capital. BRICS (the association of the five national economies of Brazil, Russia, India, China and South Africa) appears as a strong union, which rolled out the red carpet (literally) everywhere in 2018 throughout Africa and the Middle East for visits from Xi Jinping. Xi is the head of state with whom the political and business classes in BRICS regions most desperately want to make a deal in the interest of their own prosperity. In the summer of 2018, more and more countries seemed to be lining up to cooperate with China, not only motivated by their economic interests, but also symbolically, in order to take sides against Trump's discourse of American chauvinism.

Indeed, when one takes a close look at commercial centers in China, coupled with the global sway of Chinese capital, the thinness of the socialist presentation of the country's formal institutions appears only convincing to those who have committed themselves ideologically to insisting on the truth of Chinese communism no matter the reality. The productive pervasiveness of China in the West, in the form of every kind of commodity from toys to

9. Kellee S. Tsai, *Capitalism without Democracy: The Private Sector in Contemporary China* (Ithaca: Cornell University Press, 2007), 42–43.

technology, is just one of the major features of China's role in global capitalism. Consumption, however, is another aspect, and includes consumption of Western commodities like Starbucks, KFC, Pizza Hut, and Häagen-Dazs, all of which shared real estate in a close vicinity to a major Xi'an shopping center.

Some things trouble the present spectacle in China. On my way to class one day, I saw from the taxi a small protest. I asked the graduate assistant assigned to my class, "Zhao," if she knew anything about the protest.[10] She told me that the protest was by residents asked to leave their homes in an apartment building, which the government wanted to commandeer for public services of some kind (she did not know what services). She told me that the people did not want to leave their homes but that they had eventually agreed to do so after the government promised to pay them sufficient compensation, which according to the protest, had never come. The protesters were demonstrating against the government's failure to make good on its promises, especially now that the people were vacating their homes without the promised compensation.

I found the sight of the protest reassuring, despite the bad news of its making. While it is generally a good idea to take the side of protesters against any government—certainly true in this case—we in the West must be careful not to abuse such stories in order to justify any sense of relative greatness. The fact is that there are protests against governments and government policies throughout North America and Western Europe, since there, too, people are regularly evicted, homes are foreclosed, unhoused and impoverished people can be found in every city, and without any government assistance to aid them. Any honest accounting will not exploit real problems in China in order to make Western governments look better. The Chinese government, for example, has committed brutal human rights abuses against the Uyghur population, as well as other ethnic and religious minorities in Xinjiang, which many have characterized as genocide. There must be no apologetics or softening of that brutality. At the same time, we cannot simply sit back and congratulate ourselves as if our own history of slavery, ongoing mass incarceration, white supremacy, and active imperialism are kinder and gentler affairs. All governments deserve fierce and ongoing protests, and protest is

10. I have changed the name of my graduate assistant to avoid associating her with this chapter.

happening in China (though far more prevalent in major cities like Beijing and Shanghai or contested locations like Hong Kong and Taiwan).

As well, it would be unfair to retort that the protests in China do not change anything because of the government. Protest demonstrations express disaffection but very rarely lead to measurable major outcomes. We cannot say that protest in China is less effective than protest in other capitalist countries. Also, even where protest is generally ineffective, it remains one of the few substantive activities of actual democracy. For all its shortcomings and limitations, I am happy to see protest and, aside from the question of its efficacy, find its absence more worrying than its presence.

There is another side to this. Protests by impoverished workers or evicted tenants in China, no matter how ineffective, reveal that the so-called communism of China has not reached those who need the communist commitments of other people. When communism is really communist—and not merely a spectacle—capitalists target it for criticism and protest. The protests of the impoverished, evicted, and vulnerable can and do, however, target the spectacle of communism. Communism that means anything at all can be spotted because it is opposed by the rich, by the ruling class. Worker or peasant revolts are substantive activities of communism, and therefore communists take that side of class conflict. Communists do not side with the ruling class against worker or peasant revolts. In 1967, in "The Explosion Point of Ideology in China," Guy Debord reviewed political and social crises within China that undermined the government's claims of a socialist reality:

> The workers could not fail to realize what the Maoist perspective implied for them; as for the peasants, who saw their patches of land threatened, they proceeded in several provinces to share out the fields and equipment . . . Rail strikes were followed by a general strike in Shanghai (denounced, as in Budapest, as the favorite weapon of the capitalists); by strikes in the industrial conglomeration of Wuhan, in Guangzhou, in Hubei, and among metal-workers and textile-workers of Chongqing; and by attacks mounted by peasants in Sichuan and Fujian.[11]

11. Guy Debord, "The Explosion Point of Ideology in China" (1967) in *A Sick Planet*, trans. Donald Nicholson-Smith (Calcutta: Seagull Books, 2008), 57.

Debord's point here is that the uprisings of the very people who would be the active subjects of revolutionary movements explode the ideological lie of socialism in China. Every time strikes and rebellions challenge the so-called socialist state, rather than confessing its disproven and untrusted communism, the state declares the revolts "revisionist" or counterrevolutionary "capitalist plots." In 1967, with major crises in the bureaucratic government of China, Debord thought the spectacle of communism in China could be abolished. While Debord was right about the communist spectacle, he was wrong about its explosion. To this day, many still assert the peculiar and highly ideological socialist and communist identity of China from the inside and outside, proliferating a lie that continues with astonishing credibility.

In making such an analysis, we should beware a common tendency in Western political discourse to use that analysis to prop up a country like the US as enviable by comparison. I did not leave China with any clear sense that life is better in the United States. Politics in the United States is commonly associated with corruption, universities are privatized and increasingly defunded, and for all of our beloved freedom, our cities are full of homelessness, racism, and poverty; growing insecurity and antisocial violence is met with little support for psychological and other health care. This is not to say that other or similar problems do not exist in China. The point is that we cannot count on an honest consideration of China today to make Chinese life and politics look, in the main, qualitatively worse than American life and politics generally.

Comparisons of a US free-market capitalist utopia to a repressive communist regime of enforced Chinese equality are utter nonsense, ideas taken seriously only by patriotic idiots who shield their chauvinism with ignorance. Nonetheless, there are different forms of repression in the United States and China. It is always easier to condemn the repressive aspects of other peoples' societies while ignoring the normalized quotidian repression of one's own society. This is true of capitalist ideology in the US, and I think it is also true in China.

I would like to focus here on a particular repression in China. Let us consider the Museum of Education in Xi'an, one of the biggest museums in China and (I was told) the largest education museum in the country. Whole sections of the museum were devoted to different eras in the long history of China. When I say "long history," I mean stretching back to the Neolithic period and to the Han dynasty. There are fifty-five ethnic minority groups (referred to in China as "nations"), twenty-two provinces, and roughly 1.5 billion people. The Museum of Education attempts to cover all of the vast historical and cultural ground encompassed by that, and physically, the museum is massive in size. There are rooms full of the earliest money from ancient times, samples of the first writing in China, a wide array of different traditional clothes on exhibit, showcases in separate installments featuring the customs and styles of each of the distinctive nations. The museum provides close coverage of how education changed after the 1949 Chinese Revolution, what the classrooms and textbooks looked like before and after, how Russian became a second language in the schools, and even included an entire section comprising many rooms devoted to the history of women in China from antiquity to the present.

In the giant wing of the museum devoted to culture, however, I was stunned to find that the Cultural Revolution was skipped over, essentially deleted. When you get to 1966 in China, it seems that nothing particularly notable was happening. The term "Cultural Revolution" was only mentioned to me in whispers in Xi'an (perhaps especially to a foreigner like me). I cannot say if there is a different approach in other parts of the country, but in Xi'an, students spoke with marked caution about the Cultural Revolution after class, and it seemed a dangerous and guarded conversation even then. Zhao regularly cautioned students to say little to me about it. Cultural Revolution appeared to me as a forbidden subject in the sliver of China I visited, variously repressed and erased, and this requires further consideration here.

The Cultural Revolution, from roughly 1966 to 1976, was a sociopolitical movement variously encouraged by Mao and Maoists as both an official and sometimes unofficial policy of the Communist Party of China. The Cultural Revolution aimed to establish and preserve communist culture and ideology, at least in part, by eradicating any capitalist or traditional religious elements from Chinese society (more on this below).

In China today, people now celebrate traditional culture and the rich and multifarious heritages of Chinese people going back to the earliest records. Such celebration of traditional Chinese lifeways is understood as essential to a more cohesive national pride and self-understanding. Since the Cultural Revolution was hostile to the traditional culture now cherished and defended, and since it refers to a decade of hostilities and destructions throughout China, the Chinese people are not proud of it. The period of the Cultural Revolution is for many Chinese (certainly not all) a "bad chapter," and perhaps it is too soon (since the Cultural Revolution ran to almost 1980) for the Chinese people to focus on such a recent period of "bad governing," especially since Mao is still lionized as a great national hero. Mao is pictured on the currency, appears in statue form and hung portraits, and his ideas are widely taught throughout the country as those of one of the greatest philosophers. Many of Mao's ideas are still so beloved and taught that it is easy to see how a real reckoning with the Cultural Revolution may threaten to besmirch ongoing currents of Maoism.

I asked my host about this, and he confessed that it was a difficult question. He said that they only teach about the Cultural Revolution lightly and quickly in the classroom, and that what they teach is a lesson written and approved by the government. Perhaps it is something like in the United States, where it took just as long for people outside the antiwar movement to begin criticizing the imperial catastrophe of the Vietnam War. In fact, many Americans are still reluctant or unable to speak frankly about that chapter of US history in anything beyond the most patriotic apologetics. To take another example, we still have not begun to reverse inverted understandings of the Cold War in mainstream American politics. The conversation is guarded and potentially dangerous to prevailing capitalist ideology about the defeat of socialism.

These are different forms of repression. In China, repression is primarily state-instituted, whereas US repression is largely (not only—i.e., mass incarceration, consolidated and growing inequality, poverty, and other problems) a cultural and ideological phenomenon. To decide which is worse may be like choosing between one cancer and another. As Theodor Adorno and Max Horkheimer learned during their Californian exile, there are different ways of dissuading dissent.[12] German fascism was not identical to fascistic tendencies in the culture industry, but we can accept no comparison that makes either appear as good news.

Things are surely different in Shanghai, Peking, Beijing, Hong Kong, and Taiwan, but, in Xi'an, I saw no graffiti on the buildings, no young people

12. Theodor Adorno and Max Horkheimer, *Dialectic of Enlightenment*, trans. John Cumming (New York: Continuum, 1997).

dressed in political t-shirts or wearing punk styles, and I saw no visible evidence of any kind of subversive or underground culture. Perhaps I was not intended to find it or maybe it is just very well hidden. Perhaps it must remain hidden for its own existence, as some examples discussed below may suggest.

Interpersonally, some interactions with the people of Xi'an stood out. In one instance, a man approached me in the street and said, in notably good English, that he wanted to repair something for me. He was good with technology and fixing things, he said, and he would fix just about anything for 100 yuan. The problem, he said, is that he could not get a job because employers consider him too old. He was forty years old. He said to me, "I went to the university and got my training. I love my country and the Party. But, because I am forty, no one will hire me." I did not know what to make of this, how to contextualize it, but I did not need anything fixed. I told him that I could not hire him, and he was kind and grateful that I paid him attention. Was he unhoused? He told me that he was unemployed, but in Xi'an I saw no one sleeping in the streets. I saw no homeless encampments. Are there unhoused people in Xi'an? One would have to ask. It is a huge city, but in major cities across the US, the unhoused are visible on almost every corner. Even in smaller US cities like Springfield, Illinois, the unhoused gather around the library downtown and can be seen there at any time of year. Maybe homelessness is also in Xi'an, but it is not visible as in the United States. I also did not see or hear any music outside or on the streets.

There are so many people in Xi'an. Nearly every man and woman I saw was very thin. I felt like I was carrying around the largest body in China. I am six foot two. I am more than two hundred pounds. I am not fat. I am not skinny. Children pointed at me and their parents sometimes told me that their son or daughter thinks I am tall. There is no litter on the ground. The ground is old and broken.

Xi'an is an ancient city.

Theoretical-Political Collisions: Students and Lectures

Most of my young Chinese students expressed pride in their collectivist sensibility. In every discussion, inside and outside of the classroom, they were keen to shun any kind of individualism; they did this often in conversation with me largely because they associate individualism with American culture. A proud collectivist spirit may not solve real problems of poverty or exploitation. However, it does help to keep a general cultural-valuation norm in place, one regularly and effectively leveraged in discussions about education, politics, work, and social relations.

Liu Kang refers to this cultural topography as "aesthetic Marxism." In China today, an aesthetic Marxism counterbalances a certain conscious rejection of Marxism. As discussed above, the Cultural Revolution remains a sore point in China. According to Kang: "At the beginning of the Cultural Revolution, the tendency to politicize culture was evident. It then escalated into a massive 'grand cultural inquisition,' not unlike medieval Europe's Christian Grand Inquisition in its fervor and paranoia."[13]

The Cultural Revolution was catastrophic and regrettable in many ways, even if philosophically and politically it did express a certain critical insight. Mao was right to reject the classical Marxian faith that culture would invariably come to reflect the conditions of life. Mao understood that culture would remain a battlefield regardless of transformations in political economy. Indeed, as many Marxists since Antonio Gramsci understood well, culture is not reliably determined by political economy. This was visible in China. Because of the historical proximity of the Cultural Revolution to the present and current government ideology on that period of politics, the people I spoke with in China were not eager to answer my questions about this historical passage of repression. The Cultural Revolution was followed in the 1980s by a period (roughly a decade) known as the Cultural Reflection, led by the idea of a necessary reversal of the Cultural Revolution and organized as a range of coordinated efforts across China to retrieve as much as possible of what was destroyed. This was a period of recovering many ancient and traditional aspects and artifacts of China's long history and of returning them with dignity and pride to schools, museums, and public life.

What I would like to focus on in the Cultural Revolution is the way it centralizes the importance of culture to politics, a basic understanding that still pervades Chinese politics. Today, however, this understanding gives rise to a particular perversion, namely the total betrayal of culture and ideology

13. Liu Kang, *Aesthetics and Marxism: Chinese Aesthetic Marxists and Their Western Contemporaries* (Durham: Duke University Press, 2000), 155.

in political economy. For example, in China today, one finds the open promotion of global capitalist political economy within a culture of socialist ideology. Kang observes that most China scholars agree that "the CCP itself has substantially transformed from a revolutionary, idealist party into a power holder and corporate manager in a capitalist economy and autocratic political system. A consensus seems to prevail, though implicitly, in China today: revolution is dead and socialism only retains its name, insofar as the CCP still rules."[14]

This speaks to a less hopeful imaginary power than the one pursued in the present book. The example of China shows that one can imagine capitalism as already socialist, and in fact, we have seen a revival of imagining capitalists as socialists in US politics as well. While Kang agrees with most scholars on the point above about the CCP, he holds out some hope that China, haunted by the specter of revolution, may become revolutionary again. I hold out a similar hope and only disagree with the consensus in one way: whereas the consensus says that the CCP has "substantially transformed" into a capitalist power, I claim that this transformation is now total and complete.

At the same time, however, this does not mean that the aesthetic Marxism of China's cultural politics is irrelevant. I marveled with appreciation at the stunning sight of the unabashed School of Marxism at Shaanxi Normal University. The university constructed the School of Marxism building, located on the new campus, in the late 1990s and 2000s, well after what we in the West often perceive as the post–Cold War extinction of communist politics. In China, in 2018, there hung a huge poster for a recent conference dedicated to a Marxism bicentennial event held earlier in the year.

I wondered how heterogeneous and critical the discussions of Marxism might be in the School of Marxism. I asked Jinhao about this, and he reported that it was very common throughout China to discuss Marxism and to do so openly and with diverse interpretations. I did not witness this myself, but I expect that such discussions do take place in many circles throughout the country. Perhaps more interestingly, the School of Marxism at Shaanxi Normal University was a government mandate, a nationwide mandate that establishes one or two such schools on almost every major national university campus in China. Thus, this School of Marxism was not one of a

14. Kang, *Aesthetics and Marxism*, 190.

kind; Schools of Marxism throughout the country are often an expectation and mandate.

Furthermore, my understanding is that non-Marxist or even neoclassical economists in China do not receive this mandate with scorn because they appreciate that studying Marxism is necessary to studying their own history. The government in China today, which could scarcely be further removed from Marx's ideas, continues to mandate Marxist schools—not from any deep and abiding philosophical agreement—but rather, out of an obligation to understand the last two hundred years of Chinese political history. Non-Marxian liberal and conservative Americans may scoff at this notion, but we require civics courses and United States history curricula while banning studies of Marx, mostly informally, by way of stigmatization, vilification, and the professional punishment of Marxists in academia and politics.

Of course, even one such school on any public university in the United States would be scandalous and shocking. However, the fact is that it would make just as much sense to mandate studies of Marx and Marxism in the United States as in China. Can one really understand US politics in the twentieth century without studying Marx? One could only understand a history of deliberate misunderstanding without studying Marx. Americans cannot understand American history without studying the transatlantic slave trade, the history of labor struggles, Black revolt, and the women's movement, among many other struggles for and against power. Recently, Florida governor Ron DeSantis, with widespread right-wing support, worked to ban the teaching of an A.P. African American history course, in addition to the banning of critical race theory.[15] Imagine trying to understand US history without studying white supremacy and African American history. You would not be learning history. We cannot understand the Cold War without understanding Russia's side in the conflict. Understanding oneself always requires understanding the other or others from which one is distinguished.

What was it like to teach radical theory within such a school in China?

---

15. See, for example, Anemona Hartocollis and Eliza Fawcett, "The College Board Strips Down Its A.P. Curriculum for African American Studies," *New York Times*, February 1, 2023, https://www.nytimes.com/2023/02/01/us/college-board-advanced-placement-african-american-studies.html.

My class in China had sixty students enrolled. Not one of these students was required to take the course, so the fact that they were there indicated that they chose my lectures for reasons of interest. The classroom was very hot, as are most places in July in Xi'an. Chinese use air conditioning sparingly in this region, and they do not leave unoccupied rooms air-conditioned. They turn on the air conditioning only when entering rooms, but with the humid summer heat, it could take up to an hour to cool them. I was not accustomed to sweating constantly and did not like it. With a great deal of self-consciousness, I seemed to be the only one so discomforted by the heat. In the United States, I am used to the constant cooling of buildings and rooms, including even the empty ones, but here, even the airports bake in the hot sun, so that you walk out of the plane into hot, heavy humidity. This is part of a government mandate having to do with conserving energy and belongs to the country's environmental and economic policy. Indeed, it is probably a good idea to get more accustomed to living in heat.

One of the students in my class, during a discussion about nationalism and the colonial world, described how Japanese imperialism figures prominently in Chinese history textbooks and as a major feature in history lessons from grade school. These lessons connect Chinese nationalism to the story of a country moving through a postcolonial history, getting out from being bullied, beaten, and occupied by an oppressive foreign power. In my classroom, Chinese nationalism resonated with our discussion of Partha Chatterjee's analysis of distinctive non-Western nationalisms as discussed in his *Nationalist Thought and the Colonial World: A Derivative Discourse*, published in 1986. Outside of Europe, Chatterjee observes, "national identity was, therefore, a form of the struggle against colonial exploitation."[16] To some extent, the history of Japanese imperialism is necessary to understanding why China strives to remain a dominant political-economic power in the world today, including why it wants to hold economic sway over countries that previously determined China's reality. In this context, many in China understand China's global economic prowess as part of an empowering postcolonial passage.

My students frequently voiced a defense of Chinese patriotism, which they were keen to distinguish from self-interested nationalistic chauvinism.

16. Partha Chatterjee, *Nationalist Thought and the Colonial World: A Derivative Discourse* (Minneapolis: University of Minnesota Press, 1986), 8.

Students defended Chinese patriotism as essential in a country with a long history of abuse by foreign powers, where strong national identity and pride seem to them critical to the recovery of the confidence necessary to mobilize any kind of collective sensibility throughout the nation.

Some of these discussions reminded me of Frantz Fanon's analysis of the instrumental necessity of nationalism in struggles against colonization, according to which, before you get to humanism, you need a phase of emancipatory nationalism to rise to the challenges of national liberation.[17] As Fanon put it, nationalism, "that magnificent song that made the people rise against their oppressors, stops short, falters, and dies away on the day that independence is proclaimed."[18] This last part always seems to me more than a bit of "wishful thinking" on Fanon's part, as nationalism never dies away easily after a political victory. Once political culture and education build up nationalism, it is not so easy to dispense with. Indeed, it does not appear to be dying away as China sits atop global economic power. Here, we may recall Immanuel Wallerstein's essay "Neither Patriotism Nor Cosmopolitanism," in which he said we should never commit to one or the other categorically but consider which one (if either) best serves liberation struggles.[19] Wallerstein articulated a kind of Marxist utilitarianism about such ideologies, whereby we should use whatever theory is most promising to get the emancipatory outcomes we need and seek. However, China is in a different situation today than it was during Japan's imperial rule, and it is difficult to imagine that Fanon or Wallerstein would view Chinese nationalism as emancipatory for the people of China now. Nonetheless, such thinking remains part of defenses of nationalism in China.

We may observe other permutations of Chinese nationalism. Some students came to my lectures on subversion, revolt, and radical theory and wanted to talk about problems in China. There was an interest—certainly not unanimous—in sharing criticisms and concerns about China and its politics. However, as with all major public universities in China, the government

---

17. Frantz Fanon, *The Wretched of the Earth*, trans. Constance Farrington (New York: Grove Press, 1991). See especially the chapter "The Pitfalls of National Consciousness."

18. Fanon, *The Wretched of the Earth*, 203.

19. See Immanuel Wallerstein's short essay "Neither Patriotism Nor Cosmopolitanism," in Martha C. Nussbaum's book *For Love of Country?*, ed. by Joshua Cohen (Boston: Beacon Press, 2002), 122–24.

lavishly funds Shaanxi Normal University. The government spares no expense in making sure its professors live good lives, at least in terms of financial reward, housing, and esteem. Such conditions do not mobilize professors to bite the hand that feeds them, and my understanding is that most Chinese professors are treated such that incentives to bite are minimized.

My colleague Jinhao explained his incredible deal. He and his family get a home on campus by the university. When applying for promotion to full professor, the university invites him to design the home of his dreams, and this becomes part of his promotion. He may move into the home before his promotion, but after the approval of his promotion, the home becomes his. There are, no doubt, regulations restricting what he may do with this real estate. I toured his house while it was under construction and could not imagine such a posh reward for a professor in the United States as part of a promotion package. Beyond such perks as this, politics and politicians in Chinese culture enjoy a certain respectability and honor, on par with professors. There is what I would describe as a certain class solidarity between professors and politicians, so it was not surprising that Jinhao had little by way of an anarchist sensibility with which to rail against his government. It seemed to me that many (not all) of the students felt the same way. This is a different aspect of Chinese nationalism.

Still, I asked about contentious politics in China every day and was told that there are regular and fierce debates about the "best policies" on things like traffic, educational exams, pollution, etc., but that such debates are watched and listened to closely by the government. Jinhao, and perhaps a dozen of the students I spoke with, insisted that the Chinese government tries to be responsive to grievances. Part of what is happening in China is that the government pays very close attention to professors and universities (a double-edged sword, to be sure), so that the political recommendations of scholars are seen and taken seriously by the state. The Chinese government has a staff of political-academic officials charged with reading relevant research published by professors working at major national public universities. There is, then, a real sense that academics and politicians respect each other and work together without any clear class division. As to one edge of the sword, there is a feature of surveillance and biopolitical control in such government attention to academic workers, and it is something that constricts academic freedom. I do not think academic freedom is a central virtue of intellectual life in China. There is, however, another edge of the sword. Whereas in the United States, we bemoan the stupidity of a government that seems resolutely uninterested in the analyses of its scholars, China studies the work of its scholars and invests in the production of their scholarship.

This second edge of the sword appears especially sharp in the light of recent experiences with COVID-19. In the US, the idea that virologists and myriad scholars of infectious disease might actually have recommendations the government should abide, came under sustained attack during Trump's term. Rather than subordinating a coordinated response to the pandemic to the scholarship, Trump instead pointed at the uncertainty of the scholarship as a pretext for throwing it out.

Some students wanted to talk to me after my lectures about what they described as low levels of freedom in China, and in particular, the dangers of public political speech. One student told me she was directed to give me a good impression of China and not to tell me about any of the problems in the country. In fact, one of the students charged with touring me around museums and restaurants was Uyghur, and she gave me a reliably glowing impression of China, including a performance of traditional Uyghur dance at my final class session, a performance invited by my hosts. One could not help but wonder about the motivations for this. A different student told me professors are afraid to criticize China and Chinese politics because professors could be fired, denied promotions, or jailed. I could not test these claims with confidence, but even Jinhao confirmed that while he can speak freely in his classes, he does not publish anything critical of Chinese government and politics. In terms of academic writing on politics, he says that only constructive recommendations are allowed, and since everything published may be read by government officials, there have been and can be serious consequences including job loss or imprisonment. A less severe example, professors who are not members of the Chinese Communist Party cannot expect decent careers in academia, cannot work at major national universities, and/or do not get promotions. For that reason, most everyone joins the Party.

To Western ears, this sounds repressive, and, indeed, I think it is. Nonetheless, many in China insist that Western notions of repression are misplaced there because professors who follow the rules are actually and genuinely happy. Following the rules is a reliable path to personal reward and remuneration in Chinese academia, so the rules at least assure intellectuals a fruitful passage through their professional life.

Admittedly, it was bizarre to be on a university campus with so little criticism directed at the head of state. Respect for president Xi Jinping seemed to me near universal within Xi'an, and his philosophy (referred to as "Xi Jinping Thought") is heralded in economic, domestic, and foreign policy. Chinese media as well expresses total satisfaction with the direction that the government is taking the country. Once again, and to recall the idea of "bad imagination," I am troubled by peoples' ability to imagine any head of state or great political and economic power as uniformly benevolent. Idolatry calls upon imaginary power too, but for other ends.

China had its problems then and now. However, it did not seem to me a comparatively awful place to live, and in many ways and for many people, life is better in China than in the United States. Some readers may suggest that this only indicates that the propagandistic impressions planned by my hosts were successful. What about Tibetans? What about Uyghurs? Some problems in China are unconscionable human catastrophes, and not only these. We must condemn what deserves condemnation everywhere, including our own mass incarceration, imperialist foreign policy, the plight of Indigenous people throughout North America from Mexico to Canada, and white supremacy. No nation deserves romanticization.

At the same time, any university professor in the United States would love to be given a house on or nearby their campus like Jinhao's, which I estimated would be a three-to-four-million-dollar property in New York City, California, or Chicago. I would also quite like to live in a society where collective concern is regarded as a virtue and inculcated as such from preschool on up. I can only imagine life in a society where universities receive—instead of aggressive defunding, mergers, and closings—top priority and commitment of national investment. Not to mention that the food was good, there was plenty to do—especially for young children—and one could rather easily get to big cities like Beijing or Shanghai from most points in the vast geography. The question of "freedom" surely looks differently from the perspective of many (not all) Chinese who are living with rich social lives, good education, good food, entertainment, open public spaces, and rewarding family life and friendships. Of course, that experience is not everyone's in China. Yet, from the perspective of those Chinese who are living full and fulfilling lives, Western accusations of "unfreedom" appear as a predictable ideological trope of so-called capitalist democracies.

The students at my lectures were somewhat resistant to contemporary critical theory and Marxist philosophy from Western Europe and the United States, which is mostly—though not exclusively—what I was teaching. My hosts repeatedly told me that students in China would be comparatively docile and agreeable, as if that were something I should appreciate. I do not idealize docility in students, and, in fact, they were not so agreeable. My students defended Chinese nationalism against Nussbaum's cosmopolitanism, claiming that their colonial past requires them to assert national pride and patriotism. They also challenged criticisms of nationalist thought provided by Chatterjee, pointing out that Chinese nationalism is neither classical liberal nor deviant and racialized, that Chinese nationalism eludes the categories of nationalist thought in postcolonial theory. What I experienced was that, when students detected a potential criticism of Chinese culture and politics, most (not all of them but several a day and reliably at each lecture) aimed to distinguish China as an exception. Some of the students—I think rightly—observed that while Michael Hardt and Antonio Negri speak a revolutionary language, their politics appear ultimately reformist. Some defended speed as a virtue against Paul Virilio's dromological concerns. Others defended insecurity and precarity against Franco Berardi's criticisms.

I do not want to make it sound as if the students were flatly oppositional. They were not. They were critical, as they were thinking about the theories in relation to their own lives. While many students challenged the material, there were many more clearly challenged by it, who found it useful to their critical understandings of themselves and their world. Some wrote me letters and notes to that effect. My favorite one said: "What you are teaching is what I have never touched before."[20]

In short, my Chinese students were quite like students in the United States. However, unlike Americans who know little to nothing about Chinese philosophy and politics, Chinese students read widely in multiple languages and begin with conversant knowledge of Plato, Aristotle, Kant, and Hegel; they have a good idea of Western thinking and they characterize it well in their comments and questions. Also unlike American students,

20. Letter from a student in Xi'an, Shaanxi Normal University, July 2018.

and because of mandatory classes in Marxism, Chinese students speak freely about capitalism and dialectics, and they use the word "proletariat" as if it were a common Chinese term. It would have been completely out of place, for example, to write the words "proletariat" and "bourgeoisie" on the chalkboard and provide basic definitions to Chinese students, whereas I do that every semester in the US.

Perhaps the two most interesting lectures for me to give were the ones on Jacques Rancière and on my own book, *Specters of Revolt*. I learned a lot from those discussions especially.

I used Rancière's book *Hatred of Democracy* to introduce the arguments that democracy is not a form of government and that all governments are oligarchies. I explained how and why the word and image of "democracy" had come, in the twentieth century, to essentially mean "good," despite the fact that those who most proclaim to love democracy secretly hate it (something you can observe in the hostile reactions of liberals and conservatives whenever the *demos* actually rises up and asserts itself against oligarchic power).

With Rancière, students in China began with the assumption that Western democracy is a fraud. Some students pointed out that Trump actually lost the so-called "democratic" vote in 2016 yet won the presidency anyway, and others noted that Americans declare everything they do not like "antidemocratic." These basic sensibilities are much harder to develop in US classrooms, where they are not the starting assumptions of my students. In the United States, such points are destinations not starting line positions.

My lectures were all video-recorded. Some students told me after class that they preferred to say things that were critical of the Chinese government after the camera was off. I asked about this. They told me that while it was perfectly safe for a foreigner like me to say whatever I pleased, professors and students often got into trouble for speaking critically of Chinese politics. In the safe space of "off-the-record" conversation, some students told me that they wished they had term limits, as in the United States, and that they wished there was not such an unshakeable one-party rule in China. Others stressed that Chinese politics is highly collaborative with minority parties throughout the country, and that they have a less competitive and a more cooperative national politics than in the United States. For example, some students told me about annual meetings with citizens and civil society organizations and active and ongoing government solicitation of critical perspectives for them to consider.

I pointed out that, even though we do have term limits in the United States, the fluctuations between Republican and Democratic Party administrations are not radically different in terms of substance and basic commitments. I explained that the differences do matter to real people in the real world, so we do have to pay attention to our elections, but that the changes from one party in power to another do not necessarily make for more drastic changes in policy and practice than China would see over the same period of Communist Party rule. In other words, I agree with them in their opposition to one-party rule. At the same time, I tried to convey that our two-party system does not necessarily promise more and greater political change or reform than they would see under a one-party system. I tied to convey a sense of the spectacle of opposition in US electoral politics, when in fact both parties are neoliberal capitalist parties, both parties support the privatization of almost everything, and neither party is antiwar, anti-imperialist, opposed to the death penalty, mass incarceration, etc. This idea fascinated them. They had gotten the message from or about the United States that our political debates are so wildly divergent that the victors can and do take the country down totally different paths. I admitted that Trump was perhaps closer to doing that than previous presidential administrations in recent decades but that things have been largely status quo (from 2016 to 2018) in between international outrages over important issues like immigration, healthcare, and environmental policy.

At the same time, they understood that the major Western "democracies" are full of corruption and money politics, they know about US bullying in the global economy and even about the common American distrust of politicians. Therefore, Rancière ended up not as surprising in China as to US students who have only ever thought of American democracy as an actually existing phenomenon. Conversations surrounding democracy and its contradictions were utterly fascinating there. Most of my Chinese students began with deep suspicion of democracy. Others, with a more glowing idea of the United States, held that American freedom was the real virtue, not democracy: "Yes," several students said, "you don't have democracy, and you do have many problems, but at least you have freedom." Off-camera, students often returned to the idea that China does not have freedom whereas the United States, in their opinion, does.

I conceded that the United States government seems less interested in what professors and students say and think, but I questioned their idea of *our* freedom. There is repression in both countries, carried out in different ways. The Chinese government has its hands in everything. In the United States, there is instead a certain formalization of informal biases. This means that people are watching for and reporting on scandals and transgressions to the point where we have a diffuse integration of the repressive apparatus throughout the social body. There is a lot of diverse evidence of this. For one example, we have seen so many professors getting in trouble for Twitter tweets, comments spoken on radio interviews or podcasts, and "offensive" utterances dug up by white nationalist militias across the country. We have seen right-wing activists team up informally but effectively with media people like Tucker Carlson in order to formalize punishment by way of harassment, threats of violence, job loss, etc., which has recently been aimed at antifascist activists and others.[21] While professors do not need to be in the Republican or Democratic Party in order to get promotions in the United States, they do have to watch what they say.[22] Even where we do have great freedoms, we often do not make use of them. We have many formal freedoms that we do not exercise, and in the case of tenured university professors, many are terrified of touching any controversy at all, even though they are technically "free" to do so.

My own theory of revolt was surprisingly resonant in China because many Chinese students both (1) learned about the importance of revolt in their own national history and (2) see the Chinese government as a government of control and surveillance (i.e., as a government that worries about

21. See, for example, the case of Yvette Felarca: Natalie Orenstein, "Berkeley Teacher Yvette Felarca ordered to pay conservative group $20,000," *Berkeleyside,* April 4, 2019, https://www.berkeleyside.com/2019/04/10/berkeley-teacher-yvette-felarca-ordered-to-pay-conservative-group-20000.

22. Here, consider the cases of George Ciccariello-Maher, Steven Salaita, Johnny Eric Williams, Nathan Jun, and Norman Finkelstein, for just some examples from a much longer list: https://www.chronicle.com/article/Professors-Growing-Risk-/240424 (Accessed December 2, 2022). More recently, see the egregious case of Nathan Jun at Midwestern State University: https://dailynous.com/2021/12/17/what-a-cancellation-looks-like-guest-post (Accessed December 2, 2022).

revolt). For reasons (1) and (2), I suggested that the specter of revolt haunts Chinese society.

Yet Chinese students expressed concern about the specter of revolt in China today, simultaneously confessing its presence and denouncing its materialization. Some simply thought that revolt would be ineffective or destabilizing, whereas others would only sing the praises of party and state. My impression was that such praises were sincere.

Many of my students in Xi'an view the Chinese Communist Party and Xi Jinping as responsible for a high level of social and political stability, growing prosperity since the late 1970s, and much opportunity both domestically and globally. Many (if not most) view Xi and the Communist Party as looking out for the whole of the people, notwithstanding mistakes. One student told me that we should not expect to see revolt in China because people do not rise up when things are good enough that they have their basic needs met.

Nonetheless, the government does worry about uprisings and seeks to exert a certain discursive control throughout society.

For example, there was a scandal in late July 2018 about a government-owned drug company that knowingly cut corners in the manufacture of a rabies vaccine for children.[23] It was all over Chinese Global Television Network (CGTN) for days. However, the main line in the story in China was that the government was going to punish all those responsible. One student told me that this was the government's typical line aimed to keep people from directing their outrage at the state, who should have perhaps regulated this company better in the first place (and especially since this was not the company's first time in trouble).

Students also told me on numerous occasions that WeChat, the social media app most widely used throughout Asia (far more than Facebook, which did not work well in China), is under constant surveillance by the state. The WeChat app is very good, and everyone in China uses it because it not only provides free phone and video calls, but also because it serves as a digital wallet. Many stores in Xi'an, for example, did not accept credit cards and only took payment through WeChat. The app has an excellent translation

---

23. See Bill Chappell, "Chinese Company's Flawed Vaccines Draw Anger and a Criminal Inquiry," *NPR.org*, July 23, 2018, https://www.npr.org/2018/07/23/631509868/chinese-companys-flawed-vaccines-draw-anger-and-a-criminal-inquiry.

function from Chinese to English, which nearly everyone used to communicate with me; it was fast and reliable, with no advertisements, no fees, and no bugs or functionality issues, working seamlessly from one side of the globe to the other. Nonetheless, many of the students who "friended" me on WeChat did not have their pictures there. I asked them why they did not use their pictures on WeChat, which would have made it easier for me to know who I was talking with. Repeatedly, I was told, "WeChat is under surveillance, and anything you say or do there is watched by the government." One student took a picture with me, but she was traveling home to a different province later in the week and she wanted the picture off her phone because she was sure they would not allow her to travel back into her province if they saw a picture of her with a foreigner. At the very least, she would have to explain it to the authorities. Therefore, she sent the photo to a friend staying in Shaanxi Province, and asked her friend to send it when she arrived at her destination. This was part of what students meant by a lack of freedom.

During my lecture on revolt, I asked the students why they thought the Chinese government was so concerned about what people said, published, posted online, etc., if the government was not concerned about becoming the target of disaffection. Everyone agreed with my suggestion that the fear of revolt governs much of what the government does.

We could discuss many examples, such as programs like China's social credit system, announced in 2014 and well under way. The government had not yet fully implemented the social credit system during my 2018 visit, with the plan to make it nationwide by 2020, though it was already functioning through staffs of neighborhood behavior monitors who reported and publicly posted points earned and lost within the neighborhood. "Like private credit scores, a person's social score can move up and down depending on their behavior. The exact methodology is a secret—but examples of infractions include bad driving, smoking in nonsmoking zones, buying too many video games, and posting fake news online."[24] As a result of poor scores, some have had their ability to travel restricted.

---

24. See Alexandra Ma, "China's 'Social Credit' System Ranks Citizens and Punishes Them with Throttled Internet Speeds and Flight Bans If the Communist Party Deems Them Untrustworthy," *Business Insider*, October 29, 2018, https://www.businessinsider.com/china-social-credit-system-punishments-and-rewards-explained-2018-4.

We must not forget, however, that China saw major revolutions in 1911 and 1946–1950, which radically transformed the country, first from Imperial to Republican rule, and second, to one of the last nationwide "communist" experiments of the twentieth century. The Chinese Communist Revolution happened long after the Russian Revolution and just after the Second World War, so the historical proximity of Chinese people to life-altering revolt is near. Revolt and revolution are also major parts of the historical education of Chinese students and something that they proudly claim in present political culture. Though again, the Cultural Revolution is the glaring exception, which the people I spoke with wanted to avoid talking about (at least with me).

Ultimately, I cannot know what my hosts may have concealed from me. That fact reminded me of James C. Scott's theory of hidden transcripts. A foreigner such as myself should never expect to have access to "the privileged site for nonhegemonic, contrapuntal, dissident, subversive discourse."[25] Therefore, in addition to temporal, geographic, and linguistic limitations to my knowledge, there are also those pertaining to ideology and political discourse.

Tiny Little Weapons

It was a happy discovery to see the resonance and electricity of my theory of revolt in China. I suggested to the students that all "societies of control" or "control societies" (as Bernard Stiegler called them)—of which China is most certainly one—are haunted by specters of revolt that will materialize at various points in the twenty-first century.[26] We had already seen major global revolts in the decade of 2008–2018—from Greece, Spain, and the Arab Spring to Occupy Wall Street, Black Lives Matter, Nuit Debout, and Gilet Jaunes in France. I concluded my summer seminar by suggesting to these young people that they should be prepared to understand the next revolts

25. James C. Scott, *Domination and the Arts of Resistance: Hidden Transcripts* (New Haven: Yale University Press, 1990), 25.

26. See Bernard Stiegler, *Uncontrollable Societies of Disaffected Individuals: Disbelief and Discredit, Volume 2*, trans. Daniel Ross (Cambridge: Polity Press, 2013).

in China with sympathy and attention. I suggested that reading theory could help prepare them for participation in the next revolts, wherever such participation makes sense politically, ethically, economically, etc.

It was difficult to suggest as a grateful guest but also necessary: the Chinese people are being taken for a global capitalist roller-coaster ride, and while that ride comes with some thrill and excitement, and with the hope that often attends promises of prosperity and personal wealth and well-being, capital is a fatal logic to follow.

The cultural orientations of China contain much that is derived from noncapitalist sources: first, there is ancient China and its traditions; second, are basic sensibilities of socialism and communism. The latter remains a kind of quietly beating heart in the cultural politics and general ethos (*Sittlichkeit*) of the Chinese people. Socialist identifications still appear in the political rhetoric of the Chinese state. Among the young students I spent my time with, they repeatedly touted Chinese emphases on equality, collectivism, and social harmony as distinguishing features that proudly set them apart from Westerners. They wanted me to see this in their country and repeatedly asked me if I did. I did find ample evidence of this sensibility, including in the way they regarded one another and welcomed me.

I would say that the Chinese people possess a real and conscious communist sensibility but by no means a communist form of life. Imagine something like a self-consciously socialist culture aesthetically counterbalancing a capitalist political economy. I wonder what this means for imaginary power, the ability to think communism as a positivity inside a capitalist reality. This is precisely the strange permutation and legacy of Maoism into the present. However, China's capitalist commitments have only deepened since Mao's death, with Xi traveling the world in July 2018 arguing openly for the necessity of an unbounded capitalist world order, a world where it would be immoral for countries to wage trade wars or punish capital with rules and regulations. The strangeness of hearing this argument from Xi is evident to anyone who knows well or has lived through the Cold War—here is a Communist Party fully committed to the totality of global capitalism. The most profound oddity was that Xi was arguing for an unbounded capitalism against the rival vision of Donald Trump's United States.

If capitalist power is actively disfiguring of social relations and if it is destructive of the natural environment and exploitative (extractive) of human life, a socialist *culture* with communist sensibilities cannot hold up against it. This points, perhaps, to a limitation of imaginary power. At some point, the horizon meets reality. Moreover, commitments to privatization, growth, and accumulation cannot remain merely economic commitments, for they inevitably shape the commitments of the people whose lives they influence by such values and trajectories. Materialism is an imperfect and problematic philosophy, but it contains much truth. Signs of individuation in cultural life (particularly through social media and technology) are present, though students in Xi'an seemed aware of this and many expressed wanting to resist it. They seem to simultaneously take pride in socialism with Chinese characteristics and to fully endorse Xi's restructuring of the Communist Party into unequivocal capitalist power.

My students in Xi'an enjoyed reading and discussing critical theory and Marxian philosophy, and they wanted to reconcile it with the Chinese reality. I wanted to see them grapple with this as well, to see what possible uses they might make of the theories. I sensed from beginning to end a certain dangerous excitement, a more or less concealed appetite for some criticism of power in China. It was impossible, however, to separate this critical interest from an otherwise unshakeable patriotic nationalism. Perhaps matters are not so muddled in the hidden transcript I cannot see, or perhaps things not so muddled only appear so to an alien perspective. In any case, I do not think that I've ever felt such a sense of the subversive power of a lecture as I did at Shaanxi Normal University. I teach the same material in the United States, and students here know that it is subversive when they read and discuss it. Yet such theorizing is somewhat predictable in the United States. Students in the United States are essentially unworried by the fact that what they are reading is subversive, and they jump straight to analyzing, criticizing, or applying the arguments.

What is different in China is that a foreign visitor like me discovers that much of what I bring is not usually in classrooms on the mainland. Criticizing government in the United States is almost everyone's favorite pastime, but in China, it comes with some fear and trembling. I often felt that our sessions were on the line of acceptability and that an obligation to impress me restrained my hosts.

It is important here to emphasize that while the official position of the Chinese Communist Party is to claim itself Marxist, those same "Marxist" officials have been worried about the growing popularity of Marxism among Chinese students. *The Economist* reported in 2018 that Marxist student clubs in Beijing and Nanjing are struggling for institutional support and in some cases, shut down.[27] "Last November Zhang Yunfun, a twenty-something former member of Peking University's club, was arrested during a Marxist study session he had organized at a university in the southern city of Guangzhou. He was given a six-month jail sentence for disturbing public order. The country's rulers tremble at the thought of a Marxist revival."[28]

Even more recently, CNN reported that young Marxists are going missing in China. According to a student at Peking University, "The whole of Peking University is like under the white terror now, (the security guards) will come after you even if you were just at the scene where the student activists were distributing leaflets."[29] Today's young Marxists in China are "calling for greater workers' rights" and they have "become a growing problem for the Chinese government in recent years."[30]

It is interesting to see the origins of these disputes anchored to workers' struggles. In southern China, in June 2018, a group of workers attempted to form an independent union, a request that was prohibited by the government. This led to protest demonstrations that gained nationwide visibility. Around the time of my visit, in late July 2018, "a group of left-wing students, proclaiming themselves Maoists, traveled from around the country to join in the protests, drawing national attention."[31]

Protest demonstrations and social upheaval are more common and contentious in places like Hong Kong, which remains a special region of China, and maintains a separate political apparatus and identity than that of mainland China. Hong Kong was under British colonial rule from about 1841 until 1997. It returned to China on the agreed-upon premise of one country, two systems. The majority of people in Hong Kong are proud of the region's

27. See "A Spectre Is Haunting China: Officials in Beijing Worry About Marx-loving Students," *The Economist*, September 27, 2018, https://amp.economist.com/china/2018/09/29/officials-in-beijing-worry-about-marx-loving-students.

28. "A Spectre Is Haunting China."

29. See Ben Westcott and Yong Xiong, "Young Marxists Are Going Missing in China After Protesting for Workers" *CNN*, November 14, 2018, https://www.cnn.com/2018/11/13/asia/china-student-marxist-missing-intl/index.html.

30. "Young Marxists Are Going Missing."

31. "Young Marxists Are Going Missing."

relative autonomy from China and keen to defend that autonomy from mainland encroachments. Most living in Hong Kong identify as "Hongkongers," not primarily as Chinese, and there they more readily express criticism, anger, and resentment toward a Chinese government that is often seen as meddling in their affairs.

In June of 2019, massive protests broke out against an extradition bill that would allow the Chinese government to deport criminals and fugitives (and criminal and fugitive businesspeople) from Hong Kong to mainland China, to stand trial in China. Hong Kong police enforced official Chinese policy and were aggressive in a counterinsurgent response to protesters full of physical conflict, tear gas, and rubber bullets. Starting with tens of thousands of young demonstrators the uprising swelled to a million people over several days, leading to a rare small-business and workers' strike on June 12. Quentin Cheng Hin-kei, chair of a major union, told Reuters: "Even if we call off the strike, we cannot call off the anger."[32]

Indeed, one year after my trip to China, I watched from a distance as a formidable revolt in Hong Kong grew in size and intensity. By the end of July 2019, it was clear that the Hong Kong uprising had well exceeded the seemingly defeated extradition bill that triggered the upheaval in June. This confirmed what was clear from the start: the Hong Kong uprising expresses a broader disaffection. However, there have been several dominant analyses of the Hong Kong revolt that need refutation. These problematic analyses claim (1) that the West, and specifically the United States government, manufactured the revolts, (2) that the revolts are nothing more than a demand for Western-style capitalist "democracy," and (3) that the revolts are in no way a demand for Western-style capitalist "democracy." Let us briefly touch on each of the above.

First, some critics of the Hong Kong revolt portray the uprising as a program of US foreign policy. Multiple and independent reliable sources document that some of the groups involved in the uprising "receive significant funding from the National Endowment for Democracy (NED), a CIA soft-power cutout that has played a critical role in innumerable US

32. See Kate Leung and Vimvam Tong, "Hong Kong Shops, Workers in Rare Strike to 'Defend Freedom,'" *Reuters*, June 12, 2019, https://www.reuters.com/article/us-hongkong-extradition-strikes-idUSKCN1TD0TG.

regime-change operations."[33] US interest in Chinese instability is hardly surprising, and in fact, it would be far more surprising to discover that US power holders had no geopolitical or economic investments in powerful protests against the Chinese government. The US always seizes its interests in every global crisis.[34] Nevertheless, the indignation and disaffection of over a million Hongkongers is not a product of the NED. The relationship of Hong Kong to China is complex, and the extradition bill only created an opportunity to express longstanding disaffections (about many other things as well) that remain in the hearts, minds, and mouths of the insurrectionists. Most in Hong Kong have had too much of foreign government usurpation and much of the revolt is rooted in a spirit of autonomy. The young people are also not happy with their own leaders for being too beholden to outside powers. To take a close look at the diversity and ferocity of the uprisings in a range of clashes with police, the smashing of government building windows, and to listen to the young people speak openly in their own words is to recognize the agency of real people who are putting themselves (and their bodies) on the line. To claim that the NED manufactured all of that activity reveals brazen reductionist audacity, both insulting and unsupportable by the facts.

A second view: conservative and liberal onlookers from the West have been inclined to read the uprising as the people of Hong Kong demanding a spitting image of Western-style capitalism and rejecting the so-called "communist" tyranny of China. Unsurprisingly, the perspective of Western power can only see that everyone everywhere wants whatever exists in the West. However, that view is simple to the point of stupidity. Many in the Hong Kong upheaval have expressed anti-authoritarian opposition to creeping Chinese overstep, but they have also condemned their own institutions and representatives by name and have articulated an emancipatory hope for a form of life ungoverned by the rich and powerful. Moreover, participants frequently invoke their history of colonization as a source of mobilization against any foreign or outside usurpation, including ones from the West (which they have already had enough of). According to on-site reportage,

33. See Alexander Rubinstein, "American Gov't, NGOs Fuel and Fund Hong Kong Anti-Extradition Protests," *Mint Press News*, June 13, 2019, https://www.mintpressnews.com/hong-kong-protests/259202.

34. As we could see in the more recent example of the US response to (and coverage of) Putin's revanchist invasion of Ukraine.

"the mainly younger protesters think the government has robbed them of opportunity while pandering to the rich and powerful," and one protester declared, "There's nothing that we own except this city. There's nowhere to turn and nothing to lose."[35] Some of them have likened their situation to that of the Palestinians. The oft-repeated sense of a long struggle against the interests of money and political power should suffice to prevent Western capitalists and pundits from concluding that Hong Kong dreams about becoming a US city governed by a different set of moneyed interests.

Finally, we cannot simply assert that the Hong Kong revolt is a new anti-capitalist insurgency for communism against its spectacle form. Participants did not single-mindedly focus on opposing capitalism. Like any uprising, this one is heterogeneous and expresses a range of disaffections, often conflicting ones, and does not produce a simple ideological script. We cannot deny that some participants have been seen holding signs appealing to the governments of the United States and Britain for assistance, while some even "waved British and American flags."[36] By all accounts, that is not an overwhelming sight in the upheaval, but it is in there, too, along with everything else.

I spoke with one of my students about these revolts, and she told me that, even though she is on the mainland and away from the action, she "stands with those protesters," and she reminded me that she "watched the Umbrella Revolution in 2014" and "saw how the police attacked unarmed people, and how the protesters support one another."[37] Nonetheless, I would not be surprised if many of my students who lamented deficits of freedom in China were indeed hoping Hong Kong would agitate for a more Western-style capitalism.

There is complexity in the uprising, and we must resist any totalizing view of what is happening there. Yet I am inspired whenever I see young people confronting established powers in this way. Some things we can know

---

35. See Violet Law, "'Nothing to Lose': The Hong Kong Protesters Taking on China," *Al Jazeera*, July 11, 2019, https://www.aljazeera.com/news/2019/07/lose-hong-kong-protesters-china-190710062708453.html.

36. See Donny Kwok and Felix Tam, "Clashes Break Out as Hong Kong Protesters Escalate Fight in Suburbs," *Reuters*, July 14, 2019, https://www.reuters.com/article/us-hongkong-extradition/clashes-break-out-as-hong-kong-protesters-escalate-fight-in-suburbs-idUSKCN1U904G.

37. Personal correspondence with a student, July 2019.

with confidence, for example, that this revolt is an experience and realization of a certain power of young and everyday people in Hong Kong. Those in the uprising can see that the government is afraid of what they can mobilize. One of the lasting outcomes of rising up is the realization that people can generate different powers. In this case, this is an accomplishment young Hongkongers shall not soon forget. No doubt, this upheaval is the experience of a lifetime, and they shall want to return to it as they already have since the Umbrella Revolution and Sunflower Movement in 2014. This should remind us that when an uprising settles down, that does not mean it is over and done. Revolt can always pick up its unfinished business later on, and it usually does.

Much more recently, in November and December of 2022, the *New York Times* reported that the "broadest and boldest surge of protests in a generation is sweeping China, as people in cities across the country take to the streets to denounce the government's inflexible and exhausting Covid measures."[38] The long and large-scale lockdowns of Chinese people, for roughly three years, and the resurgence of the government's "zero COVID-19" policy, had pushed people to a point of outrage. Inside the protests, however, a range of disaffections were being expressed, and not only about COVID-19. In an interview, Li Yuan said that she had not "seen anything like this since 1989, when millions of Chinese students took to the streets all over China, but especially in Beijing and Tiananmen Square."[39] There was something inchoate and palpable in these protests, and it is too easy for liberals and leftists to stand with Xi on the grounds of a strong public health policy, as if the only opposition to the government must be right-wing. If we understand China's government as "communist," opposition to it may appear as anticommunist. However, we cannot accept the spectacles of "communism" as presented by dueling capitalist powers. Moreover, real disaffection can only be bottled and kept down for so long.

The 2022 uprisings quickly took on an antagonistic and disruptive demeanor, and their location and composition are of crucial importance. "Guangzhou has come under immense scrutiny after residents forcefully resisted being confined in their homes, restrictions that, in some cases, were

---

38. Jonathan Wolfe, "China's Covid Revolt," *New York Times*, November 30, 2022, https://www.nytimes.com/2022/11/30/briefing/chinas-covid-revolt.html.

39. Ibid.

to last for as long as a month. This week, hundreds of migrant workers in the district of Haizhu, a hub for garment production, tore down barriers and hurled glass bottles at riot police officers after weeks of going without work and seeing their food supplies dwindle."[40] These locations are not the usual ones, not Hong Kong or Taiwan, and the ferocious breaking of ranks with Xi in dozens of cities across China led to the government's plan to "crack down on 'criminal acts that disrupt social order.'"[41] If the conclusion was premature during my 2018 visit, we may now confirm that the specter of revolt not only haunts China but also confronts China in its active realization.

I think that current problems in China are not being—and will not be—solved within the limits of its twenty-first century capitalism. To the contrary, capitalism has exacerbated those problems. Some of China's own critics on the inside are calling for one form of capitalism over another. I am not sure that hope resides in Hong Kong as much as it does in the possibility for new contentious movements on the mainland. Such upheaval is more surprising and destabilizing on the mainland than in Hong Kong, for political, cultural, and historical reasons. Hong Kong is expected to let loose unrulier social energies than those that have been acculturated under the surveillance and reprisals of China's sole domain. There, we would find the most promising contradictions: Maoists against Maoists, Marxists against Marxists! The ones outside of power standing up against the ones inside of power! Such an opposition should come as no surprise to anyone who understands Marxism as a philosophy from below, the distinguishing feature of which is to challenge the codified state powers of capitalist society. Simply, what we may hope to witness on the mainland is that old opposition of Marxism to "Marxism," of the real thing in opposition to its spectacle form.

I refuse to overstate the significance of my China lectures for the obvious fact that they could have only affected a tiny segment of the thinking of an even smaller subset of my students in Xi'an. Nonetheless, I felt that the course could have been a tiny preparation for struggles on the horizon. We do not know what those struggles may be. The students had a better sense

---

40. David Pierson and Chang Che, "After Mass Protests, China Appears to Back Away from Harsh Covid Rules," *New York Times*, December 1, 2022, https://www.nytimes.com/2022/12/01/world/asia/china-covid-protests-restrictions.html.

41. Pierson and Che, "After Mass Protests."

than I about what may be on China's horizon, and I left them to make connections between their knowledge and experience and the texts we read.

Perhaps the only serious role of academic theory in politics is as a means of preparation for unknown struggles on the horizon. It has something to do with our imaginations. Not all imagination aims at emancipatory horizons. There are plenty of bad imaginations out there in the world, imaginations only capable of aspiring toward a tepid "socialistic" capitalism, or worse, only reproducing the mythologies of communist and capitalist spectacles. However, theory also happens elsewhere, outside of academia and outside of texts, though my context in Xi'an was to do it with books in a university classroom. Such a practice has its limitations. I told my students that they would quickly forget some—if not most—of what we studied, that some of it was probably irrelevant to their lives and to politics in China. However, I also conveyed my sincere hope that something—even if just some *one thing*—could be taken forward into future fights for a possible and desirable future as they saw fit.

Theory provides us one means by which to compare what is to what we imagine could be. Good theory may do that in words or in the critical activity of revolts. We are not in the position of choosing one to the exclusion of the other. We must marshal every helpful resource for the diverse creative activities of making new worlds. We must never forget that human beings make the worlds they inhabit. If we do not participate in world-making activities—activities that always draw on our imaginary powers—others will continue to make the world for us, and they will not change a status quo that serves their interests. We reproduce the worlds we inhabit by doing what we are expected. Recent and ongoing uprisings in China show that people are capable of breaking with such expectations, even in societies of control characterized by nationalism and loyalty.

I confess that I am partial to the old notion of theory as a weapon. I think it was therefore appropriate that my last three words to the students in China were "choose your weapon."

CHAPTER 5

How Dare We Speak of Love?

Melodie und Rhythmus: *At a crucial point in* The Communism of Love, *you write that "love politics" is not only a "field of experience" but also a "battlefield on which we must fight wars of maneuver and wars of position."*[1] *What are the most important wars a "communism of love" must fight at a time when a vast dispossessed majority of humanity finds itself in the stranglehold of a pandemic crisis—forcing us into atomization and destroying social bonds without which love cannot flourish? What is the role of a communism of love when humanity has to fight for its existence on a planet driven toward ecological collapse by an exploitative mode of production at an ever-increasing rate?*

Richard Gilman-Opalsky: First, I should explain that, according to my theory, love is not something we possess like a commodity or private property. We can never reduce love to the private affairs of two or a few people in a sexual, romantic, or familial relationship. Instead, I define love as an active practice of human relationality incompatible with the logic of capitalist exchange relations. For example, you cannot claim to love a friend if you charge a fee for your friendship. If we offer food and shelter to our children in exchange for labor, that would have to be understood as a different relationship than love. In practice, love relations seem to follow Marx's motto "from

1. A shorter version of this interview about my theory of love appeared in German in *Melodie und Rhythmus* in 2021. Susann Witt-Stahl conducted the interview. The interview has only appeared in German thus far, and never in full. The German magazine piece was a short feature on the book *The Communism of Love* (Chico: AK Press, 2020). It appears here for the first time in full and in English translation.

each according to their ability, to each according to their needs." What I find in love is therefore a certain communism that is generally not recognized as such in common understandings of love. Therefore, I am thinking of love as an activity of human relations that abides by a certain logic, a logic that is antithetical to the logic of capital. People do not typically define love that way.

Now, you were asking about my claim that love politics is a field on which we must fight wars of maneuver and wars of position. Yes! I am referring there to the terminology of Antonio Gramsci who repurposed military science for revolutionary politics.[2] A war of position is an ideological battle, and a war of maneuver is a phase of material struggle where we confront real enemies and try to change things in the world. Ideologically, I think we have to help people see that their own most cherished human relations conceal irreducibly communist commitments. It turns out that communism is not as far away from human understanding and experience as most think. If people can come to see that *the best things in their own lives* are not only *not* capitalist, but *anti*capitalist in key respects, this would mark a crucial development in ideological struggle, a victory of the war of position.

In terms of the war of maneuver, we need this more than ever and precisely because of the examples you mentioned. You are right to think in terms of pandemics and ecological crisis. I completely agree. However, the pandemic is not what has forced us into atomization and destroyed social bonds. Capitalism has been doing that for roughly two hundred years, which Marx identified already in 1844, and then later in *Grundrisse*. The pandemic has only exacerbated a competitive individualism that capitalism has been proliferating aggressively since the 1970s, since the decades of the accelerated privatization of everything—often called "neoliberalism." It is even possible to say that capitalism has prepared us for the pandemic by developing technological methods of being-together while staying apart, and by encouraging us to look out for our own health and well-being to the exclusion of that of others. The COVID-19 pandemic reveals how devastating this logic is when exacerbated, which is not to say that it was not already devastating beforehand. Now we can see, with a brutal clarity, nations competitively seizing upon vaccines, comparing death rates, and many nations hoarding

2. Antonio Gramsci, *Prison Notebooks, Volume 1*, trans. Joseph A. Buttigieg and Antonio Callari (New York: Columbia University Press, 2011), 217.

more vaccines than they can use while others scarcely have any.[3] Beyond this, the prevailing idea is that each responsible individual should be vaccinated, contributing to a society of vaccinated individuals. However, we witnessed that individualist action does not defeat the virus. The "invisible hand" is not at work here, not any more than it works in economic affairs. Massive and collective global immunity is the only sensible goal. In all of this, we were pushed to venerate and advertise, entirely for free—and to accept with virtually no criticism—the benevolence of major pharmaceutical companies that make billions by exchanging human safety for money. Moreover, the pandemic exposed existing racial stratifications of health and poverty in their naked callousness to anyone who cared to look. The disaster of the pandemic mapped out over the class and racial dimensions of capitalist societies. It is therefore catastrophic also because it is capitalist, although none of the liberal officials will say so.

As to the ecological crisis, the only hope of rising to the challenge—if it is still possible to do so—is to abandon competitive self-interest for cooperative collective and global action that rejects the logic of capital and its concern for extraction, growth, and profit. No one has made this case more clearly and powerfully than Kohei Saito.[4] How to get from here to there is another matter, unfortunately. We might possibly know how to do this if we could follow the lessons love teaches in our precarious little communes of family and friends, if we are fortunate enough to have those. The problem is that we not only have to learn the lessons of love but, a much more difficult task, to liberate its logic from the confines of private relations and make it social. A project of such magnitude will obviously require many wars of position and wars of maneuver. I wish there was a surer path, but the truth is that a communism of love may only play a tenuous part in the solutions we need.

The existential climate crisis alone means that time is running out for humankind and nature, and, as the human ecologist Andreas Malm rightly says, we urgently

3. Whether or not one wants to debate the safety or efficacy of the vaccines, the fact remains that international competition over adequate responses and public health protocols characterized the early months and years of the pandemic.

4. Kohei Saito, *Marx in the Anthropocene: Towards the Idea of Degrowth Communism* (Cambridge: Cambridge University Press, 2023).

need to "learn to fight in a world on fire."[5] *The '68 movements preached pacifism to the Western left. Its maxim "Make Love, Not War!" was not only directed against the Vietnam War and other imperialist acts of aggression but also disarmed an entire generation—a very one-sided disarmament. The mainstream of the movement, although initially oriented toward Marxists like Herbert Marcuse and considering itself revolutionary, soon ended up in a permanent state of drug intoxication, escapism, and eventually cynical affirmation of the prevailing order, revealing that this generation had pursued a false "peace and love." Such historical defeats are partly why communists do not put much faith in love. You, on the other hand, consider it a mistake that "communists have mostly ignored love as a soft and vaporous feeling unfit for materialism or militancy!" How, then, can love be used effectively as "communist power" and as a "weapon" of emancipation in the war described by Gramsci without being integrated by capitalism, and without Marxists who avail themselves of it being "hugged to death?"*

Yes, we are running out of time. Regarding ecology especially, it is not clear we can do what is necessary quickly enough. However, I really want to stress that no philosophy can teach us how to fight in a burning world. As a materialist, I often consider the possibility that the only thing that can teach us how to fight in a burning world is a world engulfed in flames. We have seen similar sad lessons with pandemics before COVID-19, such as Ebola, where a prevalent indifference around the globe took the form of a simple selfish hope: "*Maybe it will not come here.*" As long as people can turn on the tap and water pours out, there is the possibility that they will prefer immunity to community. This the important point explored by Donatella Di Cesare.[6]

The best any philosophy may hope for is to produce some epiphanies that might alter analyses and commitments as an accomplice to revolutionary activity. However, even philosophers must wait for philosophy from below, that philosophy which expresses itself in riots, revolts, and insurrections.

So, why love? More bluntly, *how dare we speak of love in a time like this*? Well, as you know, I am not thinking in terms of sexual freedom or some

5. See Andreas Malm, *How To Blow Up a Pipeline: Learning to Fight in a World on Fire* (New York: Verso Books, 2021), 142.

6. Donatella Di Cesare, *Immunodemocracy: Capitalist Asphyxia* (South Pasadena: Semiotext(e), 2020).

refurbished culture of the 1960s that proved itself ultimately compatible with liberal capitalism. Of course, we must learn from the past, but the present is a cruel reminder that we must not reproduce it. To point to the failures of the movements of '68 as a reason to abandon love is, to my mind, like abandoning communism because of the failures of the Soviet Union. No, we cannot do that. We keep our good ideas and root out the bad ones.

It is also important to say that hatred and love are not opposites. In the same way that love for a friend may mobilize hatred of their enemy, love of life on Earth may mobilize the hatred of capital. Many in the US stupidly say that the people who participated in the uprisings of Black Lives Matter hate their communities because they break windows, burn buildings, and vandalize cars, as if people do not know the difference between a community and a police car! The truth is that Black Lives Matter expresses disaffections mobilized by a real and active love of community. Capital, law, and order are the real enemies of the community. Poverty rates, police violence, and mass incarceration bear this out, among other things.

Finally, the epiphany I am after is no faith or hug but, rather, a real consideration of the material conditions of love in our lives. We have to begin there. Enrique Dussel writes in *Philosophy of Liberation* that processes of human emancipation must throw the whole system into question, "as a questioning that opens a world from itself, its own road from within itself."[7] This means that liberation must come out of practices and experiences that follow a different logic and *reveal* different ways of being-in-the-world, different possibilities. We have to find ways to make an accomplice out of our affection. At the most basic level, this may take the form of active expressions of solidarity. There are other possibilities, such as when Angela Y. Davis highlights that feelings of solidarity with Black Lives Matter can and must take the form of active expressions of solidarity with Palestinians living under military occupation.[8] That's just one example. However, it is in this way that communists must not surrender love to solipsistic poets, theologians, or to 1968, and should think again about love as a weapon.

---

7. Enrique Dussel, *Philosophy of Liberation*, trans. Aquilina Martinez and Christine Morkovsky (Eugene: Wipf and Stock Publishers, 1985), 63.

8. Angela Y. Davis, *Freedom Is a Constant Struggle: Ferguson, Palestine, and the Foundations of a Movement* (Chicago: Haymarket Books, 2016), 15.

I think Walter Benjamin was right when he accused "social democracy" of having "cut the sinew of the best strength" of the proletariat by diverting its attention from the defeated oppressed of the past. For in doing so, social democracy has at least partially neutralized the hatred of the working class against its rulers, which is fueled not least by the fond memory of the many millions of slaughtered comrades and their longing for revolution. In other words, social democracy has undermined the productive relationship between love and hate that you describe. Isn't this collective historical and emotional dissociation now becoming an even greater problem on the anticapitalist left, which is increasingly afflicted by its obliviousness to history, by ideologically sophisticated appeasement, and by hypocritical moralistic attacks from "progressive" left liberals, for example?

I completely agree with you about "social democracy." One could begin in a number of places, even with Marx's own ferocious *Critique of the Gotha Program*, but I think it is best in this context to revisit Rosa Luxemburg's refutation of Eduard Bernstein. Bernstein's idea about the evolution of capitalism into a more socialistic and democratic capitalism took root inside anticapitalist circles, and it is precisely for that reason that Luxemburg was compelled to confront it.[9] Despite Luxemburg's efforts (and Marx's before her), we are now seeing the proliferation of Bernstein's capitalist concept of socialism in popular left-wing magazines like *Jacobin* and in the so-called "democratic socialism" of capitalist politicians throughout Western Europe, the US, and variously throughout Latin America and elsewhere. While I am supportive of seeing the best ideas of politicians like Bernie Sanders or Jeremy Corbyn prevail, faith in such a politics turns out to be a kind of liberal utopianism. If we are to be utopians, why not exceed the conservative horizon of liberalism? The history of capitalism should have proved by now that capital and capitalist elections move in exactly the opposite direction. In short, we do not need a "socialism" that accepts the permanence of capitalism.

What is missing from today's capitalist concept of socialism (or what you call "social democracy") is, of course, anticapitalism. Also missing is any commitment to revolution. Your previous question about running out of time in the face of ecological crisis highlights the fact that we need revolution (by

9. Eduard Bernstein, *Evolutionary Socialism: A Criticism and Affirmation* (London: Forgotten Books, 2018).

which I always mean the structural transformation of something, including political economy, culture, social life, forms of life, i.e., ontological transformation, etc.) more now than ever. We cannot accept a theory that abandons the critique of capital and the hope of revolution.

Working-class people around the world would absolutely do well to reclaim that old hatred of the ruling class, a hatred expressed with love in the songs, art, poetry, and other writings of our comrades from the past. But beyond the ascendancy of social democracy on the left, we are now also plagued with confused talk about "class reductionism." People who speak of "class reductionism" either forget (or do not know or want to know) that some of our greatest thinkers thought about race, gender, and sexuality with a critical focus. What I find in the Marxist trajectory—from W. E. B. Du Bois, Rosa Luxemburg, C. L. R James, Alexandra Kollontai, and Sylvia Pankhurst to Walter Rodney, Raya Dunayevskaya, Angela Y. Davis, Robin D.G. Kelley, Ruth Wilson Gilmore, Vanessa Wills, and so on—is robust class analysis that does not ignore other axes of oppression. Claims about "class reductionism" are part of the current tendency to run away from class, revolution, and anti-capitalism, and all of this is aided and abetted by an increasingly fashionable "social democracy." We must not agree with those critics who like to reduce Marxism to some form of "regulated" capitalism. If we are utopians, we are not utopian liberals who invest our hopes in the triumphs of socialistic advances in capitalist elections!

A serious problem of this betrayal of the working class by "democratic socialism" is that it literally invites reactionary forces to profit from its distortions. Whether in the ghettos on the outskirts of the cities or in the structurally weak countryside: wherever the liberalized left has abandoned the impoverished population, far-right activists and politicians appear, misleading a growing number of desperate and disoriented people with slogans like "America First!" toward an identitarian love that Hardt and Negri have characterized as a "corrupt form of love." What is so dangerous about this "love"—also from a socio-psychological point of view?

Yes, this is a big problem today and the issue of so-called "identitarian love" is one that I spend a lot of time on in *The Communism of Love*. Chauvinistic patriotisms like "America First!" or other racialized supremacist declarations of "self-love" are not, in fact, problems of love at all. These are problems that stem from not understanding what love is in the world or what it means conceptually. Therefore, these are problems I think my book may help to solve. What we are talking about is a fundamental confusion that mistakes narrow self-interest for self-love. Narrow self-interest, such as the "love" of one's race or nation, is not any kind of love. If one's "love" generates indifference or worse for strangers, if it undermines basic commitments of humanism, then it is not love. Unfortunately, love has a good name that can be invoked by anything that wants to wear its disguise. Many horrific things take cover behind a mask of love. This is dangerous because abusers often tell their victims that their abuse is an expression of love, and fascists of various kinds declare that they hate no one yet have a profound love for their own kind. Such "corrupt forms of love" appear in my theory as no forms of love at all, and this has to be seen very clearly so that we do not accept the unacceptable in the name of love.

From a socio-psychological point of view, people have a hard time with ideas like cosmopolitanism and its better version, communist internationalism. Many people incorrectly think that expansive and inclusive ideas of the human community mean that they have to abandon themselves and their interests. That is not true. When we understand the communism of love, we see that love is not an abandonment of the self but a relation of the self to others that enlarges, rather than shrinks, the *Gemeinwesen*.

The most shameless exploiter of love is still the culture industry, which produces false consciousness as a mass commodity (and thus, as critical theory recognized, also reveals the fascist potential of capitalism). You say, "Lovelessness is a boon to consumerism." In light of the increasing brutalization of bourgeois society that we are currently experiencing, more and more people are seeking comfort and security in the consumption of culture industry products that kitsch up and mystify love—and thus ideologically deform it. In the process, their authentic feelings are displaced by prefabricated emotions; their love is replaced by the fetishization and desire of certain products or by the fanatical worship of show business icons, and their range of emotions is dulled and narrowed. As early as the 1990s, the sociologist Stjepan Meštrović put forward the thesis that we are living in a "postemotional age." Is that true? Is the cultural sphere not perhaps even one of the main battlefields on which we must fight to save love?

I agree with what you say about the culture industry, which refers to a specific form of capitalist society that emerged in the twentieth century. It is not surprising that capitalists would seize upon something like love. How could they resist? We regard love as a universal human aspiration and a great positive power, so there was no chance capital would leave it alone. Capitalists seize and seek to wield love as an instrument of capital, converting it into the love of a car, a kitchen, some other commodity, or a lifestyle, etc.

The Communism of Love offers sustained engagement with critical theory from Erich Fromm to Axel Honneth. In it, I also offer sustained criticisms of critical theory's insufficient attention to racism, sexism, and even to sexuality, despite its Freudian content. However, I think that critical theory was essentially correct. Thinkers like Fromm and Marcuse were among the best Marxists to take up the question of love.

If we do not resist the reduction of love to a commodity form (ultimately, the commodification of love is its obliteration), we give one of our greatest aspirations to the enemy. We cannot do that! We cannot let capital have love! Moreover, I am not convinced like Meštrović that our age is post-emotional.[10] Human beings are full of affection, emotion, longing, and feeling; this is precisely what the culture industry preys upon. We may be exhausted, anxious, confused, or hopeless but not without emotion. I think we have to resist the ongoing colonization of our emotional life and consider the ways that love exceeds commodification and exchange. That is the battle into which I send my theory. It is only one theory among many, like a stone thrown into an ocean . . . but we can nevertheless hope for ripples.

10. Stjepan Meštrović, *Postemotional Society* (London: Sage Publications, 1997).

CHAPTER 6

Pandemic *Gemeinwesen* and the Communist Secret of Love

In *The Communism of Love,* I aim to rethink the meanings of communism and love, and to understand a surprising and seemingly secret relationship between them.[1] In this chapter, I offer something I could not include in that book, exploring connections between the theory of love and the world-historical experience of COVID-19.

Our Beloved Miniature Communism

Still to this day, too many people who think of communism think about craven big government that crushes human freedom. Too many feel they know enough or more than enough about Karl Marx, too; no other author generates such strong feelings among so many who have never read his books. My students are always surprised to learn that, by comparison to what Marx wrote about social and economic realities, about exploitation and everyday life, his attention to government was minor and fleeting. Instead, Marx was transfixed by the *Gemeinwesen,* a German word meant to grasp the

1. Following the publication of *The Communism of Love,* I prepared several short pieces about the book for about half a dozen online and print-only venues. These were standalone articles intended to present the theory both in general terms and with particular applications. The best of these articles appeared in The New School's *Public Seminar* and *Ill Will* online magazine. I especially appreciated the opportunity to connect the theory of love to the reality of the pandemic, an application that did not appear in the book itself due to timing. This chapter combines the *Public Seminar* and *Ill Will* articles in a significantly expanded and cohesive application of the theory to present crises.

sensibility of human community, the actual and possible state of human relations.[2]

Marx defined communism as the movement that overturns a world of exchange relations, or more precisely, as "the real movement that abolishes the present state of things."[3] "Exchange relations" refer to the ways we relate to people when we exchange something for something else, whether that is money, labor, or some other commodity. Marx did not think a world of exchange relations made for the healthiest *Gemeinwesen*. He dreamed of that future horizon where we could one day declare "from each according to their ability, to each according to their needs."[4] What if we lived in a world where people only expected from each other what was in line with their abilities and desires? What if we lived in a world where the needs of everyone were a first priority and everything else came after?

There actually already are some places in our lives where we expect from others only what is in line with their abilities and desires and where we strive to provide people with everything that they need. That hopeful horizon can be found in miniature in the way we relate to our children. We do not give our kids food and shelter in exchange for their labor. We do not expect anything from them in exchange for what they need. Similar islands of miniature communism can be found in different love relations with others, with partners, family, friends, comrades, or anyone with whom we are happily connected for reasons other than money. We are not there for a friend in despair only if that friend pays us fifteen dollars an hour for our time and attention. Such a requirement would nullify the friendship. If you and your partner measure every chore and favor you do for one another on a spreadsheet to ensure an equal exchange, you'll both be on a fast track to resentment.

What is going on there? Why do we have these precious no-go zones for capitalist exchange relations? I believe it is because love relations motivate

---

2. Marx's focus on the *Gemeinwesen* is actually a continuation of the earlier focus of G.W.F. Hegel on the same concept. Hegel wrote often about the *Gemeinwesen* in his political and theological writings. Marx carried on and sustained interest in that concept throughout his body of work. Perhaps the best place to read Marx on the *Gemeinwesen* is in *Grundrisse: Foundations of the Critique of Political Economy*, trans. Martin Nicolaus (New York: Penguin Books, 1993).

3. Karl Marx and Frederick Engels, *The German Ideology* (New York: Prometheus Books, 1998).

4. Karl Marx, *Critique of the Gotha Program* (New York: International Publishers, 2002).

actions and commitments in a different way, and these differently motivated actions and commitments matter to us greatly. Our aspirations to love reveal a deep yearning for something greater than exchange relations.

In *The Communism of Love,* I wanted to help us understand love as something bigger than the private property of a romantic relationship. I define love as an action, as something we do, not something we give or get like a favor or a gift. I want to help us see the social and political dimensions of love. Our aspirations of love go off in search of others with whom to make common cause, in pursuit of something hopeful on the horizon. Likewise, those who struggle in the streets, in strikes, and in uprisings against racism, class inequality, and other exclusions also make common cause in pursuit of something hopeful on the horizon. To know what love does for real people in the real world is to grasp its communism and to reconcile ourselves with a communist aspiration in all of us. Yet, why bother relating any of this to "communism," such a thoroughly vilified word? As long as words and ideas offer something good and useful, something we need, we must not abandon them when they are misunderstood—especially not when they are deliberately misunderstood for political reasons.

COVID-19 and the Communism of Love

Why not just enjoy love as the private experience of family or friends? Do we really need a different society? The COVID-19 pandemic, among many other things, teaches us that we do. Gabor Maté noted, "As a speaker on stress and trauma I'm often asked what lessons we may derive from the COVID-19 pandemic. Chief among them, surely, is the indispensability of connection . . . increasingly drained from modern culture, long before the isolation imposed by the virus . . . The health impacts are immeasurable."[5] Maté adds that the pandemic "has done much to *unmask* many unflattering facts about our ways of life" and "is a powerful reminder of the interconnections between all life-forms . . . of the inequities of a system in which the most socially vulnerable are left most open to attack by a deadly virus; of how the slogan 'We

5. Gabor Maté, *The Myth of Normal: Trauma, Illness and Healing in a Toxic Culture* (New York: Avery Books, 2022), 286.

are all in this together' is a sad fiction when it comes to the economic ravages and windfalls of the public health catastrophe that has marked this decade for all time."[6]

It has been a brutal lesson indeed, and at the time of this writing, it is unclear what we have learned. Millions upon millions variously left alone, evicted, deprived of food and financial security, cut off from relationships that give their lives meaning, left without the jobs that were a prerequisite for the satisfaction of their everyday needs. Meanwhile, inside abusive homes, the old refuges of school, work, and friends were foreclosed, quarantining victims with their abusers in horrific private nightmares that we will learn about for years to come, possibly for the rest of our lives. Studies already show that people are unequally impacted by a pandemic. Wealthy countries are first in line for the vaccine, which they can stockpile, but even within wealthy counties, the poorest communities, and communities of color, bear disproportionate pains.[7] "Latino and Black Americans have been three times more likely to be infected by COVID-19 and twice more prone to dying from it. In Britain, too, communities of color were disproportionately affected, owing to deprived housing conditions, economic disadvantage, and preexistent health problems rooted in discrimination and inequity."[8]

There was also a sexist dimension to the pandemic, rooted in the ongoing gendered divisions of labor. "The self-stifling expectation of caregiving while ignoring one's own emotions and needs has only been reinforced by the COVID-19 pandemic."[9] Nancy Fraser analyzes the crisis of the pandemic as a "veritable orgy of capitalist dysfunction," claiming that "COVID-19 establishes beyond all doubt the need to abolish this social system once and for all."[10] Fraser notes that "racialized populations in many countries have been

6. Maté, *The Myth of Normal*, 494–95.

7. See Megan Twohey, Keith Collins, and Katie Thomas, "With First Dibs on Vaccines, Rich Countries Have 'Cleared the Shelves,'" *New York Times*, December 15, 2020, https://www.nytimes.com/2020/12/15/us/coronavirus-vaccine-doses-reserved.html. See also the Centers for Disease Control and Prevention, "COVID-19 Racial and Ethnic Health Disparities," *CDC*, December 10, 2020, https://www.cdc.gov/coronavirus/2019-ncov/community/health-equity/racial-ethnic-disparities/index.html.

8. Maté, *The Myth of Normal*, 317.

9. Maté, *The Myth of Normal*, 338.

10. Nancy Fraser, *Cannibal Capitalism: How Our System Is Devouring Democracy, Care, and the Planet—and What We Can Do About It* (New York: Verso Books, 2022), 160.

denied access to conditions that promote health: affordable, high-quality medical care, clean water, nutritious food, safe working and living conditions. No wonder, then, that their members have been disproportionately infected and killed by COVID."[11]

One of the most urgent lessons we should take from this experience is that money cannot be allowed to determine whether or not one's basic needs are satisfied, whether or not one receives necessary care. We don't want money to decide the enduring responsibilities and commitments of a healthy love relation, and we should not allow it to do so in society more broadly. Learning this lesson especially from the pandemic may be necessary for surviving the next catastrophe. For example, the message of the ecological crisis is not to keep extracting more from the natural world and to competitively seize the finite resources of our very small planet. What we have to do, if it is still possible to do so, is to shift urgently from competition to cooperation, from growth to degrowth, from wealth to needs. That is the urgent *Gemeinwesen* current emergencies call for.

The Communism of Love was published in December of 2020 and was written before the strain of coronavirus known as COVID-19 became a pandemic that changed the world as we knew it. Nonetheless, the connections I discuss in this chapter will be made in the minds of anyone who reads that book in the wake of COVID-19. After all, the communist theory of love sustains attention to questions of human well-being and healthy forms of being-together, all questions intensified by the global pandemic.

When the virus began to derail life in countries around the world, I was in La Plata, Argentina, where I was invited to do a seminar on the communist theory of love. The event was canceled when the Argentine government added the US to a list of countries with dangerous carriers of COVID-19 and barred anyone recently in the US from the universities. By April 2020, it was clear that this pandemic—*or a future one*—could outpace ecological or psychological crises and even world war, in posing an existential threat to life on Earth. The first order of analysis would have to keep the pandemic in the column of ecological, psychological, and imperialist crises and not in the column of social movements, revolts, and revolutions. This was not always easy to remember during early months of the virus when too many people

11. Fraser, *Cannibal Capitalism*, 163.

congratulated and cheered on the collective action and solidarity of social distancing and wearing masks.

No pandemic is "good" from a moral point of view, although some responses to it may be. A virus has no virtues. A virus has no morality, ideology, or politics. But because of it, people around the world genuinely wonder if the world as they know it is ending, and perhaps it is too soon to say it did not end in some ways already. Perhaps the pre-pandemic world was yet another casualty of the pandemic.

For some, the virus rendered all preceding reality unreal. For others, the virus only exacerbated a preceding reality of financial insecurity, anxiety, domestic abuse, and other nightmares. Everything you were doing before was miniaturized by what was happening now. Such experiences happen by other causes, as for example in Liberian civil war, Australian bushfires, Israel's genocidal decimation of Gaza, aerial bombardments on Iraq and Yemen, or in sieges on Ukraine. Reality previously included doing this or that, going here or there, but that reality gets canceled. With COVID-19, in the proliferation of quarantines and stay-at-home orders, a veritable world of workers became unemployed overnight and awoke in a new world where it was not clear how to procure food or rent.

Meanwhile, in the world of capitalist business, the big players were better positioned than all the little shops and restaurants moving rapidly closer to death. "The Swiss bank UBS reported in October 2020 that during the COVID-19–induced market turmoil the international billionaire stratum had grown their fortunes to over ten trillion dollars between April and July of that year. The world's then-richest individual, Amazon founder Jeff Bezos, had increased his wealth by over $74 billion; Tesla owner Elon Musk by up to $103 billion . . . The notion that capitalism is *meant* to provide equality and opportunity for all must be taken on faith, since history and material reality provide no evidence for it."[12] Anticapitalists have been making similar arguments for nearly two hundred years, but it seems that the pandemic experience of COVID-19 substantiated many of those arguments more widely than Marxist theorists could have done on their own.

A pandemic does not end class society; it happens within it. For those with some privilege, the preceding reality could become unreal without

12. Maté, *The Myth of Normal*, 284.

terrible consequences. However, consider those stuck in homes where there was already neglect and abuse, those who cannot leave for temporary emancipations from those abusers who, suddenly unemployed, are full of fresh frustration and anger. For many, the collective action of staying put intensifies preexisting violence and vulnerability, including the financial violence and vulnerability of the "normal" capitalist society. What hides in quarantined worlds of psychological and sexual abuse, and what happens to children in such hellish habitations? What of the elderly, who are also the most susceptible to sickness and death, when they are deprived of human contact? What of the disproportionate difficulty to flee from the virus among the impoverished and in communities of color? Photographs of New York City subways packed full of Black and Brown people in the epicenter of the pandemic, coupled with disproportionate rates of sickness and death, recall the Lower Ninth Ward in New Orleans during Hurricane Katrina.

The virus was never a simple story of social solidarity, but of asocial despair, brutal disregard, and abuse. As the horror stories make their way into the light, let's hope they make the journey with the help of the attentive love of other people. A good theory of love recommends a clear comportment and practical actions in the face of any crisis. The communist theory of love demands that we do our best to attend to the frailties and despairs of our beloved. Love materializes in active relationships of attentive care, relationships that are not governed by money, and that cannot be governed by money without becoming different relationships.

However, what is the fate of active relationships and attentive care in a socially distanced society? Indeed, pandemics require a passage of what we may call "asocial solidarity." But we should not treat such measures as if they're aimed at creating a different world. They have mostly been aimed at returning to a world that we previously wanted to abolish. Early after the first effective stay-at-home orders, right-wing groups in the US coordinated what looked like "protests" against staying home. But what is the meaning of a "protest" that demands going backward to restore a preceding normalcy? The answer to that question is part of the reason why the January 6, 2021 upheaval at the Capitol Building was a paramilitary deployment *of the state*—indeed, a neo-fascist reaction of a particular head of state and his disaffected base—and not any hopeful revolt against oppressive state power. We should not mistake the form for its content, just as we cannot mistake every marriage or family as a haven of love. An armed temper tantrum of Trump's supporters after Biden's electoral win is not the same thing as a revolt or an insurrection, despite the careless language of impeachment proceedings that constantly referred to the "January 6 Insurrection." No, we must never equivocate backward looking right-wing reactions with the future-oriented freedom struggles of women and Black people, from radical suffragettes like the Pankhurst women to Black Lives Matter.[13]

Still, one of the lessons of the virus was that, in order to overcome it, people had to break with the logic of capital that organizes so much of their lives. Of course, capitalist logic was not simply abandoned. Capitalists of the ruling class, with their emergency tax plans, so-called "stimulus" checks, and subsidies for millionaires, have long known to never let a good crisis go to waste. Nonetheless, there was a real reckoning amid the pain. Governments everywhere confessed that the capitalist logic of life could not by itself help us through the crisis. In a pandemic, the terrible and the good coexist in a complex unity. We must not surrender pre-pandemic values in a pandemic. Not exchange value, but other values are necessary for finding our way.

Is it too hopeful to think that the virus revealed the necessity of at least a little bit of communism? Remember, we only broke with the logic of capital in order to survive and, in turn, to return to its order. But even that is a crucial lesson. The virus shows that survival requires learning how to live differently. We must remember that this lesson will be indispensable for facing ecological, psychosocial, and other crises on the horizon.

One major conclusion of *The Communism of Love* is that human well-being cannot be maintained according to the logic of capital. For our health and well-being, we need relations beyond exchange relations; we need those non-monetary human relations that make our lives worth living. In all my work, including the present book, I explore the reality, desirability, possibility, and necessity of new forms of life. I look at real experiences of love in the real world in order to understand already-existing experiences of communist relations that we cherish even without identifying them as communist. Love is as close as we may get to a universal communist aspiration for a set of commitments

13. The suffragettes of the Women's Social and Political Union, an organization led by Emmeline Pankhurst, included radical women who smashed windows of government buildings, deliberately damaged property, and even made protests by means of arson.

and relationships that help us create little precarious communes. Little communes of family, friendship, comrades, artists, and colleagues shield us from the worst realities of life under the ongoing dictatorship of capital.

The pandemic strengthens old arguments about capital and human life, but that's not a pandemic's purpose. That we must defend and expand our communes beyond their narrow limits must be the purpose of communists like us.

Love and its Communist Secret

Considering the communist theory of love outlined above and the recent experience of pandemic, we need now, more than ever before, a serious inquiry into the poverty of exchange value. The capitalist mode of assessing value is incapable of appreciating what human beings—everywhere on Earth—value the most. This has to be one of the central lessons of COVID-19. Most human life is subordinated to exchange relations.

Erich Fromm was right to understand love as an activity, not a private property. Love is not a commodity but an active form of human relations ungoverned by the logic of capital (it's an active relation but not an exchange relation). In practice, love is our active participation in the various "becomings" of other people, such as in the ways we participate in our beloved becoming what they are able to and would like to be but are *not-yet*. As for communism, do not listen to conservatives (or to those anarchists who agree with them) who claim that communism is an assemblage of bureaucratic offices called "government." We can and must insist on following Marx's original definition of communism as an active abolitionist opposition to the existing world, as a struggle to create new forms of life, and as a revolutionary process. In this frame, communism must be—among other things—an effort to overthrow the rule of exchange value, a real movement toward healthy human relations.

In order to fully expose the communist secret of love, we can begin with the materiality of love relations. Human relationality is formed in our worldly intersubjectivity, and what shapes our relationships with others can be (and often is) far more valuable than the relationships established by capitalist exchange relations. Harry Cleaver observes: "Capitalists, unfortunately, try to organize this kind of relationship in ways that give them power over us. They seek to impose our relationship to them to such a degree that we come to define ourselves, and are defined by others, primarily in terms our jobs . . . In actuality, of course, we may *do* and *be* a great many things, but within capitalism the expectation is that we will identify with our work."[14] In pandemic times, many millions of people had to confront what they are and do besides and beyond capitalist work. For many, not going to work is an existential crisis in both financial terms and in terms of identity.

Capitalism, as both an ideological position and as an actual power that organizes life, cannot satisfactorily encompass the psychosocial and emotional needs of everyday people. Capitalism itself did not offer any way through the psychosocial and emotional needs of pandemic life, because its logics of profit, accumulation, and growth were hard at work elsewhere, characteristically seizing upon human needs as business opportunities.

In *The Communism of Love*, I wanted to address the major question posed by Kathi Weeks at the end of her book *Constituting Feminist Subjects*: "What are some of the different ways to conceive a collective subject, ways that move beyond the liberal model, according to which the individual is primary and authentic, the group is a 'mere' secondary construction, and a legitimate group is posed as a consensual aggregation of individuals? Given the pervasiveness of liberal individualism and its stubborn grip on our thinking in late capitalist societies, this remains a difficult task indeed."[15]

Therefore, we seek to understand the possibility of a real collective subject that is *not* secondary to the individual because—among other reasons—the individual is realized only in dialectical relations with others around her. The individual is developed within that sociality and does not precede it.

Today, I contend that Bruno Gullì has provided the best answer to Weeks's question. He writes about "singularity" to invoke individual nodal points in a social fabric of humanity that can only be *misunderstood* when treated as individuals. Following Gilbert Simondon, Gullì writes, that the "singular is precisely the 'particular being' that is 'more than an individual.'"[16]

---

14. Harry Cleaver, *Rupturing the Dialectic: The Struggle against Work, Money, and Financialization* (Chico: AK Press, 2017), 110–11.

15. Kathi Weeks, *Constituting Feminist Subjects* (New York: Verso Books, 2018), 159.

16. Bruno Gullì, *Singularities at the Threshold: The Ontology of Unrest* (Lanham: Lexington Books, 2020), 29.

According to Gullì, "All there is are fragments in search of individuation, constantly individuating, yet regularly falling short of full individuation. It is in this sense that to the concept of the individual I prefer the concept of the dividual (or rather, the gathering of dividuals)."[17] Because so many of our social relations are determined by the capitalist mode of life and work, we cannot answer the question of what ought to be in terms of what is. That is to say, we are not looking for a collectivity that is the determined subject position of capitalist society, but, rather, we are looking for a collectivity formed in our noncapitalist being-in-the-world, our relations to other human beings that maintain a sociality beyond and against exchange relations.

For Gullì, the concept of singularity is important because it moves beyond efforts to individuate toward, instead, the common. "Ultimately, the singular and the common are the same, as [Paulo] Virno stresses, the former expressing the latter each time in a different way. But the singular should not be understood as another word for the individual, which, as we have seen, does not exist. The singular is the gathering of commonalities expressed in fragments, dividuals and differences."[18] Later, Gullì says the singular is "the expression of the common."[19] I agree, as well, that each of us and our aspirations could be an expression of a common aspiration, but this can only be seen if and when we drop the fiction of atomized individuals. I suggest that already-existing love relations in the world are themselves singular expressions of the common, and Gullì might agree, for he claims in the end, "Singularity is another word for care" and "that singularity is love."[20]

Love cannot be made into a synonym for anything we like or may wish to praise. But if we don't explore the materiality of what love is and does in the world, capital will continue to do with it whatever it pleases, and for its own purposes. As Raya Dunayevskaya observed: "Capitalism tries to use everything for its power."[21] It is no surprise, then, that love has been shrunk down to a private affair, to the private property of a sexual relation or to the

---

17. Gullì, *Singularities at the Threshold*, 23.
18. Gullì, *Singularities at the Threshold*, 27–28.
19. Gullì, *Singularities at the Threshold*, 123.
20. Gullì, *Singularities at the Threshold*, 123.
21. Raya Dunayevskaya, *Women's Liberation and the Dialectics of Revolution: Reaching for the Future* (Atlantic Highlands, NJ: Humanities Press, 1985), 180.

bond of the family as an island unto itself. It is no surprise that love is marketed as something to nurture with gifts and expensive romantic getaways, or to secure through algorithmic matchmaking you can pay for. If it is not presented as these *things*, it is often presented as an ineffable, vaporous power unfit for social science, best left to theology and poetry. But we need not surrender important concepts to marketing campaigns or mystification. Indeed, we can speak of the materiality of love, of its actual existence as a human aspiration and its material reality in our own lived experiences.

According to Marx, one of the distinguishing features of life in capitalist society is alienation, which disfigures healthy human relations and the well-being of people. What kind of *Gemeinwesen* do alienated persons comprise? Alienated persons cannot comprise the communist *Gemeinwesen* because in so doing they would cease to be alienated. Thus, where alienation reigns, the common recedes, dissipates, or disappears. For Marx, capitalism exacerbates all earlier forms of alienation by multiplying processes of estrangement in work and society. For Jacques Camatte, who has done much to help us appreciate the centrality of the *Gemeinwesen* in Marx's work, the establishment of the *Gemeinwesen* would be an antithetical and oppositional movement to capital because *real community* counteracts alienation.[22]

What does love have to do with the old communist interest in counteracting capitalist alienation? Oskar Negt and Alexander Kluge understand the disposition of capitalist societies wherein "the realism of values is read economically: Is a thing or a service worth the money I pay for it? In this context, raising children, love relationships, the work of mourning, and joy are all 'unproductive labor.'"[23] Love and love relationships put us in touch with communist sensibilities and practices in the spaces of our little precarious communes. If we have some good fortune in life, we will know the joys of such "unproductive labors" as play, collective improvisation, laughing with children, friendship, comradeship, and deep and abiding affection for others. Negt and Kluge are right about the noneconomic values of the

22. See, for example, Jacques Camatte, *Capital and Community*, trans. David Brown (New York: Prism Key, 2011), 216–40.

23. Oskar Negt and Alexander Kluge, *History and Obstinacy*, trans. Richard Langston with Cyrus Shahan, Martin Brady, Helen Hughes, and Joel Golb (New York: Zone Books, 2014), 347.

most meaningful aspects of a human life. Nonetheless, the logic of capital does not stop at the boundary of friendships and families, where children are the most expensive investment of a lifetime and economic pressures put love to its test. Capital even rules over the proceedings of death, as in how to pay for death and dying or what to do about the money and property of the deceased. While we may discuss the communist secret of love, we should also consider the capitalist secrets of the death and dying industries, of the processing of corpses in the global carnage of wars or pandemics.

Striking Distance

Love participates in the creation of precarious little communes, which are necessary in a world defined by alienation, illness, and insecurity. Little communes of community centers, publishers and authors, activists, artists, musicians, forums, families with or without children, workers on strike, and other groups of joyfully gathering people give us experience (and practice) with a certain *Gemeinwesen* that counteracts feelings of isolation.

Some precarious communes, like those of a healthy family or friendship, make little stands in and against a world of insecurity. They do not change everything, but they change *some* things. In the case of strikes, occupations, friendships, social movements, and in a wide range of global uprisings, we see a little communism that does not necessarily rely on the activity of communists. This last point is important. Communism does not depend on communists. Maurice Merleau-Ponty was right to say, "It is impossible to be an anti-Communist, and it is not possible to be a Communist."[24] Most of the world's lovers would denounce communism yet seek communism in their own love relations and activities of love. For Merleau-Ponty, it was impossible to be a communist insofar as he felt communists should reject what was passing for "communism" in 1947. But communism is also something other than the "communism" of 1947. Communism is elsewhere. There is always something communist about human relationality that follows a rival logic to the logic of capital.

24. Maurice Merleau-Ponty, *Humanism and Terror: An Essay on the Communist Problem*, trans. John O'Neill (Boston: Beacon, 1969), xxi.

What I have wanted to show is that love, if love means anything at all, is antithetical to the logic of capital. Exchange relations cannot be associated with love relations, except as an opposing logic of relationality. To understand what love does for real people in the real world—and why it is crucial in times of exacerbated social isolation—is to grasp its communism. It is finally time to reconcile ourselves with a communist aspiration in all of us.

Could the experience of the pandemic have deepened this aspiration? Is it possible that we may have seen how much of a human life should not depend on capitalist exchange relations, and how damaging it is to our well-being to see every person as a threat to our health? To those of us who survived the pandemic, what is it that got us through? What care, what intimacy, what refuge? If one claims to have endured pandemic isolation all alone, then we should wonder about the long-term effects of that accomplishment. If we don't understand love as a refuge from—*as an alternative to*—the rule of capital, we misunderstand love and overlook the communism right there before us—*indeed, between us*—in striking distance.

CHAPTER 7

Horizons of a Riotous Epistemology

A Riotous Epistemology

The text of this chapter is an edited transcription of a two-day seminar offered by me and my dear friend, colleague, comrade, and publisher, Stevphen Shukaitis.[1] The seminar took place at Firstsite, an art, performance, and cultural center in Colchester, Essex, UK in March 2017. We sat in an exhibition called "#WorldsUpsideDown," which was organized by Stevphen, and we were surrounded by photographs, paintings, Xeroxed posters (and the Xerox machine they were made on), and other visual art—all of which variously aimed to capture and convey the present and past of global revolt.

The seminar occurred shortly after the publication of my *Specters of Revolt* and Stevphen's *The Composition of Movements to Come,* both of which provided the basic streams of thought that would gather in a pool of conversation.[2] But, we also conversed in loose relation to an idea I proposed

1. The first formulation of my concept of "imaginary power" appeared in the subtitle of a little lithograph booklet I coauthored with Stevphen Shukaitis, which was jointly published by Minor Compositions and the Journal of Aesthetics and Protest. That booklet, *Riotous Epistemology: Imaginary Power, Art, and Insurrection* compiled the complete proceedings of a two-day seminar based on my and Stevphen's work. This chapter presents much of the text of the seminar and *Riotous Epistemology* book, though I have edited it for length and connection to themes of the present book. The "textification" of this seminar/exhibition offered us the opportunity to lightly edit the transcriptions in order to (a) provide helpful citations for references made in the discussion and (b) clarify our ideas and intentions where such clarification seemed useful or necessary.

2. Richard Gilman-Opalsky, *Specters of Revolt: On the Intellect of Insurrection and*

early in the planning stages of this event on the subject of "riotous epistemology."

By "riotous epistemology" I meant the exploration of the kinds of "knowledge" and "knowledge production" that is carried out in unconventional practices and activities, in atypical locations of criticism and human understanding, and in the nontextual spaces in which expressions of disaffection and hope can be communicated in disruptive and moving ways. In my work, an atypical epistemology finds knowledge and knowledge production in riot, revolt, and a diversity of local and global uprisings. In Stevphen's work, such locations are found in an array of visual-sonic expressions and art experiments, as well as in diverse prefigurative practices in alter-relationality.

Despite many differences (and a few disagreements), the two of us are interested in possible and desirable ways of knowing, and we both seek to interrogate what constitutes that which is normally recognized and accepted as knowledge. We are also interested in thinking about who possesses and uses their creative powers to produce and circulate knowledge, and in this we are both especially drawn to the subversive. Together, we consider forms of knowledge expressed in radical movements, riot, and revolt, and in what Stevphen calls "the art of the undercommons."

Fifty years ago, in conversation with Gilles Deleuze, Michel Foucault commented on the uprisings of May 1968: "In the most recent upheaval, the intellectual discovered that the masses no longer need him to gain knowledge: they know perfectly well, without illusion; they know far better than he and they are certainly capable of expressing themselves . . . In this sense theory does not express, translate, or serve to apply practice: it is practice."[3] In certain moments, everyday people (workers, students, the unemployed, etc.) rise up and teach the teachers (if the latter will listen), revealing that they know more about themselves and their reality than those intellectuals who would translate and express that reality into words. There are moments when everyday people both produce and demonstrate their knowledge in the upheaval. This is a moment when theory is practiced, or, rather, when

---

Philosophy from Below (London: Repeater, 2016). Stevphen Shukaitis, *The Composition of Movements to Come: Aesthetics and Cultural Labor after the Avant-Garde* (London: Rowman & Littlefield, 2016).

3. Michel Foucault, "Intellectuals and Power," *Foucault Live: Collected Interviews, 1961–1984* (New York: Semiotext(e), 1996).

the theoretical field of analyzing social crises is undertaken directly, not in writing things but in breaking things—in the case of 1968, breaking rules and laws, windows and cars, and breaking with the expected behaviors of the usual order of everyday life.

In my book *Specters of Revolt*, I explore what it means to take seriously the intellect of revolt, uprising as thinking, upheaval as criticism, and other forms of philosophy from below. To theorize revolt as philosophy from below, I claim that we must refute the conventional vilification of insurrection as irrational and violent. And, I apply that refutation to a consideration of the communicative content of recent revolts and global uprisings.

Stevphen's *The Composition of Movements to Come* is not about revolt in the sense defined in *Specters of Revolt*, but he looks at radical art-politics and creative practice in much the same way that I look upon revolt. We both have a shared interest in different ways of doing, or in what John Holloway calls "other-doing."[4] Other-doing includes different ways of thinking and of imagining other worlds. Both of our books confront certain impasses in the revolutionary trajectories of past radicalisms, in variously anarchist, Marxist, and autonomist contexts. We both want to think about "revolutionary alternatives to revolution," as I call them in *Spectacular Capitalism*, and we both look for politics by other means than the conventionally political, looking for new forms of action large and small.[5]

I think what we both want to convey is a certain "counter-professionalization." We know there are professional artists and professional politicians, we know there are conventional forms of established art and politics that are "respectable," well-funded, officially accredited. But we are more interested in the art and politics of other-doing, and while we try to draw art and politics together, we also try to draw certain conclusions about their fragmentary and cumulative powers.

In *The Composition of Movements to Come*, Stevphen asks: "How do avant-garde practices shift what is said and how it can be said?"[6] In *Specters of Revolt*, I ask: "What is the critical content, at least paradigmatically, that

4. John Holloway, *Crack Capitalism* (London: Pluto Books, 2010).

5. Richard Gilman-Opalsky, *Spectacular Capitalism: Guy Debord and the Practice of Radical Philosophy* (Brooklyn: Autonomedia, 2011)

6. Shukaitis, *The Composition of Movements to Come*, 6.

the qualitatively different logic of revolt poses to the logic of the established order?"[7] So, each of us on our own wants to know how to say different things in different ways, and we are interested in logics oppositional to the logic of the existing order of life. Avant-garde practices and social upheaval challenge epistemological assumptions about what knowledgeable speech looks like because they are full of knowing, and thinking, and criticizing, and imagining, and yet they do not look anything like "knowledgeable speech."

But in the following seminar, there is also a reckoning with the desperation and smallness of the "other-arts" and "under-politics" we pursue. We are appropriately cynical (or appropriately "postmodern") about subjects like total revolution. The conventional is quotidian, which means that what we want to challenge is everywhere every day, while avant-garde practices and revolts only challenge the existing reality in the form of fleeting interruptions or hiatuses. To put it simply, sometimes we work from the margins not because we want to, but because the center is colonized by other things. One answer to the question "what is to be done?" is "only so much."

Maybe this is the reason why we are attracted to the Situationist praxis of disruption and interruption, of interrupting the logic and operations of capitalist power. The art of the undercommons and insurrections in the world are not even close to capable of seizing and transforming the world in any grand and lasting way. Often, the activities that Stevphen and I discuss don't even interrupt, let alone transform, so that mere interruption remains a kind of aspiration. We know that longing to interrupt normal life is rather far from the revolutionary transformation of life. One could say that we are more interested in the possible and desirable *preludes* to new revolutionary forms than we are in any revivification of the classical revolutionary idea.

From a political point of view, to be in such a position is not nothing-but-bad-news. It is more than a little bit desperate, yes, but not entirely sad. We do not stand on the same trembling ground as the 1871 Paris communards, as Rosa Luxemburg or Nestor Makhno in their lives and times, or even the FLN in Algeria at a high point in the 1950s, or the Zapatistas on the eve of NAFTA, where it must have seemed and felt like it was time to try for a total change—a life-changing attempt toward a different world. That is not our present sensibility. But that sensibility never meant success anyway, and

7. Gilman-Opalsky, *Specters of Revolt*, 245.

in each case where the ground shook with emancipatory hope there was a devastating realization and disillusionment waiting right around the bend. The fact is that there is some joy and hope in times that demand the creative and imaginative production of new thinking about desirable forms of life, artistic experiments and rebellious surprises.

We want to communicate and collaborate, but not with everyone or anyone. Both Stevphen and I are interested in the incomprehensibility of the undercommons of art and revolt, an incomprehensibility born of the narrow understanding of capitalism and its impoverished points of view. Subversive art and global uprisings *are* comprehensible as, for example, practices of radical criticism, even while our enemies declare them incomprehensible. Perhaps it is necessary to be incomprehensible in the worlds of professional and capitalist art and politics. We should not try to make too much sense in *those* worlds. Let the professional artists and politicians find us confusing, or better, totally incomprehensible. If the sense and sensibility of capital is what we oppose, let us become capital's *non*sense, its opposite sensibility.

At the end of *The Composition of Movements to Come*, Stevphen recalls an interesting discussion he had with Konrad Becker about strategy. Stevphen tells us that Becker defined strategy as something akin to wisdom.[8] In their book, *Assembly*, Michael Hardt and Antonio Negri oppose the old notion of strategy as wisdom, arguing that this notion is responsible for vindications of the wise leader, the military general, and the head of state, all of whom are given the role of long-term envisioning while the rank-and-file soldier and everyday person can only be tactical in the face of immediate obstacles. Hardt and Negri argue that this old "centaur" notion of wisdom as the strategic top half of the beast needs to be overturned, making everyday people and nonprofessionals into the new strategists.[9] They call for something like strategy from below. In this chapter, Stevphen and I think specifically about the strategic wisdom embodied and reflected in subversive art practices and revolt.

I sometimes tell students who want to read Jacques Derrida that it may be best to begin with the interviews. Stevphen interviews lots of people. He interviews musicians, and artists, and activists. I read lots of interviews.

8. Shukaitis, *The Composition of Movements to Come*, 142.

9. Michael Hardt and Antonio Negri, *Assembly* (Oxford: Oxford University Press, 2017), 5–21.

We like the conversational format. Reading interviews and transcripts of conversations offers a more informal experience than reading the typical monograph. Also, in conversational settings, authors are compelled to be more concise and clear than they may be in their writing, and if they are not, good follow-up questioning won't let them obscure anything.

Art, Revolt, Organization

Seminar Participant: *I'm interested in what you think are the potentials of moments of uprising and their limitations and how that translates into art. I mean, not just about being against the institution but the types of models that arise from spontaneous revolts. I'm interested in what we've learned from other models, from the uprisings that have been happening.*

Stevphen Shukaitis [SS]: Recently I was one of the curators of the Gee Vaucher exhibition held a few months ago at Firstsite, and that weirdly came out of a conversation with a few friends about how the university markets itself as a place for rebels and free thinking.[10] I'd like to think it was an amazing exhibition, not just for the works shown within it but also through what was created around it. What did having the exhibition create? That's not just asking what did it create for people getting to see Gee's work, but what kinds of social relationships happened through and because of the exhibition? There was a pop-up Syrian café, discussions with veterans about the nature of war, many different things came out of the exhibition. For me, that's just as important as the exhibition itself. How can art extend and develop forms of revolt, or exist as a form of revolt in itself?

Richard Gilman-Opalsky [RGO]: Those are exactly the questions that I've

10. For more information on Firstsite, see https://firstsite.uk. For more information on the Gee Vaucher exhibition see https://www.firstsite.uk/whats-on/gee-vaucher-introspective (access date April 24, 2023) or *Gee Vaucher: Introspective*, ed. by Stevphen Shukaitis (Colchester: Firstsite, 2016).

been asking, too, especially in the research for *Specters of Revolt*, and I still have a lot of these questions. Some of the answers are "to be determined." We always have to wait and see what comes out of the uprising, just as Stevphen was saying about the exhibition. One of the things you said about the so-called "spontaneous" revolts, and part of my own thinking on that, is that they are not spontaneous. They're surprising, and they *do* look spontaneous. Part of the reason why a lot of these recent uprisings look spontaneous is because we see them as discrete events—as events that start on a certain date and end on another. Whereas I see what they're doing as taking up unfinished business from within the society, from where previous revolts left off. The revolt repeats nothing. It is not a repetition but a resumption, a certain continuation. And so, when they're not happening, the possibility that they will resume to take up their unfinished business haunts the society. When these uprisings aren't happening, their specter haunts in their absence. In that sense, the revolt never really ends or goes away. There's plenty of evidence that this is true, for example in the police and military preparations that anticipate revolts before they happen. Indeed, the keepers of law and order are always counting on revolt with some confidence.

I see revolts as expressions of earlier grievances, sometimes staged and framed in new ways for the new situation. In the US, one of the realities that provoked my questioning on this very subject was the staggering number of unarmed Black people who are killed by the police every year. In total, cops killed over one thousand people in the US every year from 2013 to 2023.[11] The question is really, why is there *only* a revolt in Ferguson or Baltimore or in the George Floyd Rebellion, and not in many dozens of other cities in response to other cases of police murder? Why a revolt in some cases but not in others? Why here and not there?

Seminar Participant: *That's also the question of long-term organization, which Black Lives Matter was able to catalyze. Why do so many of these uprisings fail while others can hold for a long term and have this effective ripple, something that's actually sustained throughout time? What are the types of long-term organizational qualities that some have that others don't? Something that could perhaps relate to the structure of art, as a ripple without long-term plans. How do you*

11. See Mapping Police Violence: https://mappingpoliceviolence.org.

shift? How do you continue it? What are the logistics of a continual revolt that's not a revolution but that doesn't peak and finish?

Seminar Participant: *In certain circumstances, like in Egypt, certain revolts become almost stupid and trivial compared to the ones when there's a lot of logic—that's when they become serious. You're talking about Black people being shot by the police and talking about Egypt because there's a lot of blood. That's when it becomes, where the spontaneity is actually exploited by people who are not spontaneous. They're well organized.*

SS: One of the things Richard writes about is this idea that forms of revolt or upheaval develop as modes of collective thinking and philosophizing. The suggestion is not that you have to develop an analysis of them but to look to teasing out the analysis that is already embedded within and developed by the revolts themselves.

It's not that we have to explain to people in Egypt what they're doing; they already know. Connecting that to art, in moments where nothing appears to be happening, often times the publics being organized through other means, through artistic forms, not necessarily in content but in terms of what are the skills, the forms of cooperation, and the networks developed through artistic activity that then at a certain point blossom into something else. There are forms of social interaction, from dinner clubs to sports teams that do not appear to be political, let alone revolutionary, that can at times blossom into forms of organization that feed into full-fledged revolutionary movements.

RGO: These questions about organization and art specifically, they're really big questions and in some ways are some of the most important questions to raise, because art and organization are categories that we regard as categories for ongoing activities that don't depend upon major ruptures or disruptions of everyday life. Whereas revolts are characterized precisely in that way. So, art and organization suggest to us a modality of sustaining activities and radical criticism in between and through art, through organization.

I really like the way that Rosa Luxemburg challenged the German Social Democratic Party on the question of organization when she talked about the mass strike, by which she meant not only strikes as we think of them today but also things like insurrections, rebellions, revolts, like the uprisings we've seen in Egypt or in Occupy or when the Indignados in Spain rose up, or in many other examples in Greece. Luxemburg looked to be guided and informed by these uprisings all of the time, but what she noticed (and criticized) was how the political organization was always trying to figure out how to make use of that energy.[12]

Seminar Participant: *To control it.*

RGO: Right. The organization would always try to figure out how to take the social energies of the revolt and convert them into a platform for a political strategy, for the building of the party. And what Luxemburg said—which made her very unpopular within her own party that she ultimately left for this reason and many others—is that the organization should strive to be a durable articulation of the uprising itself. The mass strike is already saying exactly what has to be said, and the organization is at best really just a way of continuing to give voice to those disaffections when the upheaval simmers down and stops voicing them directly against the existing law and order.

Now, that's one thought on organization, but I would take it further: What if the upheaval itself is already an organization? In this way, precisely:

Consider that people hated Hosni Mubarak in the 1980s and 90s, but it wasn't until January 2011 that they actually occupied Tahrir Square and were able to push him out in eighteen days. They hated him for decades. A gathering of people so massive that is able to push out Mubarak is an organization; it's an organization of disaffection that has a decades-long prehistory in Egypt. People hated Mubarak, and parents and grandparents saw their young people in the square and in the streets and they said, "That's our aspiration." But it required a moment of organization. The disaffection needed the organization of the occupation of the square.

One of the problems may be that when we think of organization, we tend to think about some kind of an infrastructure, a building with offices and regular meetings, to keep it going. But I think that the uprising is already an organization. Consider, now, that racism exists in the US. Black Lives Matter

12. See Rosa Luxemburg's "The Mass Strike, the Political Party, and the Trade Unions," *Socialism or Barbarism: The Selected Writings of Rosa Luxemburg* (London: Pluto Press, 2010).

is not really a formal organization or a political party, it's just a name given to certain expressions of disaffection that happen in different places in different ways at different times. And yet, Black Lives Matter is a modality of the organization of that disaffection. So, in a way, stepping beyond Luxemburg's position, I think of the revolt as an organization.

Now, what if the uprising is an artwork? That's the other dimension we've been discussing. Brian Holmes has written a lot about the theatrical and artistic dimensions of social upheavals.[13] One of the first subjects I did research on was the uprising of the Zapatistas in Mexico and how they came out of Chiapas with fake guns carved out of wood and painted. They didn't have enough rifles, so they carved some props out of trees.[14] In this way and in other ways it was performance art. They read poetry from the balconies. What confounded the Mexican government was that the uprising was too artful and appealed too much to peoples' creative sensibilities with humor and charm to simply crush it as if it were a conventional guerrilla operation. There was, in a sense, too much art in the uprising to end it with a massacre, and the government didn't know what to do with that. So, there is art in the uprising that is, after all, full of creativity, creative energy, and artistic creation. I don't want to say that the revolt is everything. That's exactly not my point. The point is that maybe we should think differently about organization and art.

Seminar Participant: *I completely agree with you. I think revolt is absolutely organization. But there are different levels of organization; different types of organization happen simultaneously. If you think about evolutionary theory, drawing order from chaos, there are different types of order that work simultaneously.*

Seminar Participant: *One of the things is to try to undermine the existing organization, because obviously there is the existing organization, which can be turned around, used, and completely turned in a different direction. The actual power of the organization that exists used to be used for and by the people. Somehow the elements, the positive elements, have got to sort of completely undermine the*

13. Brian Holmes, *Unleashing the Collective Phantoms: Essays in Reverse Imagineering* (Brooklyn: Autonomedia, 2008).

14. Bill Weinberg, *Homage to Chiapas: The New Indigenous Struggles in Mexico* (New York: Verso, 2000), 189.

existing organization, so any use that it has would be completely transformed so any outlets to the media can all be used but not in the way that the actual people in charge of the so-called organization would want them to be used. The positive thing is always to turn things around.

SS: Yes. One of the interesting things is that it's easy to think of institutions as being stable, permanent bodies that are very planned out and know what they're doing. But often times they're contingent and unknown and improvised, built on the fly anyway, even as they appear to be stable and permanently structured.

RGO: The recent development of institutional politics in Greece with Syriza is worth some attention here. Syriza was really an unviable (in terms of conventional electoral politics), loose coalition of left-wing organizations in Greece. For a long time (since 2004), it didn't have any sort of formal political aspirations as a viable and cohesive national political party. But then the Greek revolts of 2008 broke out, and for several years there were waves of upheaval pressing on the political situation, pressing against a brutal regime of austerity. Syriza can of course see that they and the uprisings are making similarly radical criticisms of the relationship between Greece and the EU and many other things. Eventually, a decade after Syriza was founded, and some years after the revolts first broke out, Alexis Tsipras and Yanis Varoufakis and others associated with Syriza started to realize that it might be possible to convert Syriza into a serious contender in conventional party politics.

One of the things that's missing from most discussions about Syriza, including those on the sympathetic left, is a serious appreciation and understanding of how the revolt made the political organization possible to the point of Syriza winning the 2015 election and Tsipras becoming prime minister of Greece. People talk a lot about Syriza, about what it means and what its failures are, but what we need to be talking about is how the evolution of Syriza into a party in power was made possible through the social energies and disaffections of a revolt that compelled it to this development. So the revolt is necessary before but then again after the elections, because there's another moment, of course. There is the moment when Tsipras is himself shocked to be in the position of prime minister of Greece: "What the hell am

I doing here? This is very strange! Now I have to go to a conference with the Troika! I don't know what to do. I was a radical and an activist, but I never thought I'd be here!"

One of the things that Varoufakis quickly recognized—and I think Tsipras must have realized it, too—is that the position of power is very different from the position of the revolt against power. So many critics on the left said that Tsipras didn't have the political will to say "no" to the Troika. People were angry with Tsipras for his acquiescence as if it was a character flaw. This misses the real point. This failure was not a limitation of Tsipras's personality but rather a limitation of the political institution.

Seminar Participant: *Absolutely, yes.*

RGO: The problem is not that anybody else would've said "no" to the Troika. Tsipras went in and said "no," and the next day he said "yes." That's a feature of the institutional politics of state power, and that's "professional" politics. Varoufakis resigned and gave lectures around the world about these limitations and frustrations. But I think all of this shows us that even if we make an effort at political-institutional and formal organizational power, we should expect severe limitations and capitulations there, and ultimately, that those organizations are bankrupt.

And I interpret Varoufakis's disappointments differently than Varoufakis does himself. I see Varoufakis's experience with the Syriza victory and the politics of Europe to be telling us essentially this: What we need are totally different ways of thinking about organization and politics. We don't want their ways of organization or of doing politics. When we take on their ways of organization or of doing politics, when we get their ways into our hands, they are already their ways, not our ways of doing it. Radically different approaches to politics and organization will have no place within the limits of their ways of doing it.

What people see in the Greek situation, what we could call a recent Greek tragedy, is that what we need to do is to either think *against* the institutions or to totally rethink their meaning and structure and become very imaginative, more imaginative and creative than ever before. We cannot allow capitalist technology to monopolize the power of imagination. We need to develop our own imaginary powers. And this is precisely where art comes back to being central to the task. Inasmuch as art is about imagination, inasmuch as art is about the radical imagination, politics needs it. Art can really participate in productive ways in helping us discover what to do with our disaffection, what to make of it.

Seminar Participant: *You were talking about art actively taking a role, actively imagining a radically different future. I would see a lot of critical art, or engaged art, as doing a different kind of work. It makes that visible, all the invisible structures. I see art acting in the same way where it takes what power is and tries to make it visible. And art reflects why the world is so bad, usually; instead of actually engaging in a different way, it usually tends to just reveal power structures that are there, that are hidden.*

SS: I was thinking about this working on the Gee Vaucher exhibition, because one of the important things that was hard to convey in the exhibition is that it's not just what she produces but the very space of Dial House.[15] She's lived there with Penny Rimbaud, running it as an open house for fifty years. And that creates the possibility to live and work differently. But you can't take the house and the garden and put it in the exhibition.

And Dial House is just one example of a much longer history of how artists have organized cooperatively, whether living together or not. Justseeds, the artist cooperative who produced the "Celebrate People's History" poster series that are a part of the exhibition here now, are another good example of artists organizing cooperatively.[16] But again, you don't see that organizational process in the posters. And how could you see that, how do you make that visible? Draw a chart?

Seminar Participant: *There's been a couple of times in my artistic practice where I've asked, when is art going to actualize itself in a way that people are collectively working toward one goal? But can we all be working toward a goal?*

---

15. Dial House is a farm cottage located in Essex, England in the countryside of Epping Forest. It has been a functional and open anarchist space since 1967. The house has served as a site for diverse cultural, artistic, and political projects for decades, and was the headquarters for the experimental anarcho-punk band Crass.

16. Celebrate People's History Poster Series, organized and curated by Josh MacPhee: https://justseeds.org/project/cph.

Imaginary Power

RGO: One thing about the epiphanic role of art is that it shows you, or exposes something about, the world. That's entirely true. One of art's powers is the power of epiphany. When you see something reflected visually, or through sound, it shows you something in a different way than you're used to seeing or hearing. It's an epiphany, an exposé.

But there is another power to art that has to do with imaginary power. The imaginary power of Dial House, for example. The history of Dial House imagines such an incredible and different way of living in the world. It's almost *not in the world*. It's almost a way of fleeing the world or creating a new world—it's world-creating. This is imaginary power. In politics, it's typically discounted because who would want imaginary power? What people want is *real* power, not imaginary power. But I think that imaginary power is real power, that it is connected to real horizons. And this is where I think that art as something more than epiphany is very important, because if you can't imagine other ways of life, other forms of life, then you cannot approach them. You cannot build what you cannot imagine, and you cannot try to create other worlds, to create something like Dial House, without imaginary power. In this way, art is part of the production of power. Imaginary power can become real power, or already is real power, in the sense that it helps us to think about *real* possibilities beyond the existing realities.

Uprisings and revolts often exercise imaginary power as they experiment with new forms and possibilities. This is one of the things I like in Alain Badiou's book *The Communist Hypothesis*, where he comes dangerously close to making a certain apology for twentieth-century socialism.[17] But he says something really interesting that can help us think about what comes from revolt. One of the things he says is that we always think about collapsed and corrupted communist or socialist projects as being total failures, but what if we think of them as experiments instead? When you think about experiments, you think about trying something that may very well not work, but it doesn't mean you won't try again in new and improved ways. Badiou's claim is that the communist hypothesis depends upon trying again, in different

17. Alain Badiou, *The Communist Hypothesis*, trans. David Macey and Steve Corcoran (London: Verso, 2010).

ways with different kinds of creativity and experimentation, trying still to create new forms of life. This is how he wants us to think about extending the communist hypothesis into the twenty-first century beyond the failures of the twentieth. We can think of both revolt and art as coalescing around this notion of imagination and experimentation. Both revolt and art are very experimental, and they're both activities of exposé and epiphany, but at the same time, both revolt and art seem to grasp that imaginary power is close to real power, or maybe that imaginary power already is real power. The communist hypothesis, for Badiou, needs fresh imagination and experimentation. And in experiences like those of Occupy Wall Street or Black Lives Matter or the Arab Spring, the imagination and experimentation change people forever.

So the event comes to an end or the experiment is called "a failure," but actually, I have students who were changed very profoundly by their participation in Occupy Wall Street and Black Lives Matter. People and their understanding of themselves and their world change there and actually become something else in those movements. We know it happened in Egypt; a whole generation of young people changed their sense of what was possible, of their own power.

It's terrible that you have generations of people under Mubarak who felt that it was impossible to not have Mubarak, and now there are other problems of great severity. We cannot minimize the distinct catastrophes of Mubarak, Morsi, and of the military regime. We shouldn't minimize or reduce these catastrophes. But also, there's an imagination now, a living imagination in a generation of people that know that they don't have to accept any of this. A major military power, a UK- or US-kind of military power, couldn't change a regime as effectively as eighteen days in Tahrir Square could do it. That is amazing. And that is real power. So there is a mix, as in every revolt. You don't want to romanticize. We must absolutely not romanticize because we're talking about real lives and things that really matter to real people. So, there's no simple victory there. But also, there's no total failure either. We're talking about experiments that might become integral parts of victories.

Seminar Participant: *One of the great worries is that all the activity, all the revolt that's gone on in the last one hundred years has had an effect, has had a result, but unfortunately, it's been contained within the existing system. That's the big problem.*

RGO: Contained, yes, but also disguised.

Seminar Participant: *A hundred years of spontaneous revolt have been completely and utterly eaten by this existing system . . . I'm not saying it's a failure. I'm just saying that's what's happened, and that's what always will happen, and it is continually happening.*

SS: It's there in certain ways. For instance, in how US military strategy has adapted because of the anti–Vietnam War protests. That's why the military wants wars that are decisive and short so that people don't get angry about them. Not that it would be admitted or framed that way. This is very much how Richard describes how previous revolts haunt the decisions and workings of the state.

But back to what you were saying, there's a thing about this outpouring of creativity. The moments you're describing are valuable and powerful, but the danger is wanting that feeling of inclusivity and how it becomes a substitute for having to deal with the actual ongoing work.

Seminar Participant: *That's what I mean. If you think about it as a kind of investment . . . it's an investment that has probably no long-term rewards. Maybe. If that's what you define as success, and it's this investment in our lives that when we think about it, it's under this sort of capitalist logic. This type of investment doesn't give you anything back in terms of security. A lot of work without any kind of guarantee. It doesn't give you housing. It's a different type of investment that a lot of people are not so inclined to take because it's a difficult road . . . and it's not a sure road.*

We can do beautiful experiments. But that's what I mean about the long term. Infrastructure is maybe the wrong word, but long-term planning and that difficult investment . . . that's why I was interested in the original question, why certain things are continuing and other things are not . . . we're all affected and it really is valuable on a certain level, but also it's sort of a movement on a different level . . .

Seminar Participant: *And certainly, in the past, people have been very ambitious in situations like the bonfire of the institutions, and all that sort of grand turn, somehow, in 1968. The students in 1968 were going to completely and utterly change society. And some artists have said that, but it can't happen. It goes back to what you were saying, that you were trying to judge success on the basis of the existing criteria.*

RGO: There is success and failure, that's one frame, which I consider to be held hostage by capital. Capital only measures the success of things in terms of their exchange value, i.e., what do we win in exchange for the revolt? What I would prefer over "success versus failure" would be to think instead about "temporary versus permanent." This is where I'm critical of some of the influential thinkers on this subject. Guy Debord, for example, did not in my view take seriously enough the relative permanence of his opponent, which was basically spectacular capitalism. Debord looked at the situation, the rupture, détournement, and the dérive. These are mainly temporary derailments that understand themselves, from the start, as momentary interruptions that end very soon. Later, in the 1980s, Hakim Bey wrote a book that became very popular in the 1990s called *Temporary Autonomous Zone* (*TAZ*).[18] There are sometimes festivals of disruption that take place over the weekend, but then you have to return to normal, or as they said in France in 1968: *retour à la normale*. You have to go back to work.

The problem is that there is in fact a structural reality; real material conditions of life in the existing society, and the breaks we make are temporary when they don't lead to structural transformations. Marx thought of structural transformation as revolution. There's a difference between an interruption and a transformation. Something is transformed in an affective sense, but the material conditions of life, of society, are left just as they were. This is the sense in which I would agree that the revolt gets eaten up by the existing system.

So, what about a real revolution of the conditions of life itself? The revolution of everyday life doesn't change the actual conditions of life. And in this way, I tend to prefer Marx's idea that we have to be abolitionists, to abolish the existing situation.[19]

---

18. Hakim Bey, *TAZ: The Temporary Autonomous Zone, Ontological Anarchism, Poetic Terrorism* (Brooklyn: Autonomedia, 2003).

19. See Chapter 2 above.

Moving from temporary to permanent is the big and difficult question. It drives me, personally, back to crisis theory, where the bigger and more difficult change can only occur when the existing system enters a phase of existential crisis, where it simply cannot continue. This crisis theory also comes from Marx but has been rearticulated in very important ways by other thinkers, such as Franco "Bifo" Berardi. Bifo talks about the factory of unhappiness and the psychological crisis of our existing society.[20] We return to normal, yes, but what is normal, and can we even survive the normal situation?

What is permanent and normal is, quite possibly, an unbearable and unlivable situation. We have incredible suffering around the world. We don't see it right where we sit, perhaps, but there are billions of people living all kinds of precarity that are difficult for many of us to imagine. It really requires an impossible imagination to see it in many cases. And we also have people who aren't subject to such insufferable conditions but who are facing different dangers psychologically, emotionally, and affectively.

But the whole field of psychology is mainly *not* about changing the conditions of life but rather about changing the condition of the psyche to accept the conditions of life. The whole thing is completely backward because it's the conditions and not the psyche that has to be changed. So there's a possibility of a crisis on the horizon. We need a different version of Marx's crisis theory, because I don't think the capitalist political-economic structure is going to just break down or collapse. Marx simply didn't or couldn't understand the incredible malleability and flexibility of capitalism to deal with and survive major crises.

And there are other crises. We must speak of ecological crisis, in addition to psychosocial crisis. I have two children, and I don't know that the society they're being raised in is livable or bearable. I don't know that it's psychologically or ecologically survivable. One cannot stupidly expect that their problems will be exactly the same ones faced by my generation. A new crisis might create an opportunity for taking what we experience in temporary moments of rupture and revolt and making them more permanent. It's not a light switch; we do not go from temporary to permanent like the light goes

20. See Berardi's *Precarious Rhapsody: Semiocapitalism and the Pathologies of the Post-Alpha Generation* (London: Minor Compositions, 2009), especially Chapters 2, 5, and 6.

on and off. But I do think that we want to—that we have to—find ways to survive beyond temporary interruptions of what is killing us. We've created conditions we can barely survive.

SS: One compelling aspect of something like Dial House is that it's been there for nearly sixty years. Penny and Gee moved there in 1967. They found this farm cottage and decided to move in but want to live differently. So they took the locks off the doors. They have lived in an open house for fifty years with no locks on the doors. Even now I'm not sure I could do that . . . just realizing that anyone could walk in at any time. I want to believe in the world as a benevolent place, but that's pushing it! But they just decided that this is how they want to inhabit the world and it basically works for them. To me it's almost like taking a huge gamble and just hoping.

Seminar Participant: *Large-scale is dangerous, so this sort of experiment is positive but then, it can only be done on a small scale.*

RGO: Perhaps the question is how to move between scales: How do we go from a small-scale experiment to an experiment of longer duration and larger scale? The family, it's a small-scale thing, a tiny private home or a little gathering or a small group of people. And, the more work becomes insufferable, the more basic security and healthcare and the future itself becomes increasingly precarious, the little home—if it is a healthy place—can appear as a kind of refuge.[21] It's perhaps a little tiny thing, but Saskia Sassen points out in an essay about Latin American workers in the US, that they go back to their neighborhoods and their mothers and sisters and brothers and families and fathers and their familiar food and language after work as both a refuge from and a shield against what happens when they are out in the service sector being subjected to abuse, racism, and degradation every day.[22] What happens

21. It is important to note here that for many people the home is just another space of abuse—it is not a safe space, or a place of refuge. This has been written about by many feminist writers, such as bell hooks (*All about Love: New Visions* [New York: Harper Perennial, 2000]) and Susan Moller Okin (*Justice, Gender and the Family* [New York: Basic Books, 1989]).

22. Saskia Sassen, "Culture Beyond Gender," in Susan Moller Okin's *Is Multiculturalism Bad for Women?* eds. by Martha C. Nussbaum, Matthew Howard, and Joshua Cohen (Princeton, NJ: Princeton University Press, 1999), 76–78.

if, and when, the outside world faces a crisis that compels us to think about new possibilities, new ways?

What happens is that the logic of the family, this small thing, this tiny communist thing (when it is not itself abusive), has to extend outward. The example I think of is Cuba after the collapse of the Soviet Union. Cuban agriculture was subsidized for decades by the Soviet Union, and they had massive industrial-agricultural farming and big machinery that Cuba couldn't afford on its own. It was subsidized by the Soviet Union because the Soviet Union looked at Cuba as a satellite power and prime strategic ally during the Cold War. Then, from 1989 to 1991, that subsidy was withdrawn. By the middle 1990s, the Cuban people had to figure out how they were going to do agriculture, how they were going to feed the country. Now, that's a real crisis, and if you go to Cuba today you would see that much of that Soviet-subsidized machinery is overgrown with weeds and out of commission. They've gone to an almost anarchist and communist agricultural format but not because of ideology—because of the crisis.

What I find most interesting is that they always had this capacity to enlarge and expand, or even to "nationalize," what might have previously looked like community gardens. But those earlier gardens were tiny, trapped, small, and walled-off until the Soviet Union was no longer able to subsidize mass industrial farming. At that point, the gardens were extended out from their small spaces, and this has actually become a model for the future.

Art of the Undercommons

Seminar Participant: *The avant-garde has become the establishment, to put it in a very simplistic way. The avant-garde has been completely and utterly taken as the norm and the establishment actually embraces the avant-garde and they sell it and they buy it in business...*

Seminar Participant: *But maybe you have a different strategy than what the avant-garde art was doing. What could art do now in this day and age, in this time? Power has shifted and changed, and yet our strategies are somewhat similar to when power relations were so much different. That's also what I was asking about protest movements. We still have bodies on the streets, which is really great in some ways, but also, the power relations have changed over the last thirty years. We still have the same, or at least the left still has the same sort of tactics.*

Seminar Participant: *It takes us a long time to understand what has changed. Isn't that the problem? I don't think we understand what's changed, especially with things like the internet. Maybe art still hasn't changed in relation to the things that have changed? The gallery experience is exactly the same as it was thirty years ago.*

Seminar Participant: *At one stage the art colleges were one of the few places where people could have a little freedom.*

Seminar Participant: *I don't believe in that freedom.*

Seminar Participant: *But there was freedom . . . there were certain outlets where even people with little education could go to art colleges, because art colleges had taken on the university model. In the old days there were certain humble outlets where people could rise up, people who weren't as well educated as perhaps the average art student is now. There were more outlets. Gee Vaucher had this. She went to this place that was local to her. And she was in a very oppressive situation, and so the art college gave her an insight into the possibilities. She in turn has created possibilities for other people. Again, it's a failure, isn't it? Everything's a failure in some respects.*

Seminar Participant: *Art is in-between all the time; it's always in-between different knowledges. It's becoming less like a subject in itself and more of something that's imagined as this in-between-ness. Rather than the atomization of knowledges or disciplines, when you talk to people in different fields. . . It's different in the arts because we're a little bit here, there, and everywhere. Could you take seriously the being in-between knowledges to think about what this atomization is and how you could draw that back to integrate things more? And today we need more integration, more and more different knowledges coming together, not in a superficial way.*

Seminar Participant: *Theater comes in here. It's an integrated factor because you have the theater with stage sets. Theater and revolt present a good tradition, considering how they come together. This can still happen. I don't think there's anything old-fashioned about that. Around this town, theater is absolutely part of the establishment, with a few exceptions.*

RGO: The conversion of spaces like galleries and libraries and universities and other institutions into open spaces for nonexpert creativity ties into the earlier question about organization. Perhaps organization is such a challenge partly because existing institutions need to be cracked open and redeployed. What could we organize if we could do this? It seems fairly obvious to me that improvised music is art. When I listen to John Coltrane, Ornette Coleman, Linda Sharrock, Arthur Doyle, Matana Roberts, Virginia Genta, and others, I think: "That's art!" But galleries are not typically spaces where people go to just pick up instruments and create with them. It has happened; it's in the history. Sonny Rollins played in the Museum of Modern Art in 1965. People like the saxophonist Peter Brötzmann from Germany would get invited to blow a saxophone to smithereens in art galleries.

Seminar Participant: *That sounds like the art laboratories, the "Art Labs." It was a mixture of all different types of music, art, and theater, with no disqualification. The Living Theatre in New York, they caused quite a political stir.*

RGO: That's right, they did. But the main thing we need to get at is the artwork of those who do not have a résumé or portfolio, those "artists" who don't see themselves as such. This kind of opening is something that we really need. Marcuse talked about it as a form of democratization, and, more importantly, as an activity of the spirit of new revolutionary sensibilities.[23]

And it's not just capitalist power that blocks this. The art gallery typically wants to defend itself against an overly wide opening up, and I think the library wants to defend itself from the challenges of nontextual knowledge. It's the people we would often regard as colleagues or comrades who are sometimes the problem, because once they start to make a space for themselves to do their specialized craft they have to defend that and their specialization. So, let's say you're an artist and you declare that anybody can

23. See Herbert Marcuse, *Art and Liberation*, ed. by Douglas Kellner (New York: Routledge, 2017).

come in and produce content for the gallery walls, that any child can do it. There's actually a book in the gallery store here at Firstsite called *Why Your Five Year Old Could Not Have Done That*.[24] It's a reaction against people who see abstract art on a wall and say, "What's that!? My five-year-old child could do that!" In this way the artist becomes defensive and is put in the position of having to explain why a five-year-old *cannot* do it. The *real* artist can elucidate the different methods and history of the art and can point out a whole language that makes it the purview of specialists.

But I actually think that the really powerful possibility is that a five-year-old *can* do it. Do you know what I mean? And I think that these spaces—the art spaces, information spaces, spaces for intellectuals and highly educated people, philosophers, whatever else they are—they're often defended by rank-and-file participants, not some sort of mysterious person in an office wearing a tie with dollar signs on it. It's often your colleagues or comrades who actually say, "No, that can't be allowed here, that's not philosophy, that's not art, that's not music."

Seminar Participant: *The ideology of professionalism. This is something that has occurred to me over the years. There's a lot of stuff that goes on in these professional organizations, like in trade unions, but they actually create their own rules that are defensive and go against ordinary people who are not the professionals.*

SS: But I don't think it's about wanting to prevent autonomous creativity. Take for instance how art galleries and other kinds of cultural institutions function. It might be easy to fall back on the assumption that the people who run them don't want them to become spaces for the flowering of radical forms of creativity. The museums must remain the guardians of "high art" and "good taste." Perhaps there are some people who still buy into such notions, but these days they are far fewer. It would be much more common that you'd find people working in the arts who want to embrace the energies that come with more participatory and open-ended engagements, to open up the spaces to all kinds of activities but at the same time can only do so by putting limits on them.

24. Susie Hodge, *Why Your Five Year Old Could Not Have Done That: Modern Art Explained* (London: Thames and Hudson, 2012).

Let's say you work somewhere like here [Firstsite], and your job is to keep the space open, to organize the funding, to organize the structure, and you're highly invested in keeping this space open. It takes a lot of courage to let go of control, to let go of a thing that you're trying so hard to defend and keep open, not because you're defensive or angry but because it's hard, it's really hard. Being able to develop the courage and the trust to actually turn over spaces like that and have it work, it's not purely defensive. There are reasons why it's hard to do.

RGO: Yes. But I may have a disagreement with you on this. On a certain level I agree. I think we have to appreciate what it takes to keep a place like this running, but the question is: *Why is it so hard to do*? Why can't we have spaces that are open and not professionalized or curatorial and guarded in terms of the perspective of the craft and everything else? The answer to that question cuts deeper because, though what you say is right, it is only right in the context of cultural institutions in a capitalist society. This is the missing piece because you *must* have a whole set of concerns about operational costs. This building isn't cheap—maintenance of this beautiful building—it must cost an enormous amount of money. So you've got to be careful with every move you make, and you've got to bring people in. But I think that what really has to happen simply cannot take place within these limits. It's exactly what you said, and it is defensive. Cultural institutions have to defend themselves and their basic existence, against capitalist concerns about operational costs, work, and profit.

Let me use a very different example to make the same point. Consider the example of Socrates who would walk around the streets, and people wanted to talk to him so badly that, at the beginning of Plato's *Republic,* Socrates is actually held hostage by his interlocutors and forced into discussion. People often overlook this detail, but at the very start of the text Socrates is walking away with his friend Glaucon, and along comes Polemarchus and several others who say that they want to talk to Socrates. But he tells them that he is hurrying to get away from a festival he'd just attended. Right away, Polemarchus asks, "Do you see how many of us there are? . . . Either prove stronger than these men or stay here."[25] Socrates was surrounded by men who

25. *The Republic of Plato*, 2nd ed., trans. Allan Bloom (New York: Basic Books, 1991), 3, 327.

were much stronger than him, including people like Thrasymachus, whom Socrates was actually quite afraid of. So he stays and talks, and then comes the *Republic*! As Plato presents it, nearly five hundred pages of conversation that Socrates didn't want to have!

But, the story goes, people wanted to talk to Socrates and he hated the sophists, so he talked to people for free in the streets. He despised the class of "intellectuals" who charged money in exchange for ideas. Now here I am, a long time later, and guess what? My job is basically selling ideas. Here's where I want to make the connection to what we've been discussing. Why don't I just go out and do philosophy in the streets like Socrates did? Well, what if I do philosophy in the streets and nobody shows up to speak with me? What if they're not interested in what I have to say? Unlike Socrates, nobody will hold me hostage for my thoughts. I could offer philosophy for free, too, and yet nobody would show up, nobody wants it. And there's another problem: How will I feed my family?

This is a critical point. We need people to come, and money governs the activity and organization of everyday life. So you need to have professional philosophers, professional artists, professional musicians, etc. I have a perfectly good explanation as to why I sell ideas for a living, for why I'm a certain kind of neo-sophist. The problem is that in our existing society, I simply can't do it Socrates's way. I can't do it for free, because my family and I have needs that cost money, and even if I tried, nobody would come.

What happens is that we have a cultural situation, a "cultural apparatus" as C. Wright Mills called it, and we have an economic reality.[26] This makes it virtually impossible for us to open everything up in the ways we might like to, which I think is ultimately not a critique of the arts. It's not so much about the position or perspective of the gallery owners; it's a problem of capitalist society, and we simply have to confront capitalism. The question is ultimately about transforming the conditions surrounding these institutions so that the institutions we need can actually function without so much precarity and economic hostility.

But the fact is that we can't just create the organizations and institutions we want in the existing society. An obvious lesson: we can't always do what

26. C. Wright Mills, *Power, Politics and People: The Collected Essays of C. Wright Mills* (Oxford: Oxford University Press, 1963).

we want to do. But this is why I go to the revolt. The revolt is the only activity today that wants, and actually tries in practice, to break limitations and rethink reality. Everything else is creativity within the boundaries of unacceptable limits. We've got to go out of bounds.

But if we just open the doors and say anyone can do anything here, this place won't be here for long. That's the defense, but it's also the problem. The problem is that everything belongs to somebody. You're not allowed to go there. When I worked in New York City, they had signs in the public park at Union Square telling you to keep off the grass.

SS: What I was referring to was the idea that people actively want to prevent some things from happening in the spaces. I am suggesting that it's more complicated than that; it's a different dynamic. And that's important because if you want to move to expand the possibilities of what can happen in a space, the problems you're going to face more than likely will not be the demands of some administrator determined to stop them, but rather concerns raised by someone who has a shared desire to keep a space of possibility open.

That's a different kind of terrain. What I am saying is that moving or breaking those constraints requires us to actually consider what is the motivating factor, what led to them existing. And there's two ways of moving them. The one is trying to expand spaces gradually, and then there's another approach that wants it done right now. Both are ways to move things. But if you're trying to negotiate and expand spaces to interact in, again, it can be more possible by identifying what are the common grounds you share with those who also have a stake in these spaces—and then push them. The people who run cultural institutions aren't cartoon baddies, usually. How far can you go? How far can you push it? What is possible? Knowing what is possible is a start for understanding what it actually is that is constraining the situation—or you have some conception of it. Otherwise, you'll try to change it in ways that won't actually affect the constraint because you'll be doing something else. I definitely appreciate and value larger structural analyses, like the way that capitalism constrains cultural institutions. But I was making a point more about the micropolitics of negotiating and expanding how spaces are used. It's negotiating the constraints in the best way possible, because it's not like you can just magically imagine that they're going to disappear.

RGO: Yes, they won't disappear. I see your point, and I also don't think they're bad people. I think they're good people, but they're good people who have to defend their spaces of life and work. It's not that you're a bad person if you defend that space because you live in a world in which you're not guaranteed anything without your position. But I do think that, inasmuch as we are negotiating things, there's still a basic commitment to imagining a totally different organization. Maybe that's putting too much on art. Maybe I shouldn't urge that kind of a directive for art. But I tend to think that really powerful art that can move things, art that possesses what I have been calling imaginary power, is precisely the art that goes beyond the negotiable boundaries of the existing situation. How so? It shows us real possibilities that break boundaries.

Seminar Participant: *There probably are a lot of silent voices. Sometimes the artistic establishments try to reach out. They had this thing called "outsider art" where they recognize that there have been people who have been on the outside, and so they try to embrace them and put them on the inside.*

RGO: You then convert the outside into the inside. Years ago, the New York City subway had a whole cavalcade of people who'd go down into the subway stations and play music, turn over a hat, and get donations from commuters. But they formalized that. So now, if you're the outsider artist in the subway, what if you don't have that banner saying you're a part of the "Music Under New York" series? They've converted the outside into the inside. So you say, "I want to play my saxophone in the subway to get some money for food." That is the real political economy of outsider art.

You've got somebody who takes their saxophone down into the bottom of the F train station and maybe gets 40 or 50 dollars, maybe 150 or 200. That is the outside venue. A makeshift venue. Just a space, *not* an institution. The outsider saxophonist says, "I'm just going to make a venue wherever I can stand." This reminds me of something the great saxophonist Albert Ayler once said: "I remember one night in Stockholm, I tried to play what was in my soul. The promoter pulled me off the stage. So I went to play for little Swedish kids in the subway. They heard my cry."[27]

27. See Nat Hentoff, "Albert Ayler—The Truth Is Marching In," *Downbeat Magazine*, November 17, 1966, http://www.ayler.co.uk/html/interview1.html#hentoff.

But once the outsiders are converted into official insiders, the outside is outlawed. If you go down into the subway station and take out a saxophone, the transit authority may ask you where your badge and banner are. "License and registration?" If they seize the inside and the outside, then what is left? That's the basement. Is the person playing a saxophone? Yes, they're playing a saxophone. But they get no bread from it, and nobody hears their cry.

SS: I quite like how Theaster Gates approaches this.[28] He's an artist from Chicago who creates these collective community art projects, made with community effort. And then he brings them, sells them to the high art world, and gets money. And with the funds from that sale he buys more spaces, more infrastructure, precisely to create collective spaces where people can then make more stuff. There's this whole process of using collective projects to get resources which he reinvests back into projects and spaces. And I like that because it's neither inside nor outside, but it's negotiating back and forth between the different worlds. It's not using collective resources to make money for himself and then to say, "I'm rich, I'm so great." But rather, it's to create more capacity for people to relate and create together.

Seminar Participant: *Yes, I think there are different models that need to be thought through. The gallery space has become almost redundant on some levels. That's okay. New things can be thought of; we don't have to cling to these old forms. But we also need to survive. Theaster Gates is a really good example of someone who's done really interesting work. But I think that there are possibilities for more of that, and then there are possibilities to integrate more of this into counter-models so we can invest in a way that doesn't break us.*

Seminar Participant: *You definitely did the right thing by holding this seminar. . . What you're doing is putting into action what you're saying should happen in a small way.*

RGO: Thank you for saying that. I like what you said about Theaster Gates.

28. *Theaster Gates: Twelve Ballads for Hugenot House* (Cologne: Verlag der Buchhandlung Walther König, 2012).

Part of what I've tried to resist is the idea that the intellectual class has to answer these questions. Part of "riotous epistemology" is that, for example, when people after 1991 thought that the entirety of revolutionary hope and history was a closed chapter of the twentieth century, the re-emergence of new revolutionary activity challenged and changed that conclusion. When the Zapatistas rose up in Mexico, we had to think again. But then the intellectual class started thinking about what the *New York Times* called the postmodern revolution, new forms of post-Soviet revolutionary politics.[29] But actually, it was because of the Zapatistas that a left-wing intellectual class realized there's still a possibility and a hope there. The Arab Spring is now responsible for what will surely be generations of intellectual consideration of Middle Eastern and North African social and political movements and revolutionary possibilities. It would be really refreshing if intellectuals could admit that their own creativity in thinking about new models actually comes straight out of these movements.

So, you've mentioned Theaster Gates, and how a different model comes out of his practice. The most imaginative stuff comes from elsewhere. And that's the rub, isn't it? We have these institutions where people are supposed to gather to get their imaginations going, but that's rarely where we find it happening. Outside is where it's happening. We have to wait and see. When you go back to any revolt, we just have to wait and see what comes from it. This means *not* saying it's already succeeded and *not* saying it's already failed. We must not say that it's over when it appears to have ended. Wait a minute! It may be taken up again in new and different ways. With art, too, it has the power to teach us what we wouldn't have thought of without it.

SS: Basically, your revolt is kind of like Spinoza's notion of eternal life. Spinoza says that insofar as something a person did in the world continues to have an effect and have ripple effects, death is not the end. It's just a marking point.

RGO: Yes, I completely agree with Spinoza there.

---

29. Tim Golden, "Revolution Rocks: Thoughts of Mexico's First Guerrilla Commander," *New York Times*, April 8, 2001, http://www.nytimes.com/books/01/04/08/reviews/010408.08goldent.html.

One of the things I argue with regard to recent Black revolt in the US is to look at the upheaval as a coordinate in a long history going back to the seventeenth, eighteenth, and nineteenth centuries. You could say that slavery is over, but white supremacy lives on and relocates its racist order into different institutions, such as the criminal "justice" system and mass incarceration. Like W. E. B. Du Bois and Angela Y. Davis, I resist the idea that slavery was simply abolished. In the United States today, the racialization and demography of poverty, police brutality, and incarceration, substantiate the claim that slavery never fully ended but took on different forms.[30]

SS: The BBC did this really interesting program on the abolition of slavery in the UK. How that happened here was much different than in the US, most obviously in that there wasn't a war over it. When slavery was abolished in 1833, the government made a massive payout to slave owners to compensate them for their "loss." The BBC show was about research done by people at UCL who, using archival records, traced where the money went, how it was invested, which railroads were founded with those funds, which estates were founded, and so on.[31] And there you have an economic legacy of how all the money paid out to people for their "loss of property" created other forms of trusts, foundations, companies, family inheritances, and wealth—all of which, needless to say, became important parts of capitalism. It keeps going.

What we're calling riotous epistemology shows us another continuity, another way of keeping things going. But it's not one of property, ownership, and control. It comprises, instead, all the micropolitical activities that link and bring together moments of revolt. Or practices that draw up and reactivate those histories and memories into tools for the present.

Toward the Unprofessional

RGO: Stevphen always strives to try to think about art beyond its

30. In this regard, I agree with both Angela Y. Davis in *Abolition Democracy* (New York: Seven Stories Press, 2005) and Michelle Alexander in *New Jim Crow* (New York: The New Press, 2012).

31. For information on the Centre for the Study of the Legacies of British Slave-Ownership: https://www.ucl.ac.uk/lbs.

conceptualization as the private property of a professional class of artists. In our societies—in capitalist societies—the concept of production is always connected with economic power, money. There's a certain sense in which, for Stevphen, the de-professionalization of art production, the art of the undercommons, is a kind of open invitation to everyday people who wouldn't otherwise think of themselves as artists, as having the power to create something, to spark something, and maybe to change things.

But it is important to notice something about these recent uprisings we've seen—and they've been in and around London, too—namely, the reaction against them. The reaction against them is usually composed of the same tri-part opposition: they're (1) irrational, (2) ineffective, and (3) violent. Philosophy is supposed to like the opposite things. Philosophy proclaims rationality, objectivity, problem-solving, and calm, cool analysis. Philosophy prefers logic and order and places hope in argumentation as the effective path to change. So basically, the revolt is always condemned as the opposite of philosophy. It's a violent, irrational, ineffective, and dangerous emotional outburst.

I want to de-professionalize philosophy and politics similarly to how Stevphen wants to de-professionalize art. I don't know if that's the right way to say it. It's not that we want to de-professionalize art, politics, or philosophy in an institutional sense, but that we don't want to allow a class of professional thinkers, politicians, and artists to tell us what we can do creatively, politically, or intellectually.

When the Egyptian revolution happened in 2011, the people knew that they didn't like Mubarak, but it raised questions throughout the whole region. One of the most popular demands that emerged in that wave of uprisings was, "the people demand the overthrow of the regime."[32] So, that demand was in Tunisia, it was in Egypt, it was in Bahrain: "Overthrow the regime." There were particular problems in each place but also a sort of general and common expression of "we want something else." And that activity raises questions about the society; it raises questions about the power of everyday people, and not only of the professional class of politicians.

32. Hamid Dabashi, *The Arab Spring: The End of Postcolonialism* (London: Zed Books, 2012), 75.

SS: This is probably a pithy thing to say, but I think there's more than a few of us who looked at the election of Donald Trump and said, "This is horrible, but music is going to get really good again."

RGO: People always sharpen the knives when something really objectionable happens. I don't want to say the election of Trump was good or dialectically productive, because for real people it actually mattered what he was doing right away with those immigration bans—and also in terms of foreign policy, health, environmental, and education policy. These things do really matter, although there is another side to it, for sure. Hopefully, music takes up the problems, art takes them up, intellectuals take them up, everyday people take them up, and with any fortune, revolts take them up too; we immediately saw the occupations of airports to take on Trump's anti-immigrant position.[33] And in fact, I think about this form of activity—creative and disruptive social activity—as the activity of real power.

Previously, we discussed the nature of imaginary power as opposed to real power. And sometimes we say that imaginary power isn't what we want. We want real power! But I would put a slight twist on that, because real power is worth nothing if you cannot imagine something radically different. What good is real power without the imaginary power to think of something much better, much different? Again, art can help with power. But if you only value power by measuring how it changes government policy, our power doesn't look like real power.

Seminar Participant: *It's a force, though, isn't it?*

RGO: Yes, and I don't think we should judge power in terms of how it changes policy. I work in a School of Politics and International Affairs. What many political scientists think is that nothing is political until it is articulated at the level of public policy. I reject that. There are events that transform relationships between people. When we look at the 1969 Stonewall Uprising in New York, in the gay club down in Greenwich Village, we find real power in

33. Retrospectively, revolt against Trump was minimal and ineffective during his single term in office. US citizens who denounced Trump as "unacceptable" not only accepted him but also were pathologically interested in his every utterance.

the revolt. A power that changes things, it even changes law and policy much later on, as it participates in reshaping our thinking about sexuality, and eventually, issues like same-gender marriage. But the law only comes to reflect what's already been changed prior to the law, what's been happening outside of and against the law.

Seminar Participant: *Power isn't necessarily words, and that is important, too.*

RGO: Yes, I think this is really the point: to think beyond words and text.

SS: It also applies to a difficulty I've had. There's this sociologist I quite like, John Clammer, who wrote a book called *Vision and Society*.[34] In it, he says that he wants to create not a sociology of art but a sociology *from* art. He wants to work from the direct thought process of art itself. I find this to be very interesting and very appealing. It reminds me, again, of how we talk about revolt as philosophy, revolt as thinking. But the difficulty is in how you write about it, explain it, mediate it, in a way that doesn't fall back onto the traditional or institutional role of the intellectual who tries to explain everything in a nice pattern and a clever, tidy explanation. How do you take direct practices, whether they're artistic or political practices, and try to tease them out and explain and expand them without forcing them back into the box or format of pre-fabricated explanations?

RGO: You were asking how you can take something that is nontextual, like a revolt, and say what it means through text without somehow disfiguring or distorting its meaning. And I think some translation and reiteration have to be done, but it's very difficult to think about how to do that. The starting point for me would be at the level of definitions. There's a reason why I don't talk about ideology from below or the ideological content of revolt. Instead, I talk about philosophy from below and the philosophical content of revolt.

There's an important distinction between ideology and philosophy, and unfortunately, it's one that Marx did not fully grasp. When Marx wrote *The German Ideology*, he was criticizing German philosophy. And it was true that in

34. John Clammer, *Vision and Society: Towards a Sociology and Anthropology from Art* (London: Routledge, 2014).

the middle of the nineteenth century his generation was hobbled by a culture of sitting around in bars and cafés and talking about Hegel and having unending conversations about philosophy. Marx was making a declaration against all of that, saying that the world is burning outside, that you're all too damn philosophical. He, of course, famously wrote in his "Theses on Feuerbach" that the "philosophers have only *interpreted* the world, in various ways; the point, however, is to *change* it."[35] But he missed the crucial importance of a critical difference between philosophy and ideology. Ideology is what you get when you already have a finished worldview through which you interpret and understand the world. In German, there's a word for it: *Weltanschauung*. And if you look at the world through a particular worldview, you look at it through ideological lenses that make the world appear as if it entirely supports your worldview.

One way I saw this was in the *International Socialist Review*, a pretty popular left-wing magazine. When the so-called Arab Spring started, they had many articles about how the people in Tahrir Square were anticapitalists, how they were socialists, and how when they said, "down with the regime," they meant "down with capitalism." But this was an ideological translation of a very complicated and heterogeneous social reality that was really much messier. I recommend that people watch the really good 2013 documentary entitled *The Square* by Jehane Noujaim. The cameras go into Tahrir Square and one of the things you see is the deep disagreement there. Friends and family members fighting in their apartments, really not sure at all about what should come next. You see so many people who don't want the Muslim Brotherhood but who think that it might be the best available option. There were other people who were categorically against it and others who wanted total revolution. And actually, there were a lot of people who were just talking about opportunity and not talking about capitalism. They're talking about reforms; they're talking about democracy.

For me, this open questioning is philosophical. Ideology is the end of open questioning. With ideology, you already know how things ought to be: you're a conservative, you're a liberal, you're a radical, you're a communist, or you're an anarchist. And then you put on your ideological glasses and, through that *Weltanschauung*, you look at the world, and everything you see is confirmation

35. Karl Marx, "Theses on Feuerbach" in *Karl Marx and Frederick Engels: Selected Works in Three Volumes: Volume One* (Moscow: Progress Publishers, 1973), 15.

bias. Instead, I think we should look at revolt as a philosophical rather than an ideological activity. And when we look at these revolts, we ought to resist saying that they are communist, or Marxist, or anarchist, or liberal, or conservative. That's what I try to do—to resist giving them, in some translation, any particular ideological perspective, which I think that in fact they don't have. They're much more heterogeneous and philosophical, and it's precisely that fact that makes it so hard to translate such nontextual events. But this doesn't mean that open questioning in the philosophical activity of revolt is not saying anything at all. It's just not an expression of some *single*, cohesive ideology.

From Below

SS: Our discussion reminds me of approaches that have been developed by people working in social history, where the idea is to record a variety of experiences and perspectives—in particular, voices and stories that are usually not recorded as part of the historical record—without necessarily trying to impose a coherent or unified narrative on them. Social history, in this sense, is a process of registering the messiness of such accounting as much as the readable and communicative contents themselves.

RGO: Yes, and not to give the real movement a meaning that is external to it. It is a complex social history. The only thing I don't like about the word "history" here is its implication that certain events, or a series of events, are finished and done and part of the past. Sometimes something happens, and while it seems to be over, it is in fact far from finished.

I like the notion that history is happening. But I also think that what is happening are so many things that have already been declared finished and done. But they're *not* finished. A lot of these revolts—for example, Black revolt in the US—involve taking up very old problems in new contexts. You see this with racism, you see it with inequality. Inequality is very old. When politicians call for so-called austerity, you have antiausterity protests. New language for an old discourse. When you see the Indignados in Spain rise up, they're not addressing a new problem; it's a very old problem. Yet the problem of dignity isn't only a historical problem. Nor is an uprising ever the last act in the history of confronting that problem.

A lot of the students I've had who were part of Occupy Wall Street have told me that they miss that period of questioning the existing reality. A real period of questioning, deep down into the bone marrow of society: "Should things be this way?" I think such questioning is one of the things that goes away for a time when a revolt settles down. It doesn't go away permanently, just for a time. And I would say the same thing about art and the way it poses new questions and ways of thinking. That is the philosophical moment. Now, I wouldn't want to make art into philosophy, but it is at least philosophical. And I think that art actually does philosophy better than professional philosophers in many cases. If you go to an exhibit or watch a great documentary film, and it is jarring and hurts and puts you in a place where you just. . .

Seminar Participant: *Where you didn't want to be.*

RGO: Right. It's an affective experience. The power can be overwhelming. You leave the exhibit or the theater or the music venue, and you say, "I don't think I'll ever be the same," or "I'll never think about this in the same way that I did." And this is precisely what good philosophers aspire to do, but rarely do they achieve it. I would almost rather see the extinction of the class of professional philosophers who like to think, as Bertrand Russell argued, that everything comes from philosophy. Russell said that every open set of questions first belonged to philosophy, and once it collected enough certainty, it then broke off to become its own science.[36] But that's the ideology of philosophy. And it is possible for philosophers to become very ideological about their own practice. They find a place where it is comforting to think a certain way, so they stay there.

Seminar Participant: *Comfort is dangerous. Many just want to resolve, nurture, and come to a calm resolution of all conflict in life and society.*

RGO: Exactly. I'm glad you raised this, because we haven't talked about it yet. There's a whole chapter in *Specters of Revolt* dedicated to this, which is

36. See Bertrand Russell, "The Value of Philosophy," in *The Problems of Philosophy* (London: Oxford University Press, 1912), available on Project Gutenberg (2013), https://www.gutenberg.org/files/5827/5827-h/5827-h.htm.

called "Beyond the Old Virtue of Struggle." In politics, there's a long tradition, going back not only to Marx but also to Frederick Douglass and others, that believes the way to change the world is through struggle and agitation. Douglass famously said that there can be no progress without struggle.[37] But life is full of pain, and people struggle even when they're not doing anything political at all. They struggle to make ends meet, to make their families happy, to make themselves happy. People struggle with anxiety, with the uncertainty of their jobs and their futures. People struggle financially, psychologically, emotionally. People struggle with physical afflictions, surprise illnesses, and death, all kinds of things from abuse to hunger to homelessness. So, for somebody to say today that in order to change the world the very first thing we need to do is struggle, you want to shout back: "No! Enough struggle!" It would be inconceivable, even immoral, to tell the people of Gaza today that they need more struggle. We have got to find ways of challenging the existing reality that are not so damn miserable! Something like joyful agitation.[38]

And isn't it natural to want to be comfortable? Humans aren't looking for more stress, anxiety, agitation, and struggle. And there's been quite a bit of psychological research to show that it's damaging even physiologically to be overburdened with different forms of stress and anxiety. Alain Ehrenberg wrote a book, *The Weariness of the Self*, in which he talks about how all of these everyday things can destroy you.[39]

What's great about art—which you can also see in the recent revolts—is the way that it can be disruptive yet joyful. And the people gathering, they're not so unhappy in the gathering. They often are experiencing community for the first time, and that is disruptive to their everyday alienation. The struggle, properly speaking, is in everyday life outside of the revolt. The revolt, in this sense, is what interrupts the struggle.

Seminar Participant: *It is the element of getting together, the common body of a social gathering. It's so important.*

---

37. Frederick Douglass, "West India Emancipation," in *The Life and Writings of Frederick Douglass*, ed. by Philip S. Foner, vol. 2 (New York: International, 1950), 437.

38. Here, I recommend Nick Montgomery and Carla Bergman's *Joyful Militancy: Building Thriving Resistance in Toxic Times* (Chico: AK Press, 2017), especially Chapter 5.

39. Alain Ehrenberg, *The Weariness of the Self: Diagnosing the History of Depression in the Contemporary Age* (Montreal: McGill-Queen's University Press, 2010).

RGO: Yes, and sometimes we underestimate this, this little bit of human solidarity. That's often hard to come by in everyday life. But the feeling of connection to others who share some of your disaffection is extremely important. The surrogates we create for friendship don't actually serve the functions of friendship. In the Arab Spring, despite the diversity of views and the low confidence about how to really solve the problems, they all quite liked the aspect of coming together. They wanted to go back to the square, and I think they couldn't wait to go back, and it didn't take them long. When Morsi came in and changed the constitution they said, "Let's go back to the square!"

Why should we think it's over now? Where there is so much unfinished business, nothing is finished and done. And I insist on taking seriously "the intellect of insurrection," that the experts aren't the only ones thinking. The really radical imaginations we need, the ones confronting the existing reality and striving to exceed it, are elsewhere than the professional spheres of the ruling class. The late great philosopher of the imagination Drucilla Cornell thought about confronting what she called "the white supremacist imagination," writing that "Black Lives Matter was formed by three women who had such hair-raising, hellish stories about their lives. And what did they do? They built Black Lives Matter, and that is a classic example of capturing a public imagination against the nostalgia for white supremacy . . . Activists constantly push open spaces for the imagination."[40]

Riotous epistemology requires trusting in knowledge-production from below where, inside of the activities of revolt and inside the art of the undercommons, we find a reservoir of imaginary powers to articulate disaffections and dream of new horizons.

---

40. See "Drucilla Cornell on the Power of the Public Imagination," an interview by Rob Hopkins, accessed April 10, 2023, https://www.robhopkins.net/2021/02/03/drucilla-cornell-on-the-power-of-the-public-imagination.

CHAPTER 8

Free Jazz and Other Insurrections

Music is intimately connected with human freedom.[1] Music comes out of, and is part of, human freedom struggles. In the case of Black music in the United States, one of the best documentations of this appears in W. E. B. Du Bois's *The Souls of Black Folk*. The entire book is full of music, musical notation and lyrics, sung and played by Black people imagining a world unlike the world of suffering they were forced to inhabit. In 1903, Du Bois wrote, "They that walked in darkness sang songs in the olden days—Sorrow Songs—for they were weary at heart . . . Ever since I was a child, these songs have stirred me strangely."[2] The "Sorrow Songs" Du Bois refers to are songs born in sadness and despair, but they are not only about sadness and despair. As Du Bois put it, "Through all the sorrow of the Sorrow Songs there breathes a hope—a faith in the ultimate justice of things."[3]

I want to begin here, with the fact that slaves sang songs in fields of misery, that workers sing songs on strike, that people bring guitars and drums to protest demonstrations, to the occupation of parks and squares. In sadness and oppression, there are times when only a song will soothe. But music is not merely palliative. Du Bois again: "In song and exhortation swelled one refrain—Liberty."[4] In grief and despair, one may not be able to speak but may be able to sing, to find hope in a song.

1. A short version of this chapter was originally published as an article in the anarchist magazine *Fifth Estate* in 2009. The chapter published here is vastly expanded, updated, and revised.
2. W. E. B. Du Bois, *The Souls of Black Folk* (New York: Penguin Books, 2018), 187.
3. Du Bois, *The Souls of Black Folk*, 196.
4. Du Bois, *The Souls of Black Folk*, 8.

Human freedom struggles make music, need music, express themselves in music.[5] Music is a modality of human expression that, like revolt, exceeds normal speech. It says what only can be said in music. As John Coltrane told Frank Kofsky in an interview, "I think that music is an instrument. It can create the initial thought patterns that can change the thinking of people."[6] Coltrane's idea of his music, which at the time of that interview was very far into the freest of free improvisation, was that it could participate in the transformation of human understanding and even that it aimed to do so.

As early as 1958, when Sonny Rollins recorded *Freedom Suite,* years before we could speak of a sub-genre called "free jazz" (Ornette Coleman's landmark album entitled *Free Jazz: A Collective Improvisation by the Ornette Coleman Double Quartet* was not recorded until the last days of December 1960), Rollins situated his music in the trajectory of the Sorrow Songs so important to Du Bois. "America is deeply rooted in Negro culture: its colloquialisms, its humor, its music. How ironic that the Negro, who more than any other people can claim America's culture as his own, is being persecuted and repressed, that the Negro, who has exemplified the humanities in his very existence, is being rewarded with inhumanity."[7] Six and seven years before the Civil Rights Act and Voting Rights Act, respectively, there can be no doubt that Rollins made *Freedom Suite* as a contribution to Black freedom struggles in America.[8]

If music is an intimate part of human freedom struggles, why is so much music a rote repetition of hackneyed predictable forms produced for commercial purposes? We know what capitalism does. It commodifies everything, and if it commodifies something like love, which it destroys in the process, it is no surprise that it can commodify music, too. This leads to the question of music that resists commodification, not only in terms of content, but also of form. Some musical forms are not well suited for commodification.

---

5. For one excellent volume documenting this claim, see *Sounding Off! Music As Subversion/Resistance/Revolution,* ed. by Ron Sakolsky and Fred Wei-Han Ho (Brooklyn: Autonomedia, 1995).

6. John Coltrane in a 1967 interview, cited in Philippe Carles and Jean-Louis Comolli, *Free Jazz/Black Power,* trans. Grégory Pierrot (Jackson: University Press of Mississippi, 2015), 175.

7. Sonny Rollins, *Freedom Suite* (Berkeley: Riverside Records, 1989).

8. Aidan Levy, *Saxophone Colossus: The Life and Music of Sonny Rollins* (New York: Hachette Books, 2022), Chapter 20.

Commodification requires standardization of some kind, and songs can be and often are manufactured as units of production. They are written and sold as such. The universe of free jazz and improvisation stakes a position at the antagonistic opposite end of the capitalist commodification of music, and more than that, embodies and reflects the aspirations of human freedom in *both* form and content. As trumpet player Donald Ayler put it, "I wanted to free my mind from America, and I wanted to find my own form—not only in music but in thought and in the way I used my imagination."[9] Musicians like Donald Ayler thought a lot about the imaginary power of music and its relationship to freedom.

In this chapter, I will not describe the music of free jazz to you. For the best description of this indescribable music, you should just listen. It is easier to hear than ever, as the works of any of the musicians I mention in this chapter can be found quickly in an online search. It may not be "easy listening," but like a very good book of theory, the experience should prove rewarding in the end despite the difficulty of the challenge. This chapter will focus on the question of radical listening and its relationship to imaginary power by way of the music that moves me most: free jazz and free improvisation.

From Regressive to Radical Listening

"Free jazz reaches back to what jazz was originally, rebelling against the ultra-sophisticated art form it has become."[10] According to the great tenor saxophonist Archie Shepp, free jazz is a rebellion against the bourgeois world of "high art." It is a music that self-consciously identifies as a kind of sonic insurrection, both within and against music itself. It makes good sense to have begun this chapter with a quote from the Black radical anticapitalist jazz man Shepp.

It makes less sense to follow up with a quote from the elitist philosopher Theodor W. Adorno whose understanding of "serious" art maps out

9. Donald Ayler, cited in Richard Koloda, *Holy Ghost: The Life and Death of Free Jazz Pioneer* (London: Jawbone Press, 2022), 56.

10. Archie Shepp, cited in Valerie Wilmer, *As Serious as Your Life: Black Music and the Free Jazz Revolution, 1957–1977* (London: Serpent's Tail, 2018), 126.

dangerously close to what so many snobbish connoisseurs of Western "high culture" take to be serious. And moreover, Adorno derided jazz in particular, with a vitriol that often reproduced thinly veiled racist caricatures of both the music and musicians.[11] Still, an honest confrontation with Adorno's writing on music demonstrates that Adorno got more than a few things right, particularly in his vicious critique of the culture industry, which can only be categorically rejected to the detriment of any critique of capitalism. It is important to keep in mind that Adorno was treating jazz as the "popular music" of the day, twenty years before rock music would marginalize it anew, and his critique was largely intended to attack capitalist culture and commodified music. With regard to commercial music, Adorno said:

> The consciousness of the mass of listeners is adequate to fetishized music. It listens according to formula, and indeed debasement itself would not be possible if resistance ensued, if the listeners still had the capacity to make demands beyond the limits of what was supplied. . . . There is actually a neurotic mechanism of stupidity in listening, too; the arrogantly ignorant rejection of everything unfamiliar is its sure sign. Regressive listeners behave like children. Again and again and with stubborn malice, they demand the one dish they have once been served.[12]

This first appeared in 1938, published in Germany, where Adorno himself witnessed many of the horrifying effects of the radio broadcasts and propaganda that the Nazis used on the German population.

It makes sense, in this historical context, that Adorno was inclined to issue an indictment of the regressive impact of prepackaged, formulaic, short-form music that was broadcast widely through a relatively new mechanism of mass media. And, to be fair to Adorno, he was much less concerned with music and art criticism than he was with the manipulation of people

11. For one of many examples of such derision, see Adorno's treatment of jazz music in Theodor W. Adorno and Max Horkheimer, *Dialectic of Enlightenment: Philosophical Fragments*, trans. Edmund Jephcott (Stanford: Stanford University Press, 2002), 119–25.

12. Theodor Adorno, "On the Fetish-Character in Music and the Regression of Listening," in *The Essential Frankfurt School Reader*, eds. by Andrew Arato and Eike Gephardt (New York: Continuum, 2002), 285, 290.

through capitalist commercial culture—something, he feared, that could prepare a population for the most deceptive and dangerous programs fascists and states could think up.

Adorno was wrong about many things, but he was right that capitalism acculturates hostility toward the unfamiliar. Capitalists benefit from a field of consumers who crave standardized and mass-produced products, including songs and movie plots that can be predicted before being heard or seen in full. Most of us have had the experience, when watching a movie with someone, of congratulating ourselves for calling the outcome before it plays out. Making good predictions is rewarding, and knowing what comes next is reassuring. The opposite, unpredictability, can be frustrating and cause anxiety. The attraction of people to authoritarian personalities can be understood in this way. The authoritarian figure, in politics for example, claims the ability to hold everything firmly in place, to prevent unpredictable tumult in the economy, social life, etc.[13] As Adorno and his coauthors put it in *The Authoritarian Personality*, "It seems possible that the rebellious tendencies have not actually been outgrown but have rather been inhibited, so that the emphasis on conformity now serves as a defense against underlying hostility toward accepted authority."[14] Adorno understood that the standardization of cultural products was a dangerous development, even a reversal of the logic of "good art." Capitalist art, including commercial music, pumped out by the culture industry, inhibits rebellious tendencies and emphasizes conformity. "Good," or "serious art," as Adorno called it, ought to be challenging and provocative, and should never be so easy to take that it could be *passively* consumed. "Passive consumption" may appear as a contradiction in terms, but it can be seen wherever the consumer accepts whatever is given or buys what is sold with little thought and question.

The listener who does not *actively* listen is not much of a listener at all, and *music that does not need to be actively listened to* is potentially dangerous insofar as it promotes passive listening, predictability, and conformity. But, instead of demanding to hear something that we do not already or immediately enjoy, instead of demanding to hear something provocative and

13. Theodor W. Adorno, Else Frenkel-Brunswik, Daniel J. Levinson, and R. Nevitt Sanford, *The Authoritarian Personality* (New York: Verso Books, 2019).

14. Adorno et al., *The Authoritarian Personality*, 162.

difficult, we tend to demand more of what we have already come to like; we may even experience revulsion in an encounter with the unfamiliar. Such a demeanor, Adorno concludes, is that of stupidity. It is not a good thing for art or politics when we stubbornly reject anything that threatens to undermine our given or preexisting tastes and frustrates familiarity.

However, when it comes to radical politics, Adorno can only provide us with a diagnostic theory. He was himself relatively uninterested in radical politics, which surprised enough activist students that they disrupted his lectures in protest during the final years of his academic career.[15] Herbert Marcuse and Adorno disagreed deeply about the importance of student activism, with Adorno refusing to side with radical students who assumed—based on his critical theory of capitalism—he would take their side in the social movements of the late 1960s.[16] In any case, I am not particularly interested in Adorno here, but, rather, a question related to his critique of "regressive listening." I am interested in the question of *radical listening* as an antithesis to *regressive listening.*

If you read critical theory, you may learn how to think and write in radical terms, how to think about a better world that looks little like the one we live in. Philosophers have a long history of imagining the good as something incompatible with "the good" and goods of capitalist society. We radical thinkers articulate ideas of the best of all possible worlds that are incompatible with the existing political-economic structures of the world we now have. That is what we do. It is connected with imaginary power. Still, to think and speak beyond the bounds of what is, and, wherever possible, to act out against what is, constitutes much of the political terrain of revolutionary activity.

But, do we know how to *listen* in revolutionary terms? What might radical listening mean? Would it even matter? I begin to answer these questions by observing that most of the formats for expressing radical ideas are formally unchallenging. Our art and music come to us in forms that are, on the whole, easy to appropriate. Many of the hardcore punk bands that rage with articulate wit against capitalist social reality, that appear in terms of their lyrical

15. Stefan Müller-Doohm, *Adorno: A Biography,* trans. Rodney Livingston (Cambridge: Polity Press, 2005).

16. Müller-Doohm, *Adorno,* 478.

content to be well beyond capitalist co-optation, have had their forms appropriated and replayed on late-night television, repackaged with inane lyrical content, and circulated as background music in clothing stores, fitness clubs, video games, movies, and commercials. They were easily marketable after all, and with some minor modifications in content and style, fully compatible with commercialization. Even for the politically radical music fan, once accustomed to two- to three-minute blasts of thrashing hardcore punk, with parts A and B, and a predictable recurring chorus, listening becomes easy. There is nothing wrong with that in principle. There is nothing formally to oppose in the rock-based hardcore punk, metal, hip-hop, rap, folk, European classical, or pop music that makes people feel good. In a world of sadness, exploitation, broken hearts, and social isolation, let music function as a balm, a refuge, a feeling companion, and social connection to others.

In fact, it is important to say that I do not listen to improvised music only for its radical messages and subversive forms. I certainly appreciate its history and the ideas behind its creative forms, content, and processes, but I also listen for pure pleasure. Sometimes, the music moves me to tears; other times it dries my tears. The music helps me feel my own feelings more acutely, helps me feel what I am really feeling beneath the veneer of everyday life, and it often clears my mind in the morning. Thus, aside from all of its contentious and social dimensions, the music is for me a kind of healing force in my life, as Albert Ayler once said.[17] Playing and hearing free jazz is for me a joyful experience, and the affective impact it has on me would be enough reason to keep on listening to and playing it. Indeed, many people who love this music enjoy it on just that level and are not thinking at all about capitalism and radical listening.

However, I want to stick with the question of radical listening here, and to the juxtaposition of active to passive listening. When it comes to music, for example, we listen in very conventional ways, standardized across genres regardless of differences in content. Let us specify that *conventional listening* is linear, meaning that we listen for beginnings and ends, we anticipate a succession of parts and changes, most of which repeat for the pleasure of familiarity and predictability. By contrast, *radical listening* is spatial, not linear. It deprives the listener of a succession of parts and changes to predictably

17. *Music Is the Healing Force of the Universe* is the title of a 1969 album by Albert Ayler.

count on, and insists on being unfamiliar at every turn. Radical listening compels us to experience music more spatially than temporally, as freer and more open formally, compositionally, and thus to raise questions rather than settle them. The great bassist and philosopher William Parker said, "Freedom cannot be handed out. It is already inside of us. And most importantly it is in improvisational music."[18] Following this, I will focus on the connections between radical listening and improvised music.

As to the more difficult (and possibly more important) question of whether or not radical listening matters, I argue it does matter, although not as much as we might like it to. Surrealist anarchist writer Ron Sakolsky puts it this way: "When people ask me to name my biggest influences in forming a radical political consciousness in 1960s America, they expect me to rattle off a list of authors and books. Confounding these expectations, I immediately respond, 'John Coltrane.' Trane's expansive diasporic consciousness and his improvisational flights of exploration encouraged me to see beyond the chord changes of consensus reality."[19] Radical listening can help us think and feel beyond the narrow boundaries of conventional listening and conformist forms of life, but it holds no certain promise, no guarantees for social or political transformation.

In general, radical political art is a desperate act, which tries and often fails to transform anyone or anything. Like the best political documentaries, music, theater, or books, it can be very good but not very effective, especially with audiences who more or less share the ideological sensibilities of the works. Nevertheless, I maintain that we need the practice of taking in and processing works that are uncomfortable and unsettling, difficult to process.

I shall take free jazz music as an illustration.

Considering Free Jazz

Adorno's critique of commercial music helped me to deeply appreciate free jazz music. Therefore, I have always found it surprising that he loathed the

---

18. William Parker, cited in Cisco Bradley, *Universal Tonality: The Life and Music of William Parker* (Durham: Duke University Press, 2021), 269.

19. Ron Sakolsky, *Creating Anarchy* (Liberty, TN: Fifth Estate Books, 2005), 67–68.

jazz musician, who was, already in the 1930s, fully involved in unpredictable flights of improvisation and the active destabilizing of linear rhythms. I could never help but wonder what Adorno would have said about free jazz as a particular movement in the history of jazz, and though he did live long enough to hear it, dying in 1969, he never wrote about it.[20] The jazz Adorno wrote about was a different variety, and he refers to it as "usual commercial jazz," which he understood as an easily ignorable accompaniment for conversation and dancing.[21] Free jazz, however, was an attack on this "usual commercial jazz," and had very different motivations. According to Sun Ra, "The music comes from the void, the nothing, the void, in response to the burning need for something else."[22]

Free jazz in America began *as a movement* in the 1950s. The music culminated in international underground movements in the 1960s, and then passed through various phases and reconfigurations throughout the 70s, 80s, and 90s and still continues as a living music today. Sometimes, the music I'm calling "free jazz" also goes by the names "avant-garde jazz," "jazz improvisation," "creative music," "improvised," "experimental music," "out jazz," "new music," among several other names, none of which are as important as the music itself. Some musicians simply call it "music." Free jazz is an insurrection in the world of sound, and it seems to me to demand what I have called "radical listening." It is also important to historically contextualize the music in relation to Black freedom struggles in the US. Interviewed by Jacques Derrida, Ornette Coleman said, "I was in the South when minorities were oppressed, and I identified with them through music."[23] As Albert Ayler put it, "I think it's a very good thing that Black people in this country are becoming conscious of the strengths of being Black. They are beginning to see who they are. They are acquiring so much respect for themselves. And that's a beautiful development for me because I'm playing their suffering, whether

20. Actually, Adorno's own piano playing, which was recorded, has much in common with free jazz.

21. Adorno, "On the Fetish-Character in Music and the Regression of Listening," 288.

22. Sun Ra, cited in A.B. Spellman, Larry Neal, Amiri Baraka, eds., *The Cricket: Black Music in Evolution, 1968–69* (New York: Blank Forms Editions, 2022), 30.

23. "The Other's Language: Jacques Derrida Interviews Ornette Coleman, 23 June, 1997," trans. Timothy S. Murphy in *Genre: Forms of Discourse and Culture* 37, no. 2 (June 1, 2004): 323.

they know it or not. I've lived that suffering."[24] William Parker understood that the music was "about revolution. It's about coming to grips with the past and the now and what we will have to deal with in the future."[25]

The music was also very self-consciously responding to white appropriations of jazz, and especially to the parasitic interests of capitalists, which descended upon jazz in the 1950s and 60s, before seizing rock and roll as a bigger and better business opportunity. Sun Ra understood this with particular sharpness in 1968. "Then something began to happen to Jazz, the Jazz musician was commercialized and packaged and Jazz began to be a product of and from the white world . . . Since I was not a product of the white world, I found that I could not fit comfortably in the place they had reserved for the black musician."[26] Black radicals like Jimmie Stewart heard something more radical in the music. "Black music is guerrilla music. Terrorist music. Revolutionary music . . . The revolutionary must destroy the prison the present makes of dreams."[27] Analysts and observers outside the US, such as French jazz critics Philippe Carles and Jean-Louis Comolli, also understood the music in terms of imperialist power and white supremacy. "We think that the contradiction between white and black values—seen at work in the colonizations of jazz and in the resistance to these colonizations—is but one of the moments in the *main contradiction*: between colonizers and colonized, exploiters and exploited; between capitalism and its prey."[28] This is the context in which free jazz emerged as a form of revolt through music.

Nonetheless, it is not necessarily free jazz that we need. If not free jazz alone, which will gratify me personally for a lifetime of radical listening, we need other insurrections on visual and sonic terrains, other artworks of the undercommons that could learn something from this particular movement.

For reasons discussed in all my work, I am most inspired and influenced by thinking from below, theory from the margins of society, the philosophical

---

24. Albert Ayler, cited in Richard Koloda, *Holy Ghost: The Life and Death of Free Jazz Pioneer Albert Ayler* (London: Jawbone Press, 2022), 151.

25. William Parker, cited in Bradley, *Universal Tonality*, 181.

26. Sun Ra, cited in Spellman et al., eds., *The Cricket*, 33.

27. Jimmie Stewart (1968), cited in A.B. Spellman, Larry Neal, Amiri Baraka, eds. *The Cricket: Black Music in Evolution, 1968–69* (New York: Blank Forms Editions, 2022), 93.

28. Philippe Carles and Jean-Louis Comolli, *Free Jazz/Black Power*, trans. Grégory Pierrot (Jackson: University Press of Mississippi, 2015), 5.

content of riot, revolt, and insurrection. I am more interested in the powers, imaginary and otherwise, of everyday people presumed to have no powers, than in the powers of the ruling class.

Artists, including but not limited to musicians, can say things with more urgency and impact than a text, and this I think is truer today than ever before. We live in an increasingly visual world, text is on the decline, even in recent evolutions of social media that shorten text to tweets and supplant written content with images, as can be seen in the exodus from Facebook to Instagram and TikTok. We have to confront the fact that visual and sonic provocations may captivate people's attentions in novel ways, calling on us to listen to and see things differently. Radicals and revolutionaries have understood this for a long time. Just for example, Guy Debord's work always expressed a special appreciation for artistic and aesthetic dimensions, and as I have documented elsewhere, much of what prevented the Mexican state's efforts to vilify the Zapatista rebellion was their theatrical and poetic savvy.[29] We may look, as well, for similar aesthetic sensibilities in recent uprisings in Greece, North Africa, in Black Lives Matter, and other examples.

On the one hand, free jazz may be regarded as a footnote to this reflection on radical listening and insurrectionary art. On the other hand, it is the perfect illustration. I grew up in the 70s and 80s, and music played a significant role in my politicization. Before the lessons of great dead authors, I thought about justice, inequality, and political action through CRASS, Dead Kennedys, The Proletariat, and in the late 80s and early 90s, with bands like Born Against and the DIY punk scene of that time. In the 1990s, I shifted my focus increasingly to free jazz, and as a drummer, improvisation felt to me like the most vital and living way to approach music, to engage with other players in attentive listening and creative, sensible, responses, through an artistic practice of collective freedom.

The ideals of freedom, resistance, and uprising appeared clearly in the forefront of free jazz and improvised music, and for these reasons I have been devoted to it for more than thirty years. Albert Ayler appreciated the fact that radical developments in music can demand too much from

---

29. See especially part III, Chapter 7 of Richard Gilman-Opalsky, *Unbounded Publics: Transgressive Public Spheres, Zapatismo, and Political Theory* (Lanham: Lexington Books, 2008).

an audience. "People are going to the moon. It's time for music to change, too . . . It is undeniably time for a change, but you have to be ready for it. Everybody's not. Some people don't want to be free."[30] I think Ayler is right insofar as a listener who is not interested in radical listening will turn off the music, turn away from or react against it with hostility. He experienced this in reactions to his own music in his lifetime. I think we could explain the instinct against the freedom of the form and content of free jazz with recourse to some of what we discussed above in Adorno. There is a fascistic tendency at work, corroborated by the fact that Nazis fiercely opposed jazz music. The Nazis were worried about jazz music and its international popularity, precisely because the spontaneity, improvisation, and freedom of the music represented a challenge to the homogeneity and uniformity of Nazi ideology.[31]

Approaches in free jazz have always been shaped by many different traditions and attitudes. There is no single ideological framework that binds the players, not even, say, if we are only talking about players in New York or Chicago in the 1960s. It would be inaccurate to claim that they were all politically radical, anticapitalists, and revolutionaries. They were not. Indeed, some were Black Nationalists, while others emphasized religion and spirituality, seeing themselves as conduits and vessels for messages of the Holy Spirit. Some were communists, some were anarchists, and some believed they were playing the music of their time, a music that accompanied the civil rights movement, the anti–Vietnam War movement, and the Black Panther Party.

Even when the music was centered on apolitical, spiritual, or religious motivations, its form was enough to make it dangerous in the eyes of the mainstream jazz culture. "Critics mobilize against free jazz because it no longer plays jazz's game—a game where until then capitalism and its ideology always won."[32] And regardless of the political commitments of the players, the risks of playing free jazz were often so severe precisely because of the context of capitalist political economy and racism. William Parker understood

30. Ayler, cited in Koloda, *Holy Ghost*, 52–53.

31. Michael H. Kater, *Different Drummers: Jazz in the Culture of Nazi Germany* (Oxford: Oxford University Press, 1992).

32. Carles and Comolli, *Free Jazz/Black Power*, 173.

the political connotations of this, which would apply even to musicians who were not interested in making a political statement. "We cannot separate the starving child from the starving musician, both things are caused by the same things, capitalism, racism, and the putting of military spending ahead of human rights. The situation of the artist is a reflection of America's whole attitude towards life and creativity."[33]

To be sure, to accept everything the music claimed to represent could lead to a kind of confusion. For me, it was not the religious comportment of Albert Ayler, John Coltrane, or Charles Gayle, or the Black Nationalist claims of Amiri Baraka (then LeRoi Jones) that drew me to the music. Rather, I am attracted to the revolutionary form of the art, the joys and rewards of radical listening, and the relationship of the music to life, struggles, and imaginary power. Admittedly, I am drawn as well to the political content and revolutionary spirit of people like Clifford Thornton, The Revolutionary Ensemble, Archie Shepp, Max Roach, Paul Rutherford, Sonny Simmons, Milford Graves, Peter Brötzmann, Matana Roberts, and the Art Ensemble of Chicago, as well as to the antagonistic relation of the sound to commodified music, and its real-time creative and collective action. Art Ensemble of Chicago was not the only group to make records that were directly and explicitly about revolution, but they were not the least bit mysterious about their politics. In 1969, saxophonist Joseph Jarman offered the following inside one Art Ensemble of Chicago album: "America waiting-construct transformation construct-REVOLT-DO NOT INCITE TO RIOT-INCITE TO REVOLUTION . . . TOGETHER-we free together."[34] Indeed, there is no shortage of revolutionary poetry in Black radical music, and it could even be argued that free jazz and improvised music are themselves forms of poetry.

But if we view the music in its historical context, both in the US and elsewhere, we find there are some things that the music does claim in common. *Free jazz is generally understood as an emancipatory music of some kind, either immediately liberating in the moment of performance, for both players and listeners, or liberating in a prefigurative sense, pointing toward possible future liberations*. Sun Ra said: "Freedom to me means the freedom to rise above a

33. William Parker, in Bradley, *Universal Tonality*, 174.

34. Joseph Jarman, *Art Ensemble of Chicago: A.A.C.M., Great Black Music, "Reese and the Smooth Ones"* (Paris, France: Actuel Records, 1969).

cruel planet."[35] It seems to me that, in all of its diversity, free jazz shares that aspiration, to move beyond the cruelty of the existing reality.

The music does not merely say it is "about liberation" (as in lyrics or liner notes or spoken word) but acts out a kind of liberation in its performance. Freedom usually sounds like a good idea, though not to jailers and governments, but the sound of freedom is not so easy to endure. We could make a strained analogy in the prisoner who has lived in a cell for twenty years, for whom the idea of freedom is an aspirational beacon, but the experience of getting free may take some time to get used to. Drummer Milford Graves said of free jazz: "Some people talk of freedom but they're playing what they *think* they should play. You can't go into freedom without conditioning yourself. If you've been living a certain way for twenty years and then all of a sudden you come out and say you want to be free, it doesn't work because you're fighting yourself."[36] In this way, we could say that the music is not so much freedom itself but a kind of preparation for getting free. Jimmie Stewart understood the music in that way: "We must prepare our people through our art. Because music proceeds as movement and force music is the ultimate aesthetic equivalent of revolutionary Black thought."[37] Stewart understood the music as a way of getting people ready for revolution.

Max Roach, who died in 2007, was not strictly a free jazz player, but performed with many free jazz pioneers such as Archie Shepp (on overtly revolutionary records like *The Long March* and *Force*), with Anthony Braxton, and also with Cecil Taylor. Roach once said about his experience playing with the pianist Thelonious Monk, "Monk encouraged me to emancipate the drums from their subservient role as timekeepers."[38] For Roach, since music was inspired by emancipatory struggles in the world, why should those who make it be subservient to rigid rules and roles? Can we not transcend the repetitive and oppressive limitations of the conventional division of labor among musicians and instruments, and the rote memorization of playing compositions treated as if they were sacred texts?

Free jazz was the outgrowth of a number of things already taking place in

35. Sun Ra, in Spellman et al., eds., *The Cricket*, 28.

36. Milford Graves cited in Wilmer, *As Serious as Your Life*, 249.

37. Jimmie Stewart, cited in Spellman et al., eds., *The Cricket*, 90.

38. Max Roach, cited at the Barbados Jazz Society, accessed December 29, 2022, http://www.barbadosjazzsociety.com/category/jazz-weekly/page/3.

jazz music and in society, culture, and politics in the 50s and 60s. And some of the things that were "in the air" were a growing spirit of freedom, disillusionment with the US in light of the imperialist war in Vietnam, a powder keg of race and class consciousness, the stifling rhetoric of the Cold War, and from all of this, an impetus for something revolutionary. So, when Roach talks about "emancipating the drums from their subservient role," you hear in that statement one of the ways that spirit of freedom was transposed into the music.

Improvisation has always been a big part of jazz music. Even in Louis Armstrong's music, his wild solos were most surprising when they were improvised on the spot, demonstrating his ability to run through and create loosely associated melodies that were "ready at hand," not read off sheet music verbatim. Sonny Rollins is not only known as one of the greatest improvisers but also as a musician who played familiar popular compositions, for which he was often (and wrongly) accused of commercial motivations. But, Rollins has said, "I'm always completely improvising. I keep fresh because I'm never the same."[39] When Rollins played a standard, the familiar was rendered unfamiliar and unpredictable, as he deconstructed the melodies and turned them inside out. Decade after decade, throughout the twentieth century, improvisation took on different and increasingly central roles in the music. Until ultimately, a constellation of radical musicians including Ornette Coleman, Cecil Taylor, Alice Coltrane, Albert Ayler, Bill Dixon, Arthur Doyle, Frank Lowe, Sunny Murray, Barbara Donald, Peter Brötzmann, Joe Maneri, Dave Burrell, Linda Sharrock, Gato Barbieri, Don Cherry, Frank Wright, and many others, made group improvisation the focus of their music. Improvisation was not only about music. David S. Ware lamented, "The creative spirit, what improvisation is, is lost. It's been lost—it's a lost art. And when I say that, it doesn't mean people aren't improvising. It means that the meaning behind it is lost. Because what it really is, it's something connected with our existence . . . Life itself is improvisation."[40] So much in a life requires improvisation, and if we can ever get to it, a revolutionary situation would be especially improvisatory. A good chef can improvise, as can a good parent

39. Levy, *Saxophone Colossus*, 534.

40. David S. Ware, cited in Phil Freeman, *New York is Now! The New Wave of Free Jazz* (New York: Telegraph, 2001), 45.

or friend. Ware also made a great album called *Wisdom of Uncertainty*, which was a meditation on knowing how to deal with the unknown.[41] It is not just a question of having the freedom to improvise but also of knowing how to use that freedom. Free jazz is one of many possible exercises in that.

In addition to the cultural and political context, the music also represented—and still represents—a defiant response to the capitalist music industry. It was a severe economic risk for the original coterie of artists, most of whom lived at the boundaries of impoverishment for most of their lives. One of the earliest innovators, Ornette Coleman observed what was happening: "The way they handle the publicity on me, about how far out I am and everything, it gets to be that I'm the product itself. So if it's me they're selling, if I'm the product, then the profits couldn't come back to me, you dig?"[42] The capitalist angle was, as should not surprise anyone, to try to commodify the music. But if Ornette's music becomes a product, if he becomes the product himself, then the ones who sell him and his music get the money. The product doesn't get paid. So, it was crucial for these musicians to resist commodification, which rarely ended up being profitable for them in a capitalist sense.

Most of these musicians could have chosen to play standards and straight ahead compositions in (at least relatively) decently paid working bands, because it is worth remembering that this music began before rock music made playing jazz for a living a near impossibility in the 1970s. So the decision in the 1960s to play music for which there was no commercial market, to play music that would be banned from jazz clubs and reviewed with intemperate vitriol in the press, would often launch these musicians into even more dire financial straits, which few ever escaped.

While quite a bit can be said about the history of the music, little can be said to describe it or the experience of listening. The best way to experience it is to listen. I recommend that the listener devote some time and attention to listening and try to hear what is happening in the music. Do not listen for beginnings and ends. Listen less for a succession of parts and more for spatial interaction. I sometimes think about the music as sound painting. You can listen to the colors, to the waves, the strokes.

41. David S. Ware Quartet, *Wisdom of Uncertainty* (New York: AUM Fidelity, 1997).
42. Ornette Coleman, cited in Carles and Comolli, *Free Jazz/Black Power*, 25.

Free jazz challenges the capitalist logic of the commercialization of music. Much of it is long-form improvisation, meaning a single piece of music could be thirty minutes or well over an hour. This fact alone made the music incompatible with commercial radio play. Rhythms are jagged, or smooth and multidirectional, and there are few melodies that march along in a straightforward manner, although some musicians incorporate that into compositional aspects of the music as "heads." The music sometimes continues to swing, but rarely proceeds in a line like a tape measure that could measure term years and the hours of a corporate workday.

On first exposure, I have often heard it asked if (or declared that) the music is atonal. But it is actually the complete opposite of atonal. Inasmuch as atonal means the absence of tonality, free jazz is actually better described as "extra-tonal," for it offers more tones and more tonality at the same time than we are used to hearing—hence the feeling of chaos. This is much like the common misinterpretation of anarchism as chaotic, which only reflects an inability to identify different forms of organic and nonhierarchical order.

We should not regard as "chaotic" everything that is not a hierarchical bureaucracy. There are different forms of order. One of the wildest and freest saxophonists ever to live, Albert Ayler, said, "To begin with, we are the music we play. And our commitment is to peace, to understanding of life."[43] You have to get past reactionary listening, which is worse than passive listening. Reactionary listening precedes passive listening in many cases, and is essentially a visceral and occasionally hostile refusal to listen. Reactionary listening is also corrupting and dangerous in everyday communication because it is a form of "listening" that undermines communication. The reactionary listener hears in the music only chaos and war, whereas a practitioner like Ayler insisted that his music was striving for peace and understanding

The form of this music is also its critique. You will know what I mean when you hear it. Perhaps Cecil Taylor contextualized the music best: "Anybody's music is made up of a lot of things that are not musical. Music is an attitude, a group of symbols of a way of life, whether you're conscious of it or not—and of course, it naturally reflects the social and economic and educational attitudes of the players."[44]

43. Albert Ayler, in Koloda, *Holy Ghost*, 169–70.

44. Wilmer, *As Serious as Your Life*, 45.

But let's not soften the point. There is also something furious happening in this music. It is not a mild variation on a theme, but rather, a blistering attack on the repetition of familiar melody in repetitive song structures, and it reflects the possibilities of unbounded imagination and creativity. Full of noises like chirps, screams, squeaks, howls, scrapes, smashing sounds, and an overwhelming persistence to elude all prediction. After practice at listening, after listening more radically, one discovers an alternative conception of the tonal and the melodic, and finds that there is something more beautiful than scary about the freedom of the sounds.

Poet and trumpeter Ted Joans said of hearing Albert Ayler's group for the first time that "their sound was so different, so rare and raw, like screaming the word 'FUCK' in Saint Patrick's Cathedral on crowded Easter Sunday . . . The entire house was shook up. The loud sound didn't let up. It went on and on, growing more powerful as it built up. It was like a giant tidal wave of frightening music. It completely overwhelmed everybody . . . others shouted at the musicians to shut up. I sat shocked, stoned and amazed by what I was witnessing. Their music was unlike anything that I had heard before."[45] It is worth asking: How often do we say that about the music that we hear?

Other Insurrections

It is difficult not to think of communism and anarchism when thinking of this music. Free jazz is a subversion of every tepid liberal turn in the history of music, making the music of the 1969 Woodstock Festival (which happened simultaneous with the apex of the American free jazz movement) sound tame and conservative by comparison.

One could possibly think of anarchism and left-wing communism as part of the good conscience of the left, as the expression of the utmost logical developments of the best ideas and most revolutionary arguments found on the radical left. Anarchists and communists are always denounced by liberals as "too extreme," but our reply has been to reliably point out that the world is full of extremes of injustice, repression, and terror, so any viable antithesis must be extreme in response. I see a kind of analog for this in free jazz and

45. Wilmer, *As Serious as Your Life*, 95.

free improvisation.[46] Free jazz is a music that takes some of the best ideas in radical art and extends them to their logical conclusions, and it represents a kind of good conscience of radical art such that artists, dealing either in sound or images, might do well to measure their work against the benchmarks of this music.

One of my dear comrades and fellow free jazz fanatic, Ron Sakolsky, wrote: "Leaving the chains of realism behind involves a willingness both to plunge below the surface and to embark on rhizomatic flights of unshackled imagination. When pursued together, these acts can boldly challenge all established ideas of musicality by going deep inside and far outside the mundane chord changes of reality in pursuit of nonlinear poetic adventures in indeterminate sound."[47] For Sakolsky, the music is about unshackling the imagination, about experimenting with possibilities beyond the existing reality.

My work on imaginary power shares a deep and abiding affinity with Sakolsky's surrealism. For Sakolsky, surrealism is never reducible to paintings on a museum wall. Philosophically and politically, surrealism is about surpassing the misery of the existing reality. The surreal begins in the real yet seeks to surpass it and relies on imagination to do so. That is the connection to art. We have to imagine precisely those things that the capitalist reality declares impossible, and then set our sights on what is desirable in that so-called realm of the impossible. Revolution involves converting the desirable into the possible—rejecting the parameters of possibility in the present—which I claim ultimately requires the abolition of capitalist society. Sakolsky contends that "free improvisation represents the most direct form of surrealist expression because it taps into the 'pure psychic automatism' that is at the heart of the surrealist project."[48] In other words, free improvisation is a direct engagement with disaffection and desire, allowing us to fully and freely express our aspirations to exceed the "cruel world" that Sun Ra

46. Here, I should note that there are nonidiomatic forms of improvised music that do not seek to retain any lineage with jazz or Black struggles. Saxophonist and author Jack Wright does a good job of differentiating free jazz from other forms of free playing and free improvisation in his book *The Free Musics* (Philadelphia: Spring Garden Music Editions, 2017).

47. Ron Sakolsky, *Scratching the Tiger's Belly* (Portland, OR: Eberhardt Press, 2012), 91.

48. Sakolsky, *Scratching the Tiger's Belly*, 93.

hoped to transcend in his music. Sun Ra may have best expressed the surrealist aspirations of free jazz. "In essence, looking back on [Sun] Ra's lifetime in the service of Impossible Desire, his musical creativity can be seen as an intuitively surrealist way of expressing the utopian dreamscape as soundscape."[49]

Yes, we want a different world. In fact, and especially ecologically, we need a different world. In his last period of music-making, Sonny Rollins sought to confront ecological crisis. Aidan Levy notes that Rollins "realized that the problem was endemic to capitalism. A model of infinite growth with finite resources was unsustainable."[50] Rollins said, "Pesticide-ridden food, chemicalized air, toxic water—these are the result of greed and our reliability on technological answers to life's problems."[51] Let us listen to those who imagine different possibilities. To hear their message, we need to move from reactionary and passive listening to active radical listening. Consider how hard it is to hear the message of Black revolt as a reactionary listener. The reactionary listener sees and hears only inchoate, irrational violence in the revolt. Consider how hard it is to hear the message of Black revolt as a passive listener. The passive listener just assimilates whatever everyone else is saying about it right in front of their ears and eyes, usually on a scrolling screen. Thus, the passive listener ends up with a "hot take" on the revolt without ever bothering to think about it. Active radical listening is different. You have to go for the content, insist that Black revolt is not stupid, that it is a response to everyday violence in a white supremacist society, that it is not itself the violence. With that starting position, radical listening makes the messages appear. I say messages, not message, because there is more than one brain and analysis inside the activity of revolt. Free jazz and other insurrections can help us hear what's happening and imagine what is not. Free jazz and other insurrections can put us in touch with our aspirations for what Sun Ra called "the burning need for something else."[52]

If we are concerned with the radical transformation of the world, let us take the example of free jazz as our point of departure, as a kind of launching off point for other insurrections in art and life. We have our radical texts,

49. Sakolsky, *Scratching the Tiger's Belly*, 108–9.
50. Levy, *Saxophone Colossus*, 683.
51. Levy, *Saxophone Colossus*, 683.
52. Sun Ra, cited in Spellman et al., eds., *The Cricket*, 30.

and we have our radical theater (from The Living Theater to the International Anarchist Theater Festival). We have radical music, too, from Poison Girls and D.I.R.T. to new free jazz today, such as in the creative music of Matana Roberts, Zoh Amba, Mette Rasmussen, Virginia Genta, Isaiah Collier, and countless others. But we must always ask: Where is the challenge of radical listening, the challenge of bringing the unsettling discomfort of the unfamiliar into conflict with the static status quo? Where is this taking place? Such locations exist, but they are not always so easy to find.

When ideas, and even sights and sounds, move from the periphery to the center, the radical must reconstitute itself as something else. This is true because *to not do so* is to adopt a position of relative complicity with the status quo, a position incompatible with revolutionary sensibilities. The notion that the given state of affairs can be transformed for the better is the impetus for new music, theory, and other activities of social and political change.

Cultural peripheries are where ideas and arguments *antagonistic to the center* first gather. This is not so much a philosophical point as a historical one—the center changes over time, but the surrealist aspiration—to exceed the existing reality—always reconstitutes in the margins, on the periphery, imagining how to work toward the next real horizon.

We have libraries of radical texts to consult. An abundance of sonic and visual materials are out there, too, but all of these things taken together are only challenging and disruptive in passing moments, like saturnalias that begin and end in a festival or a performance or a reading group. The problem is that our opponent enjoys the stature of permanence even if not the actual reality of permanence. I do not believe that capitalism is the final destination, but it does not exist only in fleeting moments. Capitalism permeates human life *all of the time,* often even demarcating what we call "leisure time." Ultimately, a real countervailing force to the current order must be as constant as capitalism.

We need new insurrections of visual-sonic work to help our ideas into visibility. One can think here of the Zapatistas who only said on January 1, 1994 what they had been saying variously for over seventy years of one-party PRI rule. The difference was not their interest in liberation but the poetry, the masks, and the theatrical interventions of uprising. The aesthetic qualities of the Zapatista rebellion helped to get its words and ideas out beyond the borders of Chiapas, into the world outside Mexico.

Free jazz was an attack on the center from the periphery. Roughly seventy years later, that's still what it does. Free jazz is not a music that belongs in a historical archive but a living music that continues to evolve around the world. Sonny Rollins said, "It's very important jazz doesn't become a museum piece."[53] Free jazz and free improvisation continue to develop today. After all this time, however, free music has not subverted the center, for it is still an outlier art form in the margins of music that challenges the ways we listen. Free jazz still aims to get us listening in radical, participatory ways, to reject passive reception and reactionary listening and the fetish of familiar repetition.

Yet, in some of the major cities of the world, free jazz and free improvisation are finding fresh appreciation among young people, misfits, and even bourgeois connoisseurs. Its worst fate would be that of the precious record collectors who care less about the music than the rarity and exchange value of some obscure LP. That is exactly the museum treatment Rollins warned against. One would have hoped that some of the aging and impoverished musicians did not have to live and die poor and neglected like so many of their brothers and sisters, but alas, very few manage to secure the dignified existence they always deserved. Still, growing appreciation is a good thing for those who've been so long maligned for bringing beauty into an often ugly world.

Growing appreciation of the music is not wholly motivated by revolutionary sensibilities. A lot of the musicians, including some of the most respected practitioners, are completely cut off from the social and political dimensions of the music's history. We have to be honest about that. And, even with growing appreciation, the music is hard to find and support outside of big cities. Nonetheless, even if free jazz makes no revolutionary promises, is removed from its historical Black and revolutionary commitments, the music *still* embodies and enacts radical sensibilities, it *still* comes out of a radical tradition, and *still* challenges us to listen beyond the existing boundaries of "good taste." Even if free jazz itself is not the answer, it *does* point out one possibility for radical listening.

Other insurrections are what we need most. New insurrectionary art begins on the periphery but may do better than free jazz has done to break out of the margins of a hermetically sealed subculture to disrupt the states of affairs it so abhors.

---

53. Levy, *Saxophone Colossus*, 663.

What we may take from free jazz for now is a call to artists, musicians, and other creatives to give us something that the reactionaries of our time cannot bear. Help us listen and see differently. The periphery will be inhabited by the new, so it's never too static there. Let us send our messages out from the margins for the sake of antagonisms that aspire to abolish the present state of things and that help us to imagine collectively construed liberations.

CHAPTER 9

The Practicality of Utopianism

Forms of Life and Loneliness

Let us consider capitalism and communism as forms of life and not, as is usually the case, as forms of government or as opposing systems of political economy.[1] Of course, we can also imagine and talk about capitalist and communist logics of governmentality and economy, and these are ultimately always implicated in any discussion of capitalism and communism. However, we do not have to begin with statecraft and modes of production. We may take a different starting position, and we must if we want to focus on forms of life and experiences of loneliness. That is the overarching aim of the present chapter.

I argue that we cannot be abolitionists of loneliness. Loneliness cannot be abolished. First, loneliness will have to be defined and distinguished from solitude. Also, loneliness lies within the manifold experiences of a lifetime, and no matter the form of society, it will most certainly recur throughout the course of a human life, often without warning. Still, some forms of loneliness are dangerous. As Hannah Arendt understood with penetrating insight, loneliness can be preyed upon by fascists who offer to bring an end to loneliness in the solidarity of chauvinistic patriotism and nationalist togetherness. But we who prefer the *Gemeinwesen* of antifascist internationalism can also be stricken with the pain of loneliness.[2] There is, as David Riesman studied,

---

1. This chapter is a revised and expanded version of an article that first appeared in the volume *Left Alone: On Solitude and Loneliness amid Collective Struggle*, eds. by Hjalmar Jorge Joffre-Eichhorn and Patrick Anderson (Wakefield, QC: Daraja Press, 2023).

2. *Gemeinwesen* is a German word that means community, both that which actually exists and an aspirational community, or communal sensibility.

loneliness inside the crowd, as well as loneliness outside the crowd.[3] The question, then, is to consider different forms of loneliness and to try to understand what or how forms of loneliness emanate from different forms of life. In this chapter, we can only offer a sketch of an answer, a preliminary theorization that can hopefully clarify certain problems, as well as key terms and concepts. In so doing, I hope to make a small contribution to our understanding of forms of life and loneliness.

To begin, let us define a capitalist form of life. This is a form of life that is more or less governed by capital, which is to say, a life ruled by concerns about money. In capitalist societies, money (which is not itself capital) circulates as a power of acquisition, and most things necessary and useful to life depend upon it. I say "most things" because in a capitalist form of life, not every single aspect of life is governed by money. I studied communist relations in capitalist societies in my book *The Communism of Love*. Despite the existence of nonmonetary and even communist social relations inside of capitalism, the basic orientations of a capitalist form of life are acculturated from early childhood education. Early education and upbringing prepare young children for life experiences in a world where what they can or must do will largely be decided by the logic of capital, and they soon learn that most of their life choices will be governed by money. In short, a capitalist form of life is one where what we do with our lives is centrally concerned with or determined by the logic of capital, which organizes so much of the world.

Now, a communist form of life is a very different idea. This is a form of life which is more or less governed by a concept of the healthy community, the common *wealth*, or even by the ideal of a commune, a life ruled by an overarching concern about communal life with others. To avoid any misunderstanding, however, in a communist form of life one would be free to seek solitude and to be alone as they wish. The difference is that no one is acculturated or compelled to be alone, or to consider "competitive individualism" as any kind of virtue. A communist form of life follows a very different logic and organization than the capitalist form, which can be seen in its attitude toward the acquisition of things that are necessary and useful to life. Necessary and useful things, including care of others, educational opportunities, access to health care and well-being, recreational options, mobility, and

3. David Riesman, *The Lonely Crowd* (New Haven: Yale University Press, 1961).

support for human flourishing are regarded not as commodities but as features of a decent society available to all. A capitalist declares this "utopian." Indeed, that is exactly what it is within the parameters of the capitalist form of life. In a communist form of life, not every aspect of life would be governed by the concept of community; communism is not about having dinner parties or abandoning the peace of solitude. Rather, the basic orientations of a life, which would begin in childhood education and stretch through a lifetime of experiencing the world, would be determined by the logic of common *wealth*, which is to say, by a belief in sharing the common wealth of the human world. And so, a communist form of life—what capitalists call utopian, and therefore impossible—is one where what we do with our lives is centrally concerned with or determined by a deep and abiding regard for common sociality.

It is worth emphasizing that these forms of life can mingle to a certain extent, which can be seen in real experiences of love, kindness, the voluntary sharing of burdens, and other forms of solidarity inside of a predominantly capitalist lifeworld. Therefore, if we could speak of certain experiences of communism in capitalist societies, if we had communist societies, we would likely have experiences of capitalism there as well. Rosa Luxemburg explored this latter possibility in her essay, "The Dissolution of Primitive Communism," which presented her study of communist forms of life in ancient tribal communities—or what she referred to as the "mark" communities—of Germany, Greece, the Americas, India, South Africa, and Russia. There, Luxemburg observed that even in early communist forms of life, certain tendencies toward the subjugation of others or for the consolidation of power and resources were already present. However, such tendencies were only exacerbated to the point of the extinction of primitive communism by the spread of European capitalism and slavery. According to Luxemburg, primitive communism, for all its violence and shortcomings, "endures for centuries the strains of every form of conquest, foreign rule, despotism, and exploitation. There is only one contact that it cannot tolerate or overcome; this is the contact with European civilization, i.e., with capitalism."[4] The common *wealth* and primitive communist *Gemeinwesen* of ancient mark societies,

4. Rosa Luxemburg, "The Dissolution of Primitive Communism: From the Ancient Germans and the Incas to India, Russia, and Southern Africa" in *The Rosa Luxemburg Reader*, eds. by Peter Hudis and Kevin B. Anderson (New York: Monthly Review Press, 2004), 103.

tribes, and villages, was essentially privatized, the shared overtaken as private, human life converted by force to a source of free labor for capitalists. As Luxemburg put it, "Slavery accelerates the dissolution of the communist association and goes hand in hand with the rise of private property."[5]

This will have to suffice, for our present purposes, to distinguish between capitalist and communist forms of life. That is because I want to shift our attention to a consideration of the status of loneliness—which is not solitude—in different social settings. What is the basic position of loneliness in a capitalist society, and would loneliness take a different shape in a communist form of life?

But what is meant by this *thing* called "loneliness"? One could forgive, to some extent, the confusion of loneliness with solitude since, going back to the sixteenth century, loneliness referred to a condition of being solitary. We must be careful not to confuse loneliness with solitude. People deliberately carve out space and time for being alone. Loneliness, on the other hand, may follow you into solitude even if you do not want it to come. There is a difference between being happily in solitude and being lonely in solitude. Also, while one does not expect to find solitude in family gatherings, at meetings of friends and comrades, or even at parties or festivals, loneliness may be pervasive in such spaces. I therefore prefer a more recent meaning of loneliness stemming from the nineteenth century, which is about a feeling one may have whether they are alone on a train or deep in a crowd. This feeling is not a good one. It is a feeling of being dejected, deprived of companionship, without sympathy or human solidarity. This definition can therefore explain the lonely child or husband or wife who suffers this feeling even when sharing their bed with their nearest and dearest in life. This definition can also help us to appreciate the fact that fellow fighters and activists who join us in rallies or meet us in the streets as participants in shared movements may be suffering from loneliness despite such activity. Loneliness must be defined as something we can experience in a world of regular interactions with other human beings.

Hannah Arendt takes this further. In *The Origins of Totalitarianism*, Arendt writes: "Loneliness is not solitude. Solitude requires being alone whereas loneliness shows itself more sharply in company with others."[6] For Arendt, solitude was not a problem. A person seeks it out for good feeling,

---

5. Rosa Luxemburg, "Slavery" in *The Rosa Luxemburg Reader*, 114.
6. Hannah Arendt, *The Origins of Totalitarianism* (London: Harcourt, 1968), 476.

for the space and time to think about what one wishes to be or do, about life and society and tomorrow. Solitude, from its etymological roots in the fourteenth century, indicates a state of being alone. One can be alone without the feeling of loneliness. "What makes loneliness so unbearable is the loss of one's own self which can be realized in solitude but confirmed in its identity only by the trusting and trustworthy company of my equals."[7] This means that the company of trusting and trustworthy equals is ready at hand, and one can therefore move in and out of solitude as they wish. One cannot move in and out of loneliness that way.

What is perhaps the most striking feature of Arendt's attention to loneliness is that it appears in the final pages of a 479-page study of twentieth-century totalitarianism and not as a fleeting observation. For Arendt, the predatory regimes of fascists, Nazis, and totalitarians seize upon the loneliness of society, packaging and presenting fatal antidotes as sweet relief. Why does Arendt end her famous study of totalitarianism with an extended deliberation on loneliness? "Loneliness, the common ground for terror, the essence of totalitarian government, and for ideology or logicality, the preparation of its executioners and victims, is closely connected with uprootedness and superfluousness which have been the curse of modern masses since the beginning of the Industrial Revolution and have become acute with the rise of imperialism at the end of the last century and the break-down of political institutions and social traditions in our own time."[8] There is a lot to unpack here, but essentially, Arendt is saying that widespread loneliness in the mass societies of the twentieth century is the groundwork of totalitarian government. When people feel uprooted, disconnected from purpose, dejected, cut off from human solidarity, totalitarian government presents itself as a rallying cry against that condition. Disconnected and dejected people are called to come together under the banner of the nation's great power. I would consider the phenomenon of Trumpist white nationalism in the US, widespread throughout a disaffected white working class, as a contemporary example of this. What is missing from the example, and from Arendt's analysis, is the extent to which not only fascism but also capitalism preys upon loneliness.

7. Arendt, *The Origins of Totalitarianism*, 477.
8. Arendt, *The Origins of Totalitarianism*, 475.

Perhaps Max Horkheimer said it best in 1939 in "The Jews and Europe" when he declared, "Whoever is not willing to talk about capitalism should also keep quiet about fascism."[9] While Arendt provides sustained class analysis throughout her major study of totalitarianism, Horkheimer clarifies the dialectical and causal relationship between capitalism and fascism. Nonetheless, we could not say about loneliness what Horkheimer says here about fascism. Not unless we want to say that loneliness can have no cause outside of capitalist society. But that would be an absurd claim, so we must alter the question: What is the capitalist form of loneliness? Let us see if we can approach an answer to *that* question.

Loneliness of Capital

John Cacioppo was one of the foremost recent scholars of loneliness and dedicated much of his life to understanding the human experience we are focused on here. He wrote in his book *Loneliness* that while money may motivate people to work their entire lives doing jobs they hate, money has "a negative impact on their behavior toward others. There are data to suggest that merely having money on the periphery of consciousness is sufficient to skew us away from prosocial behavior."[10] Prosocial behavior counteracts loneliness, whereas antisocial behavior exacerbates loneliness. Research shows that heightened money consciousness tends toward the antisocial. Cacioppo's research is full of such data, supported variously by study after study. Loneliness is a big problem impacting not only psychological and social but also physical health and well-being. According to Cacioppo, one problem with loneliness is that "feelings of social isolation deprive us of vast reservoirs of creativity and energy."[11]

Despite his ability to identify social causes of loneliness in an individualist society ruled by money, Cacioppo is no socialist or communist. He

9. Max Horkheimer, "The Jews and Europe," December 1939, available at *The Charnel-House,* accessed April 17, 2023, https://thecharnelhouse.org/2015/03/20/the-jews-and-europe.

10. John T. Cacioppo and William Patrick, *Loneliness: Human Nature and the Need for Social Connection* (New York: W.W. Norton & Company, 2008), 264.

11. Cacioppo and Patrick, *Loneliness,* 269.

is no Marxist or anticapitalist. He simply wants us to try as hard as we can to respond to loneliness as the very serious problem it is but only by way of kindness and through an improved interpersonal comportment. He calls on us to make use of "individual actions, to continuously adjust the social environment toward something slightly better."[12] As director of the Center for Cognitive Neuroscience at the University of Chicago, Cacioppo was perhaps not so unhappy with the existing capitalist reality. He was wholly uninterested in the social or political transformation of the world. We can appreciate him stopping where he did, but we cannot accept a program of minor individual adjustments aimed to make things slightly better. Cacioppo's own research diagnosed loneliness as an urgent social catastrophe, such that his own recommendation appears as a mismatch for the scale of the emergency. Cacioppo tells us that there are political-economic and social causes of a present plague of loneliness, but we will have to make a more critical reading of such facts ourselves.

What I want to suggest is that, while loneliness cannot be abolished as a human experience, *and while I do not think we should want to abolish it altogether*, there is a capitalist form of loneliness that we must confront as such. Why should we do that? First, by considering the capitalist form of loneliness, we can learn something about the social tendencies of capital and their relation to human health and well-being. In fact, if we were lonely in a different world of our own making, then the same would presumably be true. We could use loneliness in that society, or in any society, to learn something about human relations there too. We cannot suggest that a revolutionary transformation of society against capitalist social relations would solve every problem. It would not. The problems would only be different, and we would have to approach them with an appreciation of those distinctions.

Roland Barthes tried to think about forms of life too. He was interested in certain tensions and difficulties of capitalist society. Barthes's idea was that people variously want or need to live together with other people, yet, at the same time, they have no faith in other people and find grief and other torment in efforts to live with others. There is, then, a paradoxical pull both toward and away from others. This paradox could be explained by the presence of a social instinct on the one hand, broken apart by a culture of competitive

12. Cacioppo and Patrick, *Loneliness*, 266.

individualism on the other. We become suspicious of and hostile to other people yet cannot easily overcome an urge to be with them. In *How to Live Together,* Barthes studied tendencies of living-alone in relation to tendencies of living-together. He wrote about "acedy," a word related to asceticism. This word indicates a form of life in which people place little faith in other people and therefore adopt a practice of avoiding the world. Barthes describes modern acedy as follows: "I can wake up in the morning, see the schedule for the week unfolding before my eyes, and feel hopeless. It's repetitive, it goes round and round: the same old tasks, the same old meetings, and yet there's no investment whatsoever . . . Acedy (modern acedy): no longer being capable of investing in other people, in Living-with-several-other-people and yet at the same time being incapable of investing in solitude."[13]

What is remarkable is that Barthes appears to have predicted phenomena like *otaku* and *hikikomori,* which I have discussed in several of my books.[14] *Hikikomori* refers to those who have opted to remove themselves from the world of other people (well over a million people in Japan), those who only want to interact with other people through screens. *Otaku* is different. *Otaku* refers to people who prefer a world of video games and comic books to the actual world, and often, *otaku* become *hikikomori.* The difference is that Barthes's concept of acedy contains both sides—the side of not wanting to be with other people but also the side of not wanting to live in total isolation either—whereas, *otaku* and *hikikomori* seem to have moved us, in the time since Barthes's study, closer to the possibility of being totally cut off from the world. One could argue that *otaku* and *hikikomori* are still within Barthes's model of acedy because these isolating and socially withdrawn people are still reaching out to others through screen-mediated relations and in imaginary worlds. But even that seems to move the situation beyond the scope of Barthes's imagination in the late 1970s.

Barthes also writes about "idiorrhythmy" and about "idiorrhythmic clusters, where each subject lives according to his own rhythm."[15] *Idios* means "particular" and *rhuthmos* means rhythm. So what we are talking about with

13. Roland Barthes, *How to Live Together: Novelistic Simulations of Some Everyday Spaces,* trans. Kate Briggs (New York: Columbia University Press, 2013), 22–23.

14. Most recently in my book, *The Communism of Love: An Inquiry into the Poverty of Exchange Value* (Chico: AK Press, 2020), 104–5, 203.

15. Barthes, *How to Live Together,* 6.

idiorrhythmy is each person establishing their own particular rhythm of life. Living together is complicated like musicians playing together according to peculiar rules; imagine musicians playing together but only following their own idiorrhythmic preferences. In such idiorrhythmic music, players would be both together and apart in the music. And this is how we are in life. Idiorrhythmic clusters do not make for a communist togetherness. The communist idea is to be responsive and attentive to the needs and abilities of the others. As Marx put it, a communist form of life would be guided by the motto, "from each according to their ability, to each according to their needs."[16] A capitalist form of life, however, encourages general indifference to the needs and abilities of others, unless or until the needs and abilities of other people obstruct one's own idiorrhythmic preferences.

But there are, as I have argued in Chapters 5 and 6 of this book, irrepressibly communist tendencies of human beings, which can be disfigured and suppressed but never totally extinguished. It is part of the reason why people who are traumatized by failures of friendship and love nonetheless seek out friendship and love: even though they have been hurt by bad experiences, they feel that they need them for their own human flourishing. This can also be seen in the direst and deepest traumas of family abuse, which nonetheless send victims off in search of healthy families of choice, which people sense that they need for their flourishing. But Barthes understood a great challenge facing the communist aspirations of everyday people. As he put it: "Living-Together, especially idiorrhythmic Living-Together, must incorporate the values of Living-Alone as its paradigmatic opposite."[17] This means that the challenge facing us today is to find ways of living together that do not threaten our dispositions of acedy. One wants to be reassured that they can be with others without having to give up any of their idiosyncratic rhythms. One wants to, in other words, ameliorate the dangers of loneliness without giving up the perks of being alone.

But this is only one aspect of loneliness in the capitalist form of life. We cannot possibly hope, or dare to pretend, that loneliness is some simple thing with singular causes and a fixed shape. It certainly is not. But at the same

16. Karl Marx, *Critique of the Gotha Program* (New York: International Publishers, 2002), 10.

17. Barthes, *How to Live Together*, 84.

time, we mustn't pretend that loneliness in a capitalist society has nothing at all to do with the capitalist form of life that defines such a society. This would make us just as stupid as those economists—and there are too many of these—who want to analyze an economic crisis as if it has no relation to the economic system in which it occurs.

In *Powers of Horror*, Julia Kristeva introduces a third term to the usual subject/object dichotomy in philosophy. We know about the subjects who perceive and the objects of their perception. But Kristeva writes about the abject, which is neither subject nor object. The abject is in the world, outside of oneself (like an object), but unlike an object, it is against oneself.[18] Abjection is an important concept because it captures the experience of feeling opposed, even detested, marked for exclusion, deportation, or death by forces around you. When we think about abjection, we may think of an abject situation, a reality in which one is abandoned, degraded, cast out.

Abjection has been the historical position of the marginalized and excluded peoples of the world, whether we are talking about transgender people, Palestinians in Gaza, gays and lesbians, or BIPOC (Black, Indigenous, People of Color) sectors of society that have been vilified, despised, criminalized, and incarcerated. Abjection is the condition of a Black teenager in the United States who walks around in middle school with a lopsided expectation that they—or someone they love—will be arrested, jailed, or killed by police. Abjection is a regular feature of the state of BIPOC life in a white supremacist society. According to Kristeva, abjection is the sphere of the worst horrors whereby some humans are confronted by other humans, for abjection is found in "a hatred that smiles, a passion that uses the body for barter instead of inflaming it, a debtor who sells you up, a friend who stabs you."[19] The sensibility of abjection is not simply that of loneliness, but of being unwanted in or by the world.

In later books like *Strangers to Ourselves*, Kristeva deals with the abjection of foreigners, immigrants, women in patriarchal societies, strangers, and aliens. Thinking about immigrant labor in a foreign land, Kristeva writes: "Since he has nothing, since he is nothing, he can sacrifice everything. And

18. Julia Kristeva, *Powers of Horror: An Essay on Abjection*, trans. Leon S. Roudiez (New York: Columbia University Press, 1982), 1.

19. Kristeva, *Powers of Horror*, 4.

sacrifice begins with work: the only property that can be exported duty free, a universally tried and tested stock for the wanderer's use. What bitterness then, what disaster is it when one does not obtain one's green card."[20] What a sad description of abjection: the immigrant worker who is regarded as nothing or invisible, who sacrifices all of their time and life's energy for survival, who is then repaid with denial, detainment, or deportation.

Let us not proceed as if this abjection were not a feature of capitalism. It is only the logic of capital that can lead to such abjection as this, the abjection of giving everything in work, yet being regarded as nothing (or not regarded at all), and then facing expulsion by the capitalist state at the very point of visibility. A communist form of life may appear as a utopian idea, but does it not offer a response to such abjection? A communist form of life would have to oppose itself to such abjection, would have to imagine an antithetical orientation, or else it could mean nothing at all. If we want to imagine, let alone to pursue, real alternatives to the capitalist form of life, we will have to think about a social reality that pushes back against acedy and abjection, and thus, pushes back against forms of loneliness bred in and by the existing idiorrthythmic reality. Remember that the original definition of communism, provided by Marx in *The German Ideology*, called "communism the *real* movement which abolishes the present state of things."[21] Communists would have to be abolitionists and that includes the abolition of the capitalist form of life. Such abolitionism does not mean the abolition of loneliness writ large but certainly of forms of loneliness bred by the existing society.

Toward an Antithetical Loneliness

What we are talking about is the practicality of utopianism. This appears as a contradiction in terms. If it is utopian, it is supposed to be impractical, impossible. But in fact, we cannot move toward a different reality unless we are willing to think about what is desirable and possible. The only other path

20. Julia Kristeva, *Strangers to Ourselves*, trans. Leon S. Roudiez (New York: Columbia University Press, 1991), 19.

21. Karl Marx, *The German Ideology*, in *The Portable Marx*, ed. by Eugene Kamenka (New York: Penguin Books, 1983), 179.

would be a path of accidents, catastrophes, or coercion. We must allow ourselves the freedom to think about what is desirable and possible, and we must demand that freedom. We must stick to some concept of agency and not simply accept that we will get where we're going like leaves in a stream.

In the world of science and technology, so many things were impossible until they were done. So many things we now take for granted, from airplanes to smartphones, would have been declared impractical and unreal until they were real and integrated into the practical activity of the world. Do not forget that a long time ago people called the abolitionists who stood against chattel slavery and the radical suffragettes utopian. They were regarded as dreamers with nothing practical to advance. The truth is that naysayers of the utopian suffer from bad imaginations, poor understandings of history, or worse, are too favorably disposed toward the status quo. But with imagination, historical understanding, and a hatred of the status quo, the utopian appears as a kind of North Star. Who would dare tell a sailor of old that the North Star is impractical?

Erich Fromm in *To Have or to Be?* writes: "*If I am what I have and if what I have is lost, who then am I?* Nobody but a defeated, deflated, pathetic testimony to a wrong way of living."[22] Yes, we can speak of a wrong way of living. That does not mean there is only one right way. However, if a person is nobody beyond what they have, if their possessions define them, then people who own little are not very much. Fromm's critique of the "having mode" of life was, for him, a critique of the capitalist form of life. But is there not a certain wisdom among the impoverished peoples of the world that they are something even when they own little or nothing? Many impoverished people know that they are worth more than their possessions, which they express especially in moments of indignation and protest. We must not assume that the "having mode" of life has totally decided the question of the value of our being-in-the-world.

Axel Honneth in *The I in We* explains as the central claim of his argument that "the 'I' seeks the 'We' of shared group experience, because even after maturity, we are dependent on forms of social recognition imbued with direct encouragement and affirmation."[23] From a position of loneliness, we

22. Erich Fromm, *To Have or to Be?* (London: Bloomsbury, 2013), 94.

23. Axel Honneth, *The I in We: Studies in the Theory of Recognition*, trans. Joseph Ganahl (Malden, MA: Polity Press, 2014), 214.

cry out for recognition, encouragement, and affirmation. These things are even necessary to our health and well-being when we are not feeling particularly lonely. For a child's sense of self-worth and human development, others must say to them, you are seen, you are good, you can be or become what you should be, what you desire to be. A child deprived of these things is not only lonely, they are subverted, undermined, their sense of self disfigured. One moment of recognition is not enough. Drawing on psychosocial research, Honneth says: "In order to maintain and perhaps even strengthen their self-confidence, subjects need to receive constant, reliable affection, which for the most part they encounter in relationships of friendship and love."[24]

We cannot speak of the "I" all alone without some yearning for the recognition and affirmation of a "We." Deprived of such social recognition, one might diagnose that they are lonely. But that is a red herring. This is not simply loneliness but a condition of life in a culture of social deprivation. Capitalists like to praise the heroic individual who needs nobody else. Capitalists chronically mistake interdependence as some despicable weakness they call dependency. However, their own lives, and the lives of their children or others beloved, refute their point of view. No infant is independent, no child. A young child would not live long without a certain communism of care, a certain dependency that is natural and necessary. Indeed, without other people, there could be no human life at all. How dare we call capitalist individualism, which forgets the child and ignores interdependency, anything but dehumanizing? We dare not. There is nothing more humanizing than being seen, heard, recognized, affirmed, and in regular receipt of the affection and care of other people.

It is not impossible to move from the "I" to the "We," even if it is utopian. Jean-Paul Sartre, who thought a lot about individuals and collectives, understood this well. When he considered the "I" becoming "We" in *Being and Nothingness,* he provided the following illustration:

> I am on the pavement in front of a café; I observe the other patrons and I know myself to be observed. We remain here in the most ordinary case of conflict with others (the Other's being-as-object for

24. Honneth, *The I in We,* 206.

> me, my being-as-object for the Other). But suddenly some incident occurs in the street; for example, a slight collision between a jeep and a taxi. Immediately at the very instant when I become a spectator of the incident, I experience myself non-thetically as engaged in "we." The earlier rivalries, the slight conflicts have disappeared . . . "we" look at the event, "we" take part.[25]

Here you have a case of seeing something together. The togetherness of the witnessing moves the "I" to the "We." But in this case, an event, an incident, makes it happen: "I" becomes "We" in the face of the collision. Perhaps we will abandon our lonely individuation when we face an unexpected, jarring catastrophe. Are there not historical events that throw us together? Indeed, there are many. Here, we could imagine a crisis theory according to which the capitalist form of life meets its limitations in the face of catastrophe. It is possible to consider that, in the face of the COVID-19 catastrophe, for example, we tested some of the limits of the capitalist form of life. So many people asked the question, both practically and rather unexpectedly: Could I live without work? Could I adapt to a different form of life? The pandemic form of life is not the one we would choose, but perhaps it reveals that other forms of life are more possible than we may have previously thought.

There are moments when loneliness is temporarily ameliorated in collective action, inside the living camaraderie and shared passions of a social movement or even a revolt. We can find many things, for example, in the George Floyd Rebellion, such as anger, sadness, hope, cynicism, disagreement, and furious indignation. However, I wonder if, in the throes of the rebellion itself, participants would have said they felt lonely.[26] In *Revolt, She Said*, Kristeva assesses the health and well-being of contemporary capitalist societies, and what she diagnoses is a measurable mass depression, widespread anxiety, and a deep feeling of being alienated from other people. It is unlikely that people will gather and rise up together in such an affective

---

25. Jean-Paul Sartre, *Being and Nothingness*, trans. Hazel E. Barnes (New York: Washington Square Press, 1966), 505–6.

26. It is worth noting here, especially, that the George Floyd Rebellion broke out during the lockdowns of COVID-19, and so it likely even served as an "insurgent togetherness" in a time of great social isolation.

state. She says that "incapacity to rebel is the sign of national depression."[27] However, Kristeva argues that such feelings do dissipate in the throes of revolt, since "people who rebel are malcontents with frustrated, but vigorous desires."[28] She worries more about the absence of revolt than about its presence, because, from a psychoanalytic perspective, a healthy society actively gathers to throw into question its own justice and reality. On the contrary, a profoundly lonely society is locked up inside, and individuals view the outside world more as a field of abjection. As a response to this, Kristeva argues for "the necessity of a culture of revolt," which she believes we must try to cultivate in art, writing, psychoanalysis, and social movements.[29] Imagine that we could find our way to a new reality through a culture of revolt.

Still, why would we want to confront a particular form of loneliness in the existing capitalist society only to discover a new form of loneliness on the horizon? I think that the answer is because utopians can and must be practical. We can say both that we want a totally different world and that we expect there will be serious and potentially intractable challenges in that different world too. The first part would be utopian, but the second part is practical. The first part is on the side of desirability, whereas the second part is on the side of possibility. Good utopian thinking traverses both sides, both the desirable and the possible.

However, is it worth the effort to aim at North Stars? Personally, I live in a world where it is not easy to find people who share my basic sensibilities about the world. To ameliorate the loneliness of thinking against the grain of my own lifeworld, I have to attend a conference for radicals, connect with social movements, or join others in musical experience. As a university professor and writer, there are those who are eager to ask for my perspective, but they are often interested only because they know I espouse a certain point of view that, behind their sociable outward kindnesses, they regard as utopian, unreasonable, or worse. Interest in my point of view does not indicate agreement with it, and I have never been unaware of the disregard that lurks behind the collegial veneer of so many people around me. We are surrounded

27. Julia Kristeva, *Revolt, She Said*, trans. Brian O'Keeffe (Los Angeles: Semiotext(e), 2002), 83.

28. Kristeva, *Revolt, She Said*, 84.

29. Julia Kristeva, *The Sense and Non-Sense of Revolt: The Powers and Limits of Psychoanalysis*, trans. Jeanine Herman (New York: Columbia University Press, 2000), 7.

by people—generally regarded as smart and sensible—who think that the only thing wrong with the capitalist reality is that some of the presidents and prime ministers could be better. The world, such as it is, is resolutely hostile to radical thinkers, revolutionaries, and people who live in the margins of society, not only because of what they think but because of who they are. For many, there is nowhere to go. It can be a lonely place for those who are nonconforming, despised, or who think about the world from the far left of revolutionary politics. After all, what does it mean to vacillate between being marginalized and tolerated? It is no kind thing or great gift to learn that you are merely tolerated. In a world such as this, I would welcome the opportunity to find out what kinds of loneliness we might find in a communist form of life. If that is utopian, it is a precarious utopianism at best.

One of the greatest defenders of the practicality of utopianism was Simone Weil. When Weil considered different possible forms of life from different revolutionary traditions, namely from Marxism and anarchism, she concluded: "No doubt all of this is purely utopian. But to give even a summary description of a state of things which would be better than what actually exists is always to build a utopia; yet nothing is more necessary to our life than such descriptions."[30] Indeed, loneliness is there in the manifold of human experience, and I think it always will be; but we can imagine and describe a world that would be better than this one. We may expect that the loneliness of a communist form of life would be better because, in a communist lifeworld, we would be oriented by a logic of interdependency, seen instead of disappeared by separation, buoyed by others instead of abandoned by acedy. I can imagine a world extrapolated from the best experiences of friendship and love, a world of being attentive to the principles of differential ability and needs. We have to fight for that world, as precarious, practical utopians, so that we might possibly move beyond the capitalist form of life, so that we may experience a different form of loneliness, the loneliness of an antithesis to everything awful in the present.

---

30. Simone Weil, *Oppression and Liberty*, trans. Arthur Wills and John Petrie (London: Routledge, 2001), 100.

CHAPTER 10

Insurgent Thoughts for Future May Days

Each year, May Day invites us to revisit and rethink revolutionary traditions from the nineteenth century for the present and the future. The annual international holiday comes out of a trajectory from the Haymarket Massacre in Chicago in 1886, when police attacked workers making demands for an eight-hour workday. At that time, the demand for an eight-hour workday was understood as a total opposition to the capitalist workplace, where employers extracted as much as possible from their exhausted workforce. The beginnings of May Day were not about better wages and working conditions but about an opposition to the whole system of life governed by capital and ruled by money. To insist on sixteen hours for play and rest every single day was understood as a real threat to capital, a fact corroborated by the hostile opposition to those making the demand.[1] Take a look at the history of May Day, International Workers' Day, and you will see that it comes from immigrants, anarchists, communists, socialists, revolutionaries of many varieties, and others disenchanted. I think one could argue that May Day is the holiday of imaginary power and real horizons.

Present and Future

I shall begin by presenting three insurgent thoughts on work and life suitable for the spirit and aims of May Day.

1. For the best account of the history of May Day, see Peter Linebaugh, *The Incomplete, True, Authentic, and Wonderful History of May Day* (Oakland: PM Press, 2016).

(1) Our first thought comes from Paul Lafargue, Karl Marx's son-in-law. Lafargue did not reproduce his father-in-law's fixation on work and the working class because Lafargue felt we were better defined by what we did *outside of work*. As Lafargue put it, "Modern factories have become ideal houses of correction in which the toiling masses are imprisoned, in which they are condemned to compulsory work for twelve or fourteen hours, not the men only but also women and children . . . Our epoch has been called the century of work. It is in fact the century of pain, misery and corruption."[2] Lafargue wanted us to reconsider the so-called virtue of hard work, which today remains a relatively unquestioned "sacred virtue" outside of radical circles. Lafargue considered the virtue of laziness instead.

Laziness remains one of the most damning character traits, despite the fact that it is one of the most common and recurring of human inclinations. Throughout history, liberals and conservatives have variously spoken of the "right to work," as if the most fundamental right we have is to go to work for capitalists. Liberals often talk about jobs and full employment as if that were the solution to every problem, and conservatives like the former Wisconsin governor Scott Walker defend so-called "right-to-work" legislation that gives workers the "freedom" to not pay union dues.[3] Liberals and conservatives agree that hard work is a virtue. May Day is an opportunity to question the religion of work, to consider our lives outside of work, and to consider the virtues of not working, of all the creative and joyful things we could do in time reclaimed from capital.

(2) I offer now a second insurgent thought, following an idea from a noninsurgent source, American philosopher Martha C. Nussbaum. Despite many shortcomings in and disagreements with Nussbaum's philosophy, I appreciate that she insists on play as a central human capability.[4] A good life is not possible without play. I would add that play—*at its best*—is an antidote

2. Paul Lafargue, *The Right to Be Lazy* (Chicago and Oakland: Charles H. Kerr and AK Press, 2011), 27–29.

3. See "Wisconsin Gov. Scott Walker Signs Right-to-Work Bill" on NPR, March 9, 2015, https://www.npr.org/sections/thetwo-way/2015/03/09/391901732/wisconsin-gov-scott-walker-sighs-right-to-work-bill.

4. See Martha C. Nussbaum, "Capabilities and Human Rights" in *Global Justice and Transnational Politics: Essays on the Moral and Political Challenges of Globalization*, eds. by Pablo De Greiff and Ciaran Cronin (Cambridge, MA: MIT Press, 2002), 130–31.

to work. At work, play is often called insubordination. We have come to think of insubordination as a bad thing, but consider that the opposite of insubordination is subordination. We cannot accept subordination as a virtue. Young children know the difference and distance between work and play and predictably express a general preference for the latter. For adults, play is often eventually abolished altogether or reserved for smartphone distractions at the end of an exhausted day. Many adults only reconnect to play when they're with young children.

One thing to notice about play, which I notice in play with children: It is an activity outside of work, and it follows a different logic. It is not governed by a profit logic but by imagination, free time, and open space. Play is a space of imaginary power. For many young people, the first direct experience of a little liberation is the end of the school day. Free jazz musicians play too. They make playful music, they play with subversive forms and approaches. On May Day, we might consider the importance of play and how work aims to abolish it.

(3) A third insurgent thought now from the feminist philosopher and revolutionary Silvia Federici, who, in the 1970s, participated in the Wages for Housework movement along with other important activists and writers, including Leopoldina Fortunati, Selma James, and Mariarosa Dalla Costa. Wages for Housework highlighted that so much of women's work is not treated as eligible for wages and is typically expected to be unpaid. But before readers demand to know who should or could pay for housework and child-rearing (often called "care work"), we should clarify the main point. Federici opposes the capitalist wage system, so winning wages for housework was not the central aim.[5] As Federici put it, "*The things we have to prove are our capacity to expose what we are already doing, what capital is doing to us and our power in the struggle against it.*"[6] If women actually won wages for housework, which would undoubtedly be an upgrade from unpaid and surplus labor, that achievement would also inadvertently prove the virtues of the wage system Federici condemns. Federici's point is better made by the impossibility of wages for housework in the current system of work and life, which is why her landmark essay is titled *Wages against Housework*.

5. See Silvia Federici, *Wages against Housework* (Bristol: Falling Wall Press, 1975).
6. Federici, *Wages against Housework*, 8 (original in italics).

Federici wants to reveal a flaw in capitalism, a system that is incapable of valuing what people value the most. Simple questionnaires about the most important functions of any society reliably return "the health and well-being of children" as among the most fundamental commitments. That commitment is near universal in terms of cross-cultural and global resonance. But capitalism shows what it values only with money. Capitalism is incapable of paying wages for housework because it is incapable of valuing the most basic human values and wouldn't survive the back pay. Even in the case where families outsource childcare to professionals, that labor is overwhelmingly done by women working low-paid, exhausting, and precarious jobs.

Now, take a look at the pathetic state of wage politics today. Liberals and conservatives today consider it "too radical" to demand $15–20 an hour for a minimum wage. We should stop to think that $15–20 dollars an hour, at thirty-five hours a week, comes to roughly $25,000–36,000 per year before taxes. One position today, then, taken up by many so-called "democratic socialists," is to demand what would be a living wage in the 1940s and 1950s for a family of two or three. Fifteen dollars an hour is far less than half of what would be a reasonable demand for a basic living wage in most any city in the US today. This highlights the fact that reason is too radical for our irrational capitalist reality. May Day is a fine time to point that out, although it is worth recalling often in between.

At what point do we realize that the solutions on offer are simultaneously the problems? Radicals, by definition, want to deal with problems at their root causes, and that requires a total transformation of the whole arrangement of work and life. Until then, the solutions will always also be problems. During the generalized insanity of a capitalist election cycle, it's especially important to point out that we cannot vote for the total transformation we so urgently need. What we need is not on the ballot. On May Day, all over the world there are people who know we need a total transformation—sometimes such transformation is called a revolution.

What is practical in these insurgent thoughts? I claim that the question of what is practical is the wrong question here. What is practical is only what can be implemented in the present situation, and when people ask the question of practicality, it is often a disingenuous way of saying that what we want is too far away from what we have. That is why we must insist on a different question, the question of what is possible and desirable, as we have considered throughout this book. The possible and desirable is also practical, something that is easier to see after we start doing it. Many things (*including a living wage*) are declared impractical in the world today. Today's practicality answers nothing. Neither did yesterday's.

Past and Future

Earlier May Day speeches illustrate the crucial importance of reaching for the possible and desirable beyond the so-called practicality of the capitalist reality. Let us consider the speeches of two revolutionary women and one Ukrainian anarchist and see what lessons we may draw out for the present.

Consider Eleanor Marx, youngest daughter of Karl and Jenny Marx. In 1890, on the occasion of the first May Day, she said: "We have not come to do the work of political parties . . . We believe that the eight hours' day is the first and most immediate step to be taken, and we aim at a time when there will no longer be one class supporting the others . . . This is only the beginning of the struggle . . . We must speak for the cause daily, and make the men, and especially the women we meet, come into the ranks to help us."[7]

May Day was never for the expressing of what comes through the major political parties. In the US, we do not speak on May Day for Democrats or Republicans, nor for the Green Party or socialist parties, all of which invest too much in the rigged game of capitalist elections. We do not speak, in other words, for what gains we might extract from the world bell hooks called an "imperialist white supremacist capitalist patriarchy."[8] No, we have to create space for a critique of all that. The eight hours' movement was about the reclamation of space and time from capital for the possible and the desirable, which is to say for the flourishing of the human being. So many great figures of history fought for eight, eight, eight, and today, we give it away without thought or resistance through screen-mediated lives that, beyond eating up all of our shrinking leisure time, offer employers total access to us all hours of the day. May Day was for gathering people for the imagining of

7. Rachel Holmes, *Eleanor Marx: A Life* (London: Bloomsbury Press, 2014), 332–33.

8. bell hooks, *Feminism Is for Everybody: Passionate Politics* (New York: Routledge Books, 2015), 46.

hopeful horizons and rival visions. Eleanor Marx notes, as well, the special importance of bringing women into revolutionary movement. Women have experiences and perspectives unique to their lives. This has always been true. Women have shown that living in a sexist, misogynistic, and patriarchal society matters for women's experiences and lives, and that revolutionaries need to be especially attentive to the perspectives that come out of such experiences. For the same reasons today, we have to be especially attentive to the experiences and perspectives of transwomen. Transwomen and transmen, as well as those with nonbinary gender identities, have to confront not only gendered discrimination but also transphobic and transmisic gender essentialisms that cisgender men and women cannot simply claim to already appreciate.

Let's jump forward in time now to Elizabeth Gurley Flynn on May Day 1941.

> May Day traditionally celebrates victories won; makes new demands; presses forward slogans of immediate action . . . Ten million organized workers in America today and more to come. Skilled and unskilled, black and white, native and immigrant, man and woman, young and old—shoulder to shoulder. Let the war mongers shout; let the profit-mad rave. "We shall not be moved!" retort these millions of American workers on May Day . . . Against all imperialism and fascism, including American! . . . Lower the cost of living. Resist wage cuts and longer working hours. Free all fighters against imperialist war . . . End Jim Crowism and anti-Semitism . . . peace and socialism are in the hearts, in the minds, on the lips of millions around the world May First, 1941. The "sun of tomorrow" shines upon us. The future is ours.[9]

You can see that Gurley Flynn wrote in 1941 about racism, fascism, antisemitism, immigrant and Indigenous workers, and classism. She was an early radical feminist, a member of the IWW. She thought a lot about sexism, racism, and patriarchy. Segregation was alive and raging in 1941, and the

9. Elizabeth Gurley Flynn, "May 1st: The Sun of Tomorrow," in *New Masses* 39, no. 7 (May 6, 1941).

US had no official position against fascism in May 1941 either. It is worth remembering that the US did not enter World War II until December of that year, and previously had no qualms with the rise of fascism in Spain. The US entry into World War II in December of 1941 did not indicate any opposition to fascism in principle. It is a horrific fact that we must continue to stand up against racism, sexism, antisemitism, classism, and fascism today, but worse, they are even resurgent. Perhaps we can now finally conclude that we cannot reform them out of existence. Slavery could not be reformed into a kinder, gentler institution. The abolitionists were right. Slavery had to be abolished. The same goes for mass incarceration today. The same goes for capitalism. We have to add new things to the list. We have to add transphobia, new permutations of white nationalism, patriarchal masculinity, and the latest developments in neocolonial thinking and imperial power. We have to retain Gurley Flynn's abolitionist hope, because to abandon it is to accept the unacceptable, to tolerate the intolerable.

I want now to move backward to a moment in between the words of Eleanor Marx and Elizabeth Gurley Flynn to Nestor Makhno, a Ukrainian anarchist on May Day 1928. "The first of May is considered the Labor holiday. On that date, toilers all over the world should come together in every village, every town, and organize mass rallies, not to mark that date as statist socialists as especially the Bolsheviks conceive it, but rather to gauge the measure of their strength and assess the possibilities for direct armed struggle against a rotten, cowardly, slave-holding order rooted in violence and falsehood."[10]

Indeed, Makhno himself participated in armed struggles against early imperialist adventures of the Russian state in Ukraine. The USSR could have been called "state socialist," but I prefer the analysis of thinkers like Raya Dunayevskaya, Cornelius Castoriadis, C. L. R. James, and Guy Debord that it was really "state capitalist," essentially a state-administered capitalist country, even going back to the first days of the Cold War.

In 2022, Putin's regime appeared as a revitalized revanchist state seeking to reclaim territories the Putin government considered rebel, NATO-related threats, or otherwise subversive to the interests of the Russian state. Notice

10. Nestor Makhno, *The Struggle Against the State and Other Essays*, ed. by Alexandre Skirda (San Francisco: AK Press, 1996), 59.

that I say "Putin," or "Russian state," and not "Russia." That is because we must never mistake any head of state for a whole people. Makhno understood this well. Many in the US would easily say that Trump or Biden do not represent us, and we are telling the truth. Why then should we conflate Putin for the entire people of Russia? There are many in Russia who oppose Putin's war on Ukraine and who protested against him and his regime long before the military escalation in 2022. We should listen to what everyday people in real struggles, in both Russia and Ukraine, may articulate as possible and desirable, and we should never choose heads of state as allies, never Putin nor Zelenskyy. Likewise, we cannot categorically take the side of an entire civil society, of a whole nation of people, because in every nation there are fascists, neo-Nazis, racists, conservatives, sexists, and capitalists. Who says we must choose to take sides with any head of state? Who says we cannot take sides, instead, with real emancipatory struggles against imperialism, colonization, fascism, and capitalism wherever we find those struggles? Whoever says so is wrong.

In the US and throughout Western Europe, we should especially beware the tendency to ask one imperialist state, like that of the US, to deal with another imperialist state, like that of Russia. Sometimes, in the midst of heated conflicts, even leftists forget that imperialist states do not oppose imperialism. Imperialist states do not have a critique of colonization, never in principle and especially not when they are the ones doing the colonizing. That is also why the US government scarcely bats an eye when the Israeli government actively pursues the genocidal murder of Palestinians in Gaza.

Problems of international conflict under the leadership of state power and capitalist interests are not easy to solve. Not theoretically, not practically. If there were easy solutions, we would not have needed so many May Days for the future. If there were easy solutions, May Day would have become a commemorative holiday for recalling and honoring past victories. But the issues raised by Eleanor Marx, Elizabeth Gurley Flynn, and Nestor Makhno—among so many others—are still before us, and in new and pressing ways.

As we have seen throughout this book, the possible and desirable are also practical. Asking someone what they desire is a dignified and appropriate question. It is not always easy to answer. The question of possibility is also difficult, because that which is not possible immediately may be deemed "impractical" up to the point it starts happening. May Day is fundamentally about imaginary power and real horizons. It has always been, and must continue to be, for that is the basic orientation of *all revolutionary aspiration.* Often, the first struggle is to learn that what we desire can actually be realized. There are countless examples of this happening.

What does it mean for us in the here and now? It means that we must search our talents and desires and place them in the service of the world that we want. I am a writer, a philosopher, a teacher, and some other things too. You are many things, also, and maybe you are many different things. What do you like to do and how can you place your joyful activity in the service of revolutionary aspirations? To answer the question, one has to consult their imaginary powers, and from there we speak out, teach, gather, protest, write, paint, perform, drum, care, subvert, and sing for the sun of tomorrow.

CONCLUSION

Dreaming Their Nightmares

People speak too much about the power of imagination. Capital has captured the power of imagination, holding it hostage, as some kind of entrepreneurial engine. But that was never anything more than an appropriation and exploitation (or, as Marx would call it, an expropriation) of a great human capacity for narrow, self-serving deployments. We know that an incredible screenplay, a marvel of a movie, and awe-inspiring technological gadgets existed first in the human mind before they were things in the world. If not one of the things I have mentioned, look at something else and you will be awestruck by the power of imagination. For me, it is often architecture. I look at a new building and wonder, because of my utter ignorance of engineering, how it could possibly exist. Such buildings are surely less mysterious to an architect.

In this book we have considered imaginary power as, variously, a real power, a power to be realized, and an activity connected with social transformation. As Drucilla Cornell argues: "Through critique, we can identify the limitations imposed upon us and thereby come to adequately know what we are up against. But the future can never be *known*, it can only be imagined and created."[1] I don't want to live in a world that makes generations of the greatest jazz musicians and creative artists in other milieus vacillate between precarity, destitution, and death. I don't want to live in a world where colonial-racial capitalism is not understood as such. I don't want to live in a world where we are told that we can only ever choose between different evils, because every other choice is impractical. I don't want to live in a

1. Drucilla Cornell, *Today's Struggles, Tomorrow's Revolutions* (Lanham: Rowman & Littlefield, 2023), 30.

world where psychosocial health and well-being are always on a razor's edge of anxiety, panic, and despair. I don't want to live in a world where the natural world—and all life on Earth—is ruled by money and the logic of capital, i.e., by extraction, growth, accumulation, and private wealth. To say that we need a different world is to say that we need a rival vision for life on Earth. Different ideas for different forms of life are one of many prerequisites for living differently. We cannot do everything, and it seems we can't do anything fast. But we do have the power to imagine different forms of life for a society organized by a different logic than that of capital. Our enemies will call what we imagine impossible, but we may reply that it is "not yet." Moreover, by way of imagining it, it is already *present* in the world and can be shared and proliferated by and in diverse activities of art and political action.

Imaginary power is necessary but insufficient for creating a new world. That is to say that we need it, but it alone is not enough. Imaginary power can be world creating, world making, so that the idea of the abolitionists against slavery, of the colonized against colonization, of Black freedom struggles, of women's and workers' movements, or of gays and lesbians and transgender and nonbinary people have both ideational and world-making dimensions. It is simply not true that Black people *merely* imagined freedom in slave revolts or that today they *merely* imagine a world without white supremacy, racial profiling, and police brutality. Following Orlando Patterson, Cornell argues "that it could only have been slaves who *imagined and created* freedom: enslaved people who could not *know* what freedom 'is,' but who, through a critique of the limits imposed by their enslavement came both to know what had to be overcome and to *imagine* an otherwise that they called 'freedom.'"[2] These ideas make their ways into the world through activities of emancipatory struggles that are intimately connected with the imaginary powers of the so-called "powerless," the variously oppressed, exploited, marginalized, and colonized.

Politics, including my own decrepit discipline of political science, typically dismisses the concept of imaginary power because people interested in politics are told to focus and fixate on the affairs of the ruling class. Ask the ruling class if they want to wield imaginary power, and they will tell you their preference for *real* power instead. Imaginary power is not for them, but for those who do not have the resources of the ruling class. So be it. Let us claim

---

2. Cornell, *Today's Struggles, Tomorrow's Revolutions.*

it. Let us agree with them that imaginary power is ours. In fact, those who are the beneficiaries of the existing capitalist reality do not want to think about a different reality. Why should they? This explains, in part, why their politics and culture are so unimaginative. We would do well to remember where the most exciting and innovative challenges to politics and culture come from. Always from the margins, like Black feminist theory, free jazz, art, and global uprisings from anticolonial struggles to the mountains of Chiapas to the occupations of workplaces and public spaces.

Imaginary power is in fact real power, or at the very least, always a part of it. If we cannot imagine different forms of life and society, the ruling class stands uncontested in the war of ideas. If we cannot imagine other forms of life and society, then we cannot aspire to their realization. We cannot aim to create what we cannot imagine. The creation of another world demands imaginary power, among other things. As we have seen in this book, there are important implications of this. It certainly means that art is part of the production of power. Art includes stories, music, film, theater, protest, visual art, and many other creative practices. The imaginary power of art can become real power, or already is real power, inasmuch as it helps us think about possibilities beyond existing realities. Moreover, it means that global uprisings and revolts exercise imaginary power inasmuch as they too experiment with new forms and possibilities. It is not hard to think of revolt and art as coalescing around practices of imagination and experimentation.

In Occupy Wall Street, the Arab Spring, and Black Lives Matter, human imagination is charged, and the experiences of gathering and active uprising change people forever. Participants, their self-understandings, and the world as they know it change, and for a time, everything appears to become something else. It happened in Egypt. A whole generation of young people changed their sense of what was possible, changed their sense of their own power. We have to reckon with the fact that generations of Egyptians living under Hosni Mubarak felt it was impossible to get rid of him. Now that he is gone, there are other problems of great severity throughout Egypt. We cannot minimize the various catastrophes of Mubarak, Morsi, and the military regime. We cannot tell simple success stories of recent revolts. At the same time, the active imagination is that of a living imagination in a generation of people who know that they do not have to accept the unacceptable in perpetuity. *That realization is a part of real power.*

We have also explored the practicality of utopianism, an apparent contradiction in terms. The utopian is impractical, impossible. Nonetheless, to move toward a different reality we must be willing to think about what is desirable and possible beyond existing conditions. The only other paths would be those of accidents, force, or coercion. We must exercise the freedom to think about what is desirable and possible. We need not be leaves in a stream following where the currents take us, as if that were all we could do. There are other ways for us to get to different destinations, a point that recognizes not only the history and agency of emancipatory struggles against colonization and exploitation but also recognizes the importance of the idea that people can get free.

People called the abolitionists who stood against chattel slavery, and the radical suffragettes, utopian dreamers. They were regarded as impractical. We have no choice now but to conclude, finally, that those who declared with categorical hostility that such freedom struggles were impractical were, to say the least, people with bad imaginations. If we are generous, we could say they simply have poor understandings of history, but unfortunately, it is often because they take sides with the status quo. With imagination, historical understanding, and a healthy hatred of the status quo, the utopian appears, as we have seen, as a kind of North Star, and we know the North Star was never impractical to sailors of old. Even here on the shores, we will not stay put. We can have an idea of where we are, where we are going, but also, of where we should like to go. If we don't utilize imaginary power to work out that latter idea, our enemies will do it for us.

So then, we have some imaginary powers, while efforts to seize our attention are ramped up with sophisticated algorithms that aim to steer our imagination through screen-mediated expropriations of our cognitive resources. Human attention is not an unlimited resource. We cannot attend to everything that clamors for our attention, and we enlarge everything to which we give our precious attention. A crucial part of politics today requires that we defend our imaginary powers for the conceptualization of new horizons beyond the capitalist reality, the latter of which has its own imaginary domain of foreclosed possibility, immediate practicality, and acquiescence to the quotidian reality. Capital would constrain imagination within the boundaries of its own interests.

In our sleeping dreams, many beautiful things transpire, which we hate to wake and lose. In our sleeping dreams, many sad and frightening things also transpire, which we wake and curse as nightmares. For too many on Earth, for billions of children and billions of adults everywhere, the present and the future are nightmarish in the wakeful state. Marx famously said that people "make their own history, but they do not make it as they please; they do not make it under circumstances chosen by themselves, but under circumstances directly found, given and transmitted from the past. The tradition of all dead generations weighs like a nightmare on the brains of the living."[3] Hence, and once again, the urgent theoretical and practical importance of our ability to dream the enemy's nightmares.

3. Karl Marx, "The Eighteenth Brumaire of Louis Bonaparte," cited in *The Marx-Engels Reader*, 2nd ed,, edited by Robert C. Tucker (New York: W.W. Norton & Company, 1978), 595.

Index

"Passim" (literally "scattered") indicates intermittent discussion of a topic over a cluster of pages.